Going the Distance

going the distance

distance

Piecing Together a Life of Adventure

Elspeth Kate Ronnander

BEAVER'S POND PRESS

Going the Distance: Piecing Together a Life of Adventure
© 2020 by Elspeth Kate Ronnander

Book Design and Typesetting by Mayfly Design
Cover illustrations by Susan Ronnander
Managing Editor: Laurie Buss Herrmann

ISBN 13: 978-1-64343-859-7
Library of Congress Catalog Number: 2020911002
Printed in the United States
First Printing: 2020
24 23 22 21 20   5 4 3 2 1

Beaver's Pond Press
939 West Seventh Street
Saint Paul, MN 55102
(952) 829-8818
www.BeaversPondPress.com

To Dad, for implanting in me the idea that I can walk, bike, run, ski, or canoe wherever my little heart desires;

to Mom, for providing the means to make this idea successful;

to Leif, for living, inspiring, and providing me wisdom about this idea;

to Reid, for his comic relief and encouragement;

to Erik, for his love and companionship and for sharing my desire to make the idea happen;

and to Kathryn, for her hot pinkness.

Contents

Going the Distance

Chapter 1

Just Another Nerdy Jock

My freshman year of college, I got called both a nerd and a jock by different people. My good high school friend Anna remarked this made me a nerdy jock.

But I wasn't always a nerdy jock.

In kindergarten we made a directory. We wrote our names and phone numbers and drew pictures of ourselves. Only I hadn't learned my phone number yet, and when the directory was published, my friend made fun of me for not knowing my seven digits.

I didn't learn to read until first grade. The summer before that school year, my cousin, who was the same age as me, came over to my house. We got out a Berenstain Bears book, and he proceeded to read it word for word without making any mistakes. I could only make out the letters, and when I tried to write my name, I put extra curves in the s.

Then, in first grade, my observational skills took over, and I realized I wasn't in the reading or math groups with the smart kids. And that wasn't OK with me. I told Mom. She talked to the teacher, and I got moved to the highest math group. The math was just a bit harder; I still didn't understand money or word problems. The former would come, the latter I would never comprehend. But I adjusted well, being with the overachievers.

In fourth grade I took the gifted and talented test—and failed. That was a big hit to my ego. Maybe I wasn't gifted and talented, but I started playing the flute in band and tested into the advanced math and reading classes. That year we made a human body using a Ziploc bag with acid and graham crackers to emulate the stomach. I thought it was so cool that I kept that human body and its stomach contents under my bed for months.

I grew up in the 1990s, by which time it was widely accepted that girls and boys could both play sports and do math well and women were continuing to gain prominence in the workforce. In school there were just as many girls in my accelerated math classes as boys. I never thought, as a girl, I should stop performing and let the boys catch up.

As the eldest of three children, I encountered life's events before my brothers and set a high standard for them. Leif, being only two years younger than me, was my best playmate growing up, although I made it clear I was the boss. My youngest brother, Reid, was seven years my junior, and we struggled to play together due to the awkward gap in the stages of psychosocial development. I was in the room when Mom gave birth to Reid at 2:05 a.m. and had really wanted to see him be born, but I slept through it 10 feet away on the floor despite my family's attempts to shake me to wakefulness. When I did wake up, I flew into a fit of rage and howled for a good hour, disappointed to have missed the opportunity to see a live birth.

My lack of athleticism was apparent from an early age. When I was five, my parents encouraged me to try T-ball; I hated it and declared I would never go back. I loathed gym class, where I couldn't throw or catch in any of the various ball sports we did. When we jogged in place to the theme from *Chariots of Fire* my muscles cramped throughout my torso.

Outside of organized sports, I was a beast on the playground, climbing and swinging. I walked and biked places with my parents and brothers.

In third grade we started running the mile, three laps around a Minneapolis city block, twice per year in gym class. The Friday night before our first mile, I did a practice run. After three laps I was feeling so good I did a fourth. After the fourth lap I sat on my front lawn with hot saliva filling my mouth, my chest heaving, fighting the urge to vomit. It was the first real run of my life, and the accompanying pain made me wish it would be the last. By Monday I had recovered enough to run a 10:36 mile at age eight, but the same sick feelings overwhelmed me, and I dreaded having to do it again in May.

For my ninth birthday party I invited nine girls to my house for a sleepover. Our house was so small and there were so many of us that we spread across the entire living and dining room floors. In the morning I declared we would go on a walk. It became an epic walk of sorts in late-winter melting conditions. At each turn I pushed us farther, my physical stamina manifesting. We walked several miles total. My friends complained, and we all came back soggy, but I loved the physical exertion. I was gratified to have led what felt at the time like an expedition.

In fourth grade, after a summer of monkey bars, I did two pull-ups. This was good for girls—very good for girls. The power of pulling myself up on that bar stuck with me.

Throughout the remainder of elementary school, I ran the mile in ten minutes, dipping down into the nines twice. Then I surprised myself in the spring of sixth grade by running 8:44 without training, but I still felt as if all the symptoms of flu had been suddenly thrust upon my young body. After finishing, my chest labored as I struggled to get in enough oxygen, and I drooled like a baby.

Meanwhile, I was never picked for our classroom volleyball team, in which someone else determined my skill. In contrast, with running I could control my effort and, hence, my destiny. While I was never an outstanding runner, I had the tenacity to top most of my peers.

In later elementary school, I continued improving in the academic setting, now ahead of my grade level in reading and math. We had a program at our school called Accelerated Reader in which the objective was to read a book and then take a computerized test about it. The program assigned points based on the length and difficulty of the book—for example, Nancy Drew books were worth 5 Accelerated Reader points each, and the monstrous *Anna Karenina* was worth 73 points. We only got full points if we attained 100 percent on the computerized test; otherwise we got a fraction of points for lower scores. Going into my sixth-grade year, the school record for Accelerated Reader points earned in one year was 600. I decided I wanted to shatter it by 100 points. This effort required four hours of reading per night, the equivalent of one Nancy Drew book. By the end of the school year I had racked up over 700 Accelerated Reader points and one big trophy.

When I was ten I played recreational volleyball. It was a disaster. Even serving underhand, the ball dropped before getting two-thirds of the way to the net. This led me to spend hours in our backyard using the house as a backboard while chipping the paint and trying not to break the kitchen window. I was afraid of the ball, and so, to help, the coach threw it at me.

Whack! It hit my arm.

"See, that didn't hurt," my coach said with a smile. My arm stung in pain.

The next two years, following my brother Leif despite him being two years younger than me, I played soccer. It was a recreation league and we all got equal playing time, so the team stars weren't as obvious. I scored a goal, but I remember more the halting pain from getting a soccer ball kicked into my gut.

In eighth grade I gave up on soccer and gave volleyball another try. This time, instead of the rec league, I played for my middle school. Things were better. I could now serve over the net underhand. Being short, I took to the setter position and got my bumping skills down. It was going so well, I decided to do it the next year.

Inspired by the high school athletes at the basketball games Dad took me to as a kid, I wanted to be on varsity to have my name called and "Charge" played for me.

The summer before high school, however, my family moved from inner-city Minneapolis to Bemidji, a town of eleven thousand people nestled in the Northwoods of Minnesota. Bemidji was serious about athletics. All the freshman girls served overhand, and all made it over the net. When I served the ball overhand, it dropped just short of the net. After a week I could successfully serve overhand, but this alone could not make up for my lack of ability to move to the ball before it dropped to the ground. It soon became clear I would never make varsity. Meanwhile, back in Minneapolis, some of my former teammates made varsity as freshmen at their respective schools. So I decided to go back to playing soccer. I'm not sure why I thought I could evade my poor athleticism. I was not much better at soccer than I was at volleyball, and before long I realized I wasn't destined to make the varsity soccer team either.

But my persistence took hold, and I refused to give up. I joined the running team. All those feelings of running the mile in elementary school came back, and I wallowed in air hunger, cramps, nausea, and the mental consequences of pushing myself into such a state.

It wasn't only in sports that things were more competitive at my new school. My middle school back in Minneapolis was ranked one of the lowest in the state for standardized test scores. What it lacked in academic rigor, however, it made up in cultural diversity. I had the rare opportunity as a white person to feel like a minority within a student body made up of an almost equal proportion of European Americans, African Americans, Asian Americans, and Latinos.

Most of the time I felt like the smartest kid in the school. I was in all the advanced and accelerated classes. I was the star pupil in my French class. I challenged for the top band chair. I was the first one done with the vocabulary tests. I took algebra in eighth grade, which put me on track to take calculus my senior year of high school.

In Bemidji I finished near last on vocabulary tests. I didn't make the top chair in band. I didn't double up on math classes. At this point in my life, I stopped wondering who would make up the next generation of lawyers and doctors and teachers. I stopped guessing how many of my peers would graduate high school. College was the mainstream thing to do. I was surrounded by smart kids.

And I wasn't about to not be a smart kid. I enrolled in Advanced Placement (AP) classes and double-checked all my math test answers until I was competing for the top grade in Algebra II. I learned to write well. I always finished my assignments on time. At the end of freshman year I was ranked sixteenth in my class—good, but still not good enough.

I finally learned how to be a student and how to study in sophomore AP European History. This was the first class in which I actually read the textbook. In addition to my class notes, I took meticulous reading notes so as to increase my chances of getting every test question correct. All this was required to fight for the top grade in my class. The teachers posted our grades publicly next to our ID numbers, so we all knew where we ranked. I wasn't happy unless I was first.

While I performed well on achievement tests, I never did as well as I wanted on aptitude tests. To my disappointment, my ACT score placed me in the 85th percentile.

By high school it had become clear to me that I needed to exert myself both physically and academically each day. Without one I couldn't achieve the other—I needed both to be complete. After school I went to sports practice. This provided an opportunity for physical exertion. It cleared my mind; I usually either thought about nothing except for the effort at hand or else had some great conversation with myself. On days when I didn't have sports practice, I would do my own form of exercise, either playing volleyball with Dad or going for a run or skiing. Only after I had exerted myself physically could I devote myself to my studies. At the same time, I was striving to have the top grade in all my courses and on all my tests and be number one in my class. This put incredible pressure on me, but having a physical outlet improved my concentration on my schoolwork. My athletics complemented my academics. Without both, I was lost.

This pursuit to dominate in both areas culminated in one award. By senior year I ranked in the top 1 percent of my graduating class and had also made the varsity cross-country ski team. For the combination of these two achievements I earned the coveted Academic All-State award. At the state banquet, four-time cross-country skiing Olympian Nina Kemppel shook my hand as I was presented with this award. It was a good summation of my achievements.

After high school I went to the College of Biological Sciences at the University of Minnesota because I was fascinated with the idea of dissecting cadavers and learning more about DNA and proteins. I didn't want to major in plain biology, so I majored in biochemistry even though I wouldn't learn what biochemistry was until my junior year—it just sounded difficult and impressive.

My obsession to earn all As continued through college, as did the countless hours spent studying and the meticulous reading notes. My dedication resulted in two *summa cum laude* baccalaureate degrees with accompanying GPAs greater than 3.9.

By the time I started my master's degree at age twenty-four, it seemed well overdue. Then I got 10 out of 20 points on a paper in Advanced Physiology, and a revelation occurred: for the first time in my life, I took a bad grade as hurting my pride rather than proving my lack of intelligence.

I had an epiphany.

Ever since not being placed in the highest math and reading groups in first grade, I had been trying to prove I was smart. Since my performance on aptitude tests never showed I was the smartest, I had tried to make up for it by outperforming everyone on achievement tests. And outperform I did—on algebra tests and spelling tests and calculus tests and organic chemistry tests and microbiology tests. Once in junior year, I got a higher grade on a test than the Rhodes Scholar in a graduate-level chemistry class. By the time I got the 10 out of 20 on the paper, I had enough *summa cum laude* degrees to no longer doubt my intelligence. I had finally convinced myself I was smart, something I suspect my peers knew long before I did. It took several more years, however, to convince myself I was an athlete.

Chapter 2

BS

My parents, Bryce and Susan, met on a Sierra Club canoe trip in the Boundary Waters when he was thirty-four and she was twenty-nine. By this point in his life, Dad had spent many days adventuring by canoe or foot in the wilderness, while Mom was just starting out. Both were living in Minneapolis. Within a year of meeting, my parents were married. The wedding was at the neighborhood park; the reception was at their house. It was a low-budget affair.

～～～

Dad was born to stoic Swedish American parents in a rural hospital in the northwesternmost county in Minnesota three years after the conclusion of the Second World War. He spent the first years of his life on a farm where the gumbo, a type of soil that holds moisture well, was abundant and made farming decent. By the time he was seven, the farm life proved too difficult, and Dad's family uprooted and moved to the "big city." Dad spent most of his school years in Minneapolis and graduated from South High in 1966. During high school, he played football in the fall, taught himself to cross-country ski in the winter, and played tennis in the spring.

After graduation he attended Bemidji State University for one year. He was a varsity tennis player, but his poor writing skills made it evident he was not cut out for college, and since it was the Vietnam War era, he enlisted before his draft number could catch up with him. Dad spent the next three years working as a radio operator for the United States Army in Iran and Korea.

His parents were great users of the automobile. This lifestyle—driving to town for coffee twice a day and driving to visit relatives and friends and driving to town to get the paper and driving to town to go to the grocery store—was in part the result of living several miles from the nearest stores and cafés. Sometime during Dad's childhood, he diverged from his parents' automobile dependence. He championed the bicycle decades before Critical Mass rides became popular. Not only did he ride for leisure, but he rode to work almost every day of his working life. When it was too cold or snowy to bike, which it wasn't for him unless the mercury dipped to –25 degrees Fahrenheit or there was a foot of new snow, he walked.

Dad, who had grown up 30 miles south of the Canadian border, loved it when it got cold outside. He also loved watching the weather. One morning in middle school the temperature was well below 0, so I asked him whether I could have a ride instead of walking the mile to school.

"What? Are you serious, Elspeth? The body can handle the cold much better than the car," Dad chastised.

I should've known better. This was the man who talked about the good old days when the kids had spit-rolling contests at recess. It has to be something like 40 below for spit to freeze before it hits the ground. Even my journal entries reflect Dad's hardiness.

March 3, 2002
It was very cold this morning: −20°F. I think Dad loves this
kind of weather because he went out real early and got the
paper. Then later he took Mika [our dog] on a very long walk.

Dad shared his great love of the outdoors and human-powered transportation first with Mom and then with us kids. He believed the body is a machine, and gradually I adopted this philosophy as well. He hauled us all over to the great state parks, carrying each of us on his back while he hiked or skied when we were little and later walking or biking alongside us. We biked almost 4 miles from our home to Minnehaha Falls as a family many times. I even remember walking 3 miles round trip to and from the library on nice summer evenings.

Dad had taught himself to canoe during his bachelor years, going for several trips in the Boundary Waters, and as a family we also spent time in a canoe. We bought property on the Rum River in central Minnesota. We took family canoe trips near our cabin, shooting rapids and occasionally the dam flowing out of Lake Onamia. In Minneapolis we canoed Minnehaha Creek.

Dad was into all kinds of human-powered transportation, but especially biking. Dad belonged to the Human Powered Vehicle Association, which each summer held a world championship in which people came from all over to race their human-powered bikes and watercrafts. Dad traveled to Michigan and Wisconsin to race his watercrafts, named the Rubber Ducky and the Agassiz Queen. The Rubber Ducky was a recumbent bicycle built on an inflatable raft with a paddle wheel to generate power. Dad steered with a paddle. Its less-than-sleek profile and high center of gravity meant it was slow and tippy. The Agassiz Queen came next, with a sleeker wooden boat base more resembling a canoe, to which Dad mounted a bike and put some sort of paddle wheel on the back. I spent hours in the backyard helping him paint the wooden structure. It leaked like a sieve.

Dad had worked various jobs throughout his life—railroad signalman, night hotel auditor, county human services clerk, assembler—but his true passion was building and creating bicycles. When I was seven he experimented with two types of bikes designed for him, Leif, and me to ride. The first model would have three separate bikes welded together in succession. This proved too unstable, so next he tried a side-by-side version. Besides being too wide for the streets, this style had no easy way to steer. Dad disassembled it, and we went back to our single-speeds.

When I was ten and Mom was staying at home with three-year-old Reid, Dad quit his county job, took out a loan, and opened a recumbent bicycle shop, marketing one model that came in one color and one size. When he first opened his shop, he made ten of these bikes. He was open for three months and never sold a single one. He gave one to Mom and gradually used up the other nine over the next decade as the winter salt corroded each of the metal frames in succession.

Several years after that venture failed, Dad built himself an arm-and-leg-powered lean-steer tricycle. He had dreams of selling this machine, too, even though we told him there was no market. It was an odd contraption with two wheels in the front and one in the back. While the legs pedaled like they would a normal bicycle, the arms went around together. The steering shaft was based in the seat. Although Dad called it a lean-steer, it was really a butt-steer—to go left, the seat needed to lean to the left while the frame remained in an upright position. Dad took this contraption around Lake Bemidji. We never went with him because we didn't want to be associated with the weird-looking thing, but Bemidji is a small town, and everyone knew the eccentric guy on the strange bike was Bryce Ronnander.

∿

I do not come from a succession of strong women. Just one, my Mom, who is enough.

Mom was the fourth child born in four years to my grandparents, who began their cohabitation in a prairie town in western Minnesota with the appropriate name of Fertile. They eventually had eight children. While this was not uncommon during the era—hence the baby-boom generation—Mom grew up amid severe poverty and parental indifference.

Similar to Dad's story, when Mom was five her family moved from Fertile to the Iron Range in northern Minnesota for a better life. Among her and her siblings, horror stories about their childhood abound. On summer days, they played in the active open-pit iron ore mines.

"Take the baby!" Mom's mom would holler after the grade school–aged kids as they left in the morning. This made them run away faster. "Just wait till your dad gets home!"

When their dad got home, they got a beating.

I grew up petrified of my grandpa. He always threatened to give us a knuckle sandwich, in which he dug his knuckles into our scalps, or a hook lock, in which he wrapped one of his arms around our neck, if we misbehaved.

At thirteen, while visiting my grandparents, I took a long walk with my cousin on a hot summer day. Upon returning to their house I poured myself a big glass of water from the purchased jugs of water in the fridge, since my grandparents' well water wasn't potable.

"You better drink all that water. I'm not gonna see you pour that down the drain," Grandpa scolded when he saw my glass. While I had every intention of drinking all the water, as my own parents had taught me not to waste anything, I now feared a knuckle sandwich for even pouring the water in the first place.

We visited Grandma and Grandpa for dinner one time when I was fifteen. They had bought chocolate milk, something they deemed a real treat. We were all excited to drink it, but our first sips revealed the milk was sour. As we ate, the milk stayed full in our glasses. We were scared to say anything about the sour milk, too afraid to be accused of "wasting" it and potentially receiving a hook lock.

It was Mom who noticed we weren't drinking it.

"What's wrong? Why aren't you kids drinking the chocolate milk?" Mom asked.

"It's sour," we muttered.

"What, sour? I just bought that milk yesterday!" boomed Grandpa. He then tried some and confirmed it was sour. To our relief, he poured out our glasses.

When Mom was seven she got burned after standing too close to the barbecue when her dad was adding more lighter fluid to get the grill going faster. She had just enough time to cover her face with her hands; her dad threw a blanket over her to smother the flames, then tossed her in the back of the family station wagon and drove to the hospital. Mom spent the summer of 1960 in the hospital pulling her skin grafts off the sticky sheets. This was northern Minnesota, before air conditioning or intensive care burn units. I grew up with Mom's scarred hands and face and the oddly rectangular, lightly pigmented patches of skin on her thighs from her skin grafts.

After Mom got out of the hospital the accident was never discussed. This is what she refers to as the lack of emotional support from her parents, who couldn't have a civil conversation without indictment.

Mom stopped taking math after her freshman year of high school. Her parents were neither encouraging nor supportive and didn't even attend her high school graduation. Hobbies and outdoor pursuits were not fostered. Mom never played sports. She grew up in an era before Title IX, when women were expected to become housewives; hence, she never went to college. She found some of her own hobbies, mostly sewing and painting, until she met some friends who brought her to the Boundary Waters. Like Dad, she worked odd jobs—in a fabric store, in a bank, as a nanny.

While she never maximized her potential in the work-force, she was our unwavering rock at home. She was there to send us to school every morning and to greet us at the door every afternoon. We sat down to dinner as a family every night. She never missed a school conference, music performance, or home athletic event.

Mom ruled the roost. Even though she might have said no, we always asked her permission because Dad's response lacked validity; he was scheming in another world.

She always encouraged us to keep going and do what we loved, no matter our ability. She let us know it was OK if we didn't excel in everything, showing us unconditional love and demonstrating we would always be winners to her. She had always wanted kids and was more than willing to be a stay-at-home mom. This meant that while we saved on day care, we were a single-income household. And that single income put us well below the poverty line.

As a self-proclaimed domestic goddess, Mom made bread from scratch, sewed doll and people clothes and slipcovers for our couches, and cut hair—Dad's, us kids', my cousins', her own.

Still searching for the recognition she had been deprived of in childhood as her parents could never string together the three simple words, "Good job, Sue," Mom reinvented herself when Dad quit his government job. She enrolled at Minneapolis Technical College, where she got a diploma in upholstery, the art of refinishing and refurbishing furniture. But although the domestic goddess had no shortage of talent in art, she had little desire to work for a living. And so we continued on in poverty.

∿∿∿

From both my parents I learned the art of living simple. We weren't about to borrow money to keep up with the Joneses. Instead my parents prided themselves on trying to stay ahead despite their minimal earnings. We had one car, shopped at thrift stores, and rarely went on vacation. Mom once borrowed a book from the library entitled *How to Live on $15,000 a Year*. It recommended things like renting movies instead of going to the theater and biking to work. She could have written it herself.

It wasn't always easy, and it wasn't always so simple. My parents took no shame in reminding me I "had it good" in comparison to their meager upbringings. While this was undoubtedly true, some thirty years had passed since my parents' childhoods, and I was sure times had changed. Compared to the houses of my friends and cousins, our house in Minneapolis on a 20-foot-wide lot was tiny. True, at age eight, after sharing a room with Leif for three years, I moved into my own room. But it was only 10 feet by 6 feet, not including the space occupied by the chimney, and didn't even have a closet or door.

Looking back, the sacrifices of living below the poverty line hurt. They cut deep. When we went to the grocery store, we had a set amount of cash to spend to feed our family of five. If we went over budget, we'd have to put back items in the checkout line. Growing up, I sensed early on Dad was not content. He was restless in his job, which became his jobs, and he railed against the working-class structure of America. He embodied what he perceived to be his failure in the workforce: his inability to succeed at being his own boss. A part of my heart is still heavy with his sense of failure.

Mom was different. She sought a few key priorities in her life and then made the best of her situation by relying on her ingenuity.

I desperately wanted to travel. Most of all I wanted to see

the mountains, but we had neither the money nor a car that could make the journey, nor did Dad have enough vacation time. Instead Mom filled the void by giving me a journal with a map of the world on the inside cover, as if this journal somehow replaced an actual trip. Another year, for Christmas, Mom got me a pin of a woman carrying a suitcase. "For the traveler," she scribbled on the paper scrap in the box.

"It's the same everywhere, and we'll just come back home again anyway," she told me.

As a family we rarely went on vacations, and when we did we almost always stayed within the state of Minnesota and went camping. When I was eleven Mom decided it was time to take us kids to the Boundary Waters. She figured we would go on a three-day, two-night trip. We brought one of our own canoes and rented a second.

The trip was in August. We lucked out with perfect weather, save for some wind. We put in at Sawbill Lake, Mom and I in one canoe with all the gear and Dad, Leif, and Reid in the other. There was a terrible wind, which pushed the canoe; Mom wasn't very good at steering, and she yelled at me to paddle harder and harder and told me when to switch sides. By the time we got to the campsite my arms were so tired I couldn't paddle for the remainder of the trip. I made sure to pick Dad's canoe when it came time to head back.

That was one of our only vacations, hence one of the best family vacations I had as a child. It involved human-powered transportation, lots of hard work, family time together, and minimal expense. It provided me a model for vacations to emulate throughout my life.

Sometimes one of us kids made the mistake of declaring our boredom in Dad's presence, to which we always got the same response: "Do you know what would've happened had I said I was bored when I was a boy? Grandpa Ronnander would have gotten out the belt."

"Yeah, Dad, that was the fifties, and we're in the nineties now," we'd banter.

"How can you be bored?" Dad would continue. "You have so many toys. You have so many puzzles. You know what I did when I was a kid? I had one puzzle, and I put it together upside down with my eyes closed."

To be fair to Dad, we had enough puzzles to provide us a challenge, and if we finished with the puzzles we could always build with LEGOs or color or play dolls. Sometimes Dad called us spoiled, although I hardly felt spoiled compared to all the kids in the United States who had showers in their houses and real closets in their bedrooms and pools in their backyards and vacations to the mountains.

Our family rarely ate at restaurants. Eating out was reserved for trips and birthdays, and then the chosen restaurant was usually Subway. However, by the time I was in high school we were making even less money than we had when I was in grade school, and we stopped even these birthday outings.

Not having much money for luxuries wasn't always a disadvantage. We didn't get the internet until after I moved away from home, so I never spent time surfing the fledgling net or chatting online with friends. But instead I practiced flute and piano half an hour a day each and read books and did my homework.

Each year as Christmas approached, Mom declared there would be "slim pickings." Yet every year a huge pile of gifts appeared under the tree, and we spent hours unwrapping toys. Mom had stories about her Christmases growing up. One year she only got a little red toy iron. Other years her dad took the family to the dollar store and let each child pick one item less than or equal to one dollar. Mom could only try to make up for those disappointing Christmases by spoiling her own children.

After my junior year in high school I tried to get a job. I applied to several downtown businesses within walking distance of our house, but Burger King was the only establishment to call me for an interview, which was my first ever. I imagined the types of questions I would be asked, like why I wanted to work at Burger King and how I liked the food. For a brief moment I worried the manager might inquire into my parents' jobs, but I thought that question was inappropriate. Little did I know during the interview I would get that dreaded question. I felt rather embarrassed to reply that Dad stocked shelves at Target alongside college students and Mom dabbled in upholstery but was mostly a domestic goddess.

I came to realize that while it's important to have enough money to meet basic needs, making enough money for affluence costs time. This was something I learned from my parents, who wanted to spend time with their children rather than working. Sure, we never went to Disney World or the mountains, but we did go to the park together nearly every day. My parents were around to read us books and tell us bedtime stories.

This philosophy became apparent when we got our dog, Mika, a Siberian husky–Alaskan malamute mix, from a musher living in a trailer on the reservation. Mika was skittish of people and vomited on me on the car ride home. She tried to bite us, and out on walks she pulled and pulled and chased anything with four legs. Dad believed, as he had with raising children, that if dogs are given time, they will turn out well. He gave Mika a lot of time, walking her and skijoring her for hours, and eventually she stopped running away so often and would even come if we called her.

Since we didn't have a lot of money to buy things, I was taught to value and preserve the life of the objects I owned. When I started driving the family car at fifteen, Dad commented when I did things that he thought were bad for it, such as accelerating too fast or cranking the wheel too hard.

We only owned one vehicle, something almost unheard of

in the United States in the 1990s. While we frequently used it for such errands as groceries, Dad often walked or biked to these stores, which were some 3 miles away. The lower the mercury dipped on the thermometer, the more likely he was to not use the car.

My parents had an amazing ability to prioritize their spending, likely due to their humble beginnings. They owned their belongings for decades. Knowing they had minimal prospects for gainful employment, when we moved to Bemidji my parents didn't try to live above their means. They bought a house they could afford, with cash, thus providing for financial stability regardless of their future income. I believe it was this ability to prioritize that often made me feel we were financially secure and part of the middle class despite so much evidence to the contrary. As I grew up, this lesson to prioritize followed me and made me content to have grown up below the poverty line.

Chapter 3

Leaving the City

For the first fourteen years of my life, I lived in a little yellow two-story house in the Powderhorn Park neighborhood of south Minneapolis. To the south of us was a middle-class neighborhood where it was safe to be outside after nightfall. To the north was an impoverished neighborhood where drive-by shootings and drug deals were the norm.

Our neighbor's garage was permanently graffitied. After the first offense, the neighbor painted over it; soon the same sign showed up in the same place. This time the neighbor gave up repainting.

One time my parents forgot to lock our garage. Several bikes were stolen. Another time we watched as a group of kids raided our back porch and stole our plastic sleds. Still another time, Leif had biked to a local fabric store while I walked with Mom, who pushed Reid in a stroller. Leif locked up his bike in front of the store with a cable lock. Later, when he went to check on his bike, it was missing. Mom was pissed. She found out what direction the kids who had stolen it had gone, chased them down, and got my brother's bike back.

There were more serious issues. On three separate occasions, while walking home from school, I witnessed the FBI performing drug busts on my block in full bulletproof vests and helmets. The three-story, twenty-one-unit white stucco apartment building across the street from our house—dubbed "the Alamo" for its castle-like facade—was the source of several police calls due to domestic disputes, drug deals, and loitering. My parents, whose bedroom faced the Alamo, had many sleepless nights listening to the ruckus going on outside. It was no doubt the reason Mom found many used syringes in our front yard and why plainclothes police officers knocked at our door.

A few nights before Christmas when I was ten, we were having a sleepover with our cousin. As was typical with cousin sleepovers, she and I were sleeping downstairs on the living room floor. I had a bad cold and woke up in the middle of the night for a coughing fit, so I got up to use the one bathroom in our house. I was halfway up the stairs when I heard a gunshot. It was close, but I thought it must be several houses away, so I continued with my business. Dad was pretty worked up, though, and I didn't understand why. He went downstairs and called 911.

The cops came. It turned out our neighbors next door to the north were having a party, and one friend had shot another in the front yard. I fell back asleep to the bright lights of the police and media. The next night we saw our house in the background of the TV news report.

One month before we moved away, there was a drive-by shooting down the block at five in the morning. It woke my parents, and they heard the screech of the getaway car. The bullet was lodged in a 2×4 in the house on the corner. Another time there was a loud gunshot that sounded like it was in front of our house. It echoed off the nearby houses, breaking the silence of the morning. My brothers and I were playing downstairs, and Mom was upstairs. We sat motionless, afraid to move for a while, then carefully crept upstairs to be with Mom while trying to avoid all the windows. And once when Leif and I were walking home from school we almost had a gun pulled on us.

Two years after we moved, one of the older kids who lived down the street was fatally shot in his driveway in our alley. They interviewed a guy for the five o'clock news who had been sleeping in my former bedroom at the time of the shooting and had awoken at the noise.

∿∿

To many of those who grow up in the city, there is comfort in the blocks upon blocks of houses, the constant noise from the surrounding eight-lane freeways, all the people, and the skyscrapers dominating the landscape. But for many bred in the country, the city is stifling in a way not even the biggest parks can ease. Dad, born and raised in one of the least populous counties in the state, felt like he was gasping for air in the city. He always talked about relocating our family north, for the snow, the fresh air, and the clear streams. For him, this was as much a part of his life's dream as human-powered transportation.

As a child I enjoyed looking out the window as the trees went by when we drove north to visit my grandparents. When we passed a bog, Dad would point out the tamaracks and then go on a long tirade about how although tamaracks look almost like pine trees, they are in fact deciduous, and their delicate root system is finely suited for the wet bog conditions. Personally, I liked the poplar trees up north the best. I was fond of watching their leaves turn over in the wind and catch the sunlight. Both my maternal and paternal grandparents had ample poplar trees in their yards, making them evoke feelings of nostalgia in me as I got older.

When I was five my parents bought their 3-acre parcel of land on the Rum River at the end of a street in Onamia, about two hours north of Minneapolis. They bought the property with the intention of Dad building us a house so we could move there.

First, Dad tried to put in a well. His hand-powered drill didn't go deep enough down, and we never could get any water. He also built a tiny plywood shed for our lawn tools. Then, on a 12-by-12-foot slab of concrete that Dad mixed and poured himself, we erected a cabin. The cabin was a simple design, two stories on the south side sloping down to just one story on the north side. Dad raised the north wall himself. His brothers and an uncle came to help him raise the other three. The cabin had no running water. Leif and I climbed a ladder to sleep in the loft.

During my childhood we often made the 350-mile trip by car to visit my paternal grandparents, who owned 80 acres of woods just west of Halma, 35 miles south of the Canadian border. Grandpa heated their home with wood he harvested from his property using a series of trails he built wide enough for his riding lawn mower and an attached trailer. I spent time walking and skiing and exploring these trails and saw my first wild moose. In the fall, Dad, his brothers, Grandpa, and other relatives hunted here, so deer stands and hunting blinds were scattered throughout the woods. I loved Grandpa's trails and even spent time making maps of them. When we were really lucky, Grandpa loaded us in his trailer and took us for a ride behind his lawn mower.

The Cabin, as we soon began calling our property in Onamia, became my microcosm of Grandpa's 80 acres. Dad mowed a trail to the brush dump and another to the Rum River. But I wanted to build more, so much that I acquired my first case of poison ivy while wandering the woods in a skirt scouting new trails.

The Cabin was built when I was seven. The next spring, we put our house up for sale. It being the early '90s, Minneapolis was a buyer's market; houses were cheap and ubiquitous, and ours, small and located in a bad neighborhood, was overlooked. My parents used a realtor, and Dad was convinced the asking price was too high. If it sold, the plan was for Dad to build us a house on our property, where he had built the Cabin. On weekend mornings when I woke and went downstairs, he was busy drawing house plans. I asked him for some graph paper and went about making us a house plan, too.

After a few months our house still hadn't sold. My parents, discouraged, decided this wouldn't be the year to move, and so the For Sale sign came down. Two years later, when I was ten, they tried again. This time they didn't use a realtor and lowered the price from a few years before, to $35,000. It was still a buyer's market, and we were once again skunked.

In the ensuing years Mom got smart. My uncle Curt, Dad's brother, had been working on a house addition for several years. He'd made little progress, and every time Dad called him, the joke was to ask him how the new addition was coming along. Mom realized Dad, like his brother, wasn't capable of building a house himself. She didn't want to live in a half-done house and decided that if we moved, we would buy a house. Dad agreed.

A couple years later the housing market flipped. The Twin Cities and surrounding suburbs were expanding. Companies were relocating, and housing became scarce, thus driving up the price of real estate.

My parents capitalized on this seller's market. This time, our house sold in one day, for almost twice as much as we had tried to sell it for four years earlier. We began considering which town in northern Minnesota to make our new home.

After living my first fourteen years in a big city, northern Minnesota seemed rural to me. After all, in Minneapolis we lived just 6 miles from the Mall of America. I felt a certain comfort that our house stood only 3 feet from its neighbor to the south and 7 feet from its neighbor to the north. While I found the idea of relocating to a new community exciting, I largely resisted moving north.

We were also moving just at the time my parents were finally allowing me some freedom to discover the city on my own. I began biking, as it enabled me to go farther than walking. This exploring by bicycle coincided with the worst storm of my childhood. Straight-line winds had taken down lots of big trees a couple miles south of our house—huge trees growing on the boulevard had been uprooted and were lying on their sides, blocking entire streets. Leif and I surveyed the damage by bike, which allowed us to make our way around the big trees. Discovering the big city on my bike was exhilarating, and I was not looking forward to moving to a small town.

My parents decided on Bemidji, the first city on the Mississippi River, because it had a four-year university. While driving around Bemidji looking for houses for sale, my brothers and I coined the city "broken-up shack town" in reference to the many small houses to which one or more additions had been made. My parents had plans to buy with the cash from selling both our house in Minneapolis and our cabin in Onamia. Therefore, what my parents considered an affordable house left us with few options. Mom and I wanted charm. Dad only cared about a roof over our heads and a place to scheme; he cared little about size or looks. He insisted we live in town, in keeping with his philosophy of being able to use human-powered transportation to get most places. Bemidji had few houses for sale in our price range. One possibility was a characterless rambler. Well, quite frankly, that seemed like our only possibility.

Reid, bored of driving around, was screaming and trying to jump out of his seat.

"Reid, look at that bridge ahead. That's a tall bridge. Let's drive over that bridge and see what happens!" Mom exclaimed, attempting to provide some distraction.

"Susan," Dad grumbled, "What are you thinking having me drive over that bridge? That will waste gas."

But Mom glared at Dad, and Dad drove over the tall concrete bridge over the railroad tracks.

As we reached the other side we noticed a gray three-story house with a cupola on top. In the front yard was a yellow and brown Century 21 For Sale sign. The house, adorned in gingerbread-like designs, even had a white picket fence. There was no garage, but there was a shed, also garnished in gingerbread decorations. Later, the realtor told us this house was nicknamed "the Painted Lady."

After a few negotiations, my parents bought the Painted Lady for $61,500 in cash. It had been built in 1910, but, like most houses in Bemidji, it had had several additions, including the cupola. While the gingerbread looked good from the street, closer inspection revealed rotting wood. And we soon discovered the cupola provided a nice home to squirrels. Hence why the Painted Lady, which had such good curb appeal, was affordable for my parents.

Being plucked from an inner-city school and dropped into a rural one required several adjustments. I didn't fit in. I was angry at my parents for a long time and rejected my new life.

Over the next two years I struggled to assimilate into the bland northern Minnesota culture. I struggled to remember names; in the sea of white faces, everyone looked the same. I struggled to find my niche athletically. I struggled to work my way to the top of my class academically. I struggled to accept what seemed to me the minimal worldly experience of the people of this small town. I struggled to not feel stifled by the wilderness and the lack of mall options. I struggled with the lack of city to explore on my walking and running and biking routes.

In tenth grade, after I won an essay contest sponsored by the Bemidji Area Race Relations Council, I wrote an essay about Dr. Martin Luther King Jr. for the holiday named after him, which we didn't have off from school in Bemidji as we'd had in Minneapolis. I read my essay during the morning announcements over the intercom, and afterwards King's "I Have a Dream" speech was played. I felt, for two minutes, like I was back where I belonged, in an inner-city school.

Eventually, I made my way to the top of my class. I joined track, started running in the country, and discovered mountain biking. In the end, I decided moving to Bemidji had expanded my horizons and afforded me new experiences; however, I was deeply impacted by living in the inner city. The paralyzing nightmares of someone trying to shoot me persisted. And occasionally when a car drives past, I panic, fearing it will be a drive-by.

Chapter 4

Up North

My freshman year of high school, the first year we lived in Bemidji, I went out for the volleyball team. I had held my own the previous year on my middle school team but was in no way prepared for what my new school had to offer.

Practice in Minneapolis had been an hour and a half. We ran three laps around our one-court gym. Practice in Bemidji was four hours. We ran 2 miles and did several jumping and agility drills. Before freshman year I could barely run a mile, and that mile left me gasping for air with sore muscles, a metallic taste in my mouth, and a strong desire to vomit.

After two days of volleyball practice I was sorer than I had ever been in my entire life. Every muscle in my legs hurt when I moved. I learned about muscles I'd never known existed. And at practice I still had to run and jump and sprint and squat. I made a pact then to never get so out of shape ever again in my life.

Since I was new to town, I didn't know anyone on the team. Freshman players didn't get cut, and therefore of all the grades represented, the freshman girls made up half of those trying out for volleyball. Because of this rule, there was a varsity team, a junior varsity team, a C team, and a C-2 team, with the latter two made up almost entirely of ninth graders. All the other freshman girls knew each other and already had predetermined cliques. Nobody seemed interested in the new girl. I was alone except for one girl, Alison. She knew all the others but didn't belong to any one clique. Alison was as out of shape as me, so I hung out with her, except she sprained her ankle and for a few days after she couldn't do the workouts.

Only I wasn't so sure Alison had actually sprained her ankle. It seemed almost like an act to me, like a good way to get out of doing the work. I was so sore, and it hurt so bad to walk, let alone to run and jump and squat, that I thought about spraining my ankle, too. But I was determined to try hard and show off my talents, or lack thereof.

By my second day of practice it became evident who the varsity and junior varsity girls were. They were good! They could all overhand serve wherever they wanted and bump even the hardest balls. The setters set perfectly every time and could even set backwards; at 5 feet tall, I couldn't even reach the top of the net to spike. I was just learning to overhand serve, and my serves barely dropped over the net, but more often than not they went directly into the net or fell just short. I was admittedly afraid to bump a ball, and besides, I could never get to the ball in time. I was a setter and merely so because I was too short to be a hitter.

After coming home from practice on the second day, having seen how good the varsity and even junior varsity girls were at volleyball, I knew I could never be that good. Suddenly I burst into tears knowing what I wanted so badly, to be a varsity volleyball player, was never going to happen.

That season I made the second freshman volleyball team, the C-2 team. We lost all our games and only got to travel twice. I proved to be a steady server, sometimes scoring my team several points by getting the ball over the net, where the opposing team watched it drop. One Friday practice, after we had lost a game on Thursday, our coach was particularly hard on us. We had to run extra and do all the hardest drills that required the most agility and stamina. It didn't help, and in subsequent years all of us on the team either quit, like Alison, or got cut.

Heading into my sophomore year of high school I gave up on volleyball and started playing soccer again. More girls made varsity in soccer than in volleyball, so I would have better odds. In the beginning it worked well. I was the underdog, which meant that if I performed well I was exceeding expectations. In the traveling summer league between my freshman and sophomore years, I scored a goal and became a temporary hero. I made junior varsity my sophomore year and was ecstatic. I was getting lots of playing time and was excited to feel like an athlete.

Being the underdog continued to work to my advantage for about three weeks as I took to the left midfield position, which required lots of running and little pressure, and as my endurance improved it became more enjoyable. Then the junior varsity coach, Adrienne, caught on to my limited athleticism. The first two games of the season I started and played over half the game. Then something happened during the third game, even though I'd worked hard and hadn't missed practice.

When we arrived for our game in Saint Cloud after a three-hour bus ride, the weather was unusually warm, around 90 degrees, and the girls needed subs and water often. I didn't start the game. A quarter of the way into the game, I still wasn't in. Girl after girl chorused that they needed water breaks, but each time Adrienne looked right through me and picked somebody else to go in the game. It felt like I was invisible.

During the second half our goalie got injured, and Adrienne scrambled to find a new goalie and fit positions. But even down a player, she continued to look past me. After traveling six hours total, I never got to see any playing time. A knot settled in my stomach, and I felt chilled despite the heat of the day. Adrienne thought me an unworthy soccer player. My self-confidence was shattered. When I got home, my stomach was still too upset to eat dinner, and I went for a run instead.

I didn't understand what I had done to not get any playing time. I could only assume Adrienne had decided my ball-handling skills weren't up to par. And I wasn't one of her favorites. This made me angry. This made me feel incompetent. And I thought I ought to confront my coach, but I didn't know what to say or do.

It took me a few weeks to approach her.

"Adrienne," I ventured one evening after practice, "I haven't been getting very much playing time lately."

There was silence on her end. My words hung in the air.

"To get better I need more playing time," I continued.

"OK," was all she said, flatly.

The remainder of the season she let me play five to ten minutes of each of our eighty-minute games. She didn't give me any reason why she wouldn't let me play.

Meanwhile, she favored some of the other girls on the team who had similar athletic ability to mine but whose parents were people of note in town. We were a friendly team, and the girls were always nice to me, but no one spoke up for me. We were all vying for a few prized varsity positions for the following year.

September 23, 2000

Today we went to Saint Cloud for a soccer game. As expected, I only got to play for about 10 minutes. This was a team we could have beaten . . . but we lost 2–0. Adrienne was mad. She'll still be mad on Monday. Just because they are my team doesn't mean I should be held accountable for the way they played. That makes me mad. What also doesn't make any sense is that Adrienne pulled up three players from C team—they all got more playing time than me. What else am I supposed to think about myself other than I really suck?

<u>October 3, 2000</u>
Our home game was tonight against Grand Rapids. We played really good, totally dominating the first half considering the score was 0–0. The second half we slacked a little but kept up the pressure enough to score three goals with no response from Grand Rapids. I didn't get to play at all in the first half and only for about five minutes in the second half. When I went on the field I played as hard as I could. In the last five minutes when we were ahead 3–0, Adrienne still didn't put me in.

Adrienne is pulling up four C team girls to finish the season with us. We have two games left, and I wonder if I will see any playing time. I wonder and want to know why Adrienne snubs me on the playing time. I would like to know what she has against me.

Dad didn't understand why I wasn't athletic. He came from an athletic family—he and his brothers had played their share of varsity football, basketball, tennis, and baseball.

Mom wasn't about to make a fuss to the coach because she didn't believe I should get undeserving special treatment; that would only perpetuate the problem. Mostly she lamented that while Title IX was designed to empower women, due to the limited varsity spots available, we girls were pitted against each other. Instead of learning the principles of hard work, teamwork, and confidence, we got trapped in the politics of team selection. Had Mom been coach, we all would have had equal playing time, with emphasis on healthy exercise and cooperation, not winning.

October 5, 2000
It snowed this morning but melted as it touched the unfro-
zen ground. Our soccer game in Detroit Lakes didn't get
canceled. I sat on the sidelines the whole first half freezing
to death. I moved around while I was on the sidelines in the
second half. Then I got to go in for 10 minutes or so. I played
really hard during that time and really well. I played the
least of anybody—both on JV and C team. That sucks, but
it is the cards I am dealt. I guess I'm just happy I made the
most of my 10 minutes of playing time.

I still desperately wanted to make varsity in a sport, so I
didn't give up. The next summer I played in the local traveling
league for the second year. This time was different. I was no
longer the underdog, and my self-confidence had vanished.

I was extremely critical of myself.

June 7, 2001
I am not athletic. I lack the coordination and speed. I have
always admired athletes and have always wanted to be just
like them. This is hard for me.

June 11, 2001
I should not give myself such a hard time for not being the
best soccer player. Not everyone can reach a professional
level. Yet it seems I should be able to make high school var-
sity. The good soccer players make the booting and trap-
ping and those quick passes look so easy. From somewhere
comes the phrase "give and go." That is what I need to do.
Receive the ball, gain control by giving it a couple taps,
then send it on to an open teammate. First, I have to go to
the ball. There is no waiting for it to come to me. I have to
go to the ball and always be open. Why is this so hard for
me? And why do I not have any power behind my shots?

My veins pop out of my legs because they are so muscular. My strength is obviously not the problem. I think I have the same problem when I play tennis: I have the upper body strength—I can do thirty push-ups—but I can't put any good spin on the ball. I have major problems perfecting my game, one could say.

During this time I continued to feel my soccer skills were lacking. I was still afraid of the ball. After all, it hurts to get hit by a flying soccer ball, and, being human, I tried to avoid pain. I had never done a header in a soccer game or practice, so one night I had Dad throw me balls to practice. For half an hour I continuously headed the balls he threw me. Some hurt, some didn't. It was as if I were punishing myself for being a bad soccer player, as if somehow practicing headers would make me less afraid of the ball and increase my chances of making varsity.

Two days later I developed a mother of a headache. My head hurt all the time. For a couple days I was afraid something had really gotten messed up and I was about to die—head injuries are serious. The pain came right out of my forehead and radiated around my entire head. Mom was pissed at Dad for acquiescing to my demands. When I tried to run, my head throbbed each time one of my feet struck the ground. I tried playing a soccer game with this terrible head pain and wasn't able to play very well.

"Elspeth, get in the game!" my summer coach yelled at me. I realized I was playing poorly, and from then on, despite the head pain, all I thought about was how he was thinking I was playing badly and so I couldn't focus on the game. All I could do was focus on his thoughts. He had no confidence in my playing ability, and it was reflected in my performance.

Coming into fall of my junior year I was determined to keep playing soccer, although the idea of running cross-country nagged on my mind, especially as I convinced Leif to do cross-country. I stuck with soccer figuring it was much more fun than pure running and knowing I could run the rest of my life, while my opportunity to play soccer was limited. After a hard week of tryouts, I was downgraded to C team.

August 25, 2001
Like so many other dreams that once existed as possibili-
ties but have been transformed into unfulfilled desires, like
the family trip out west and a date for Winter Formal, my
being a varsity soccer player has also been shot to hell.

~~~

I called Barney, the cross-country coach, and asked him whether I could try running with the team. I tried doing both sports for two weeks.

August 21, 2001
I have major confliction going on right now. I keep digging
my hole deeper in this whole soccer versus cross-country
deal. I went to cross-country practice yesterday morn-
ing and it kinda sucked 'cause we had to run 4 × 700 me-
ters, but it left me feeling initiated. Then I went to soccer
practice and once more felt compelled to my team. This
morning I ran 6 miles with the cross-country team and
finished with three of the top runners. I also decided to go
to cross-country camp, which means missing two soccer
practices. Then this evening I go to soccer practice, get more
excited and the number jersey I wanted. Now I feel like I'm
committed to both sports. I want to do both sports and I
have enough dedication to boot.

During those two weeks I felt torn and deceitful. I lied to my soccer coach, telling her I was going on vacation with my family. In reality I went to cross-country running camp and ran 30 miles in three days. Being at camp meant I missed soccer team pictures. I figured that was good—I wouldn't be in the yearbook as a junior on the C squad.

At cross-country practice I kept up with the top girls. We did lots of intervals, which hurt; I ran hard and at the end wanted to collapse, but instead I put my hands on my hips and just sucked in the air. At my first meet I ran 2.5 miles in 18:26 and finished fourth for our team. I had beaten one of the best runners on our team in the finishing kick, which had seemed effortless.

Meanwhile, soccer practice was degrading. I was a junior on a predominantly freshman team. Half the time I forgot the objective was to go for the ball, and I found myself mindlessly running down the field. I wasn't a good ball handler. No matter how many sprints I ran or how many agility or ball drills I performed, the genetics were missing, and this kept getting me down.

At the same time, I didn't like the cross-country running races, even when I ran well. The whole race I was fighting my conscience, which begged me to quit or at least to slow down. I had to work hard to ignore that voice, to keep pushing the pace and to breathe faster and try to stay relaxed.

August 28, 2001

Cross-country meets suck. I had that predetermined. OK, the meets aren't that bad, my attitude just needs to change. Instead of wanting to quit while I run, I need to shift my focus. The whole race sucked for me today. It really wasn't that bad, nor did I ever doubt I could go the distance, it is pushing myself to keep up a fast pace. At one point in the race I thought about slowing up my pace, but it wouldn't have been any easier, so I just kept going. For the first mile I stuck with Cadie [a fast girl on my team], then I let her pass me; however, I always kept her within catch-up distance. A few girls passed me. One coach told this girl to pass a whole line of us 'cause we were more tired and breathing heavier. The whole race I was kinda tired and didn't think I would have a kick. But from nowhere and without my deciding to I started kicking it in. I passed this girl from Fergus Falls who had just passed me, and then I passed Cadie, too. It was crazy and it felt so good. Yeah, I got fourth place for the Bemidji girls.

After the race I didn't feel too good. My stomach was stable but tense, and food was not an option. My quads were tight. My mouth was hot and I wanted water, but my stomach didn't want to take in water. It was hot. Mostly I was just restless, and I wanted to get out of my body. I think it might have been the result of my mind and body being opposing, reactionary forces during the race.

Then I go to soccer practice tonight and totally suck it up. If I really have to pick between sports, I have to choose cross-country. It's more natural and a lot less frustrating to me. Sure, the meets suck, but I am more in control, the standards more defined, the finish line more obtainable. I've worked my ass off both physically and mentally for soccer, and though I have improved, I have not improved enough to do anything with the sport. Too many girls, all better than me, are out for the same sport. Dad asked me why I'm not good. It's simple: I don't have speed or agility. I am not fiercely aggressive, and above all, I have never gotten over my fear of the ball.

So I quit soccer. As soon as I did, I stopped racing so fast and lost my varsity position. But I was free; I no longer shared punishment for my team performing poorly when I hadn't even gotten any playing time. Running is not subjective. The times, the results, tell it all.

I was my own master. Running a slow time, no matter how mentally degrading, was a million times better than being sidelined because a coach decided my skills were unworthy of play time. Even when I finished last in a race, I never regretted quitting soccer.

Chapter 5

The Classic Love-Hate Relationship

M y decision to join the track team came after earning a devastating A– in French my freshman year. The French teacher, who was also a track-and-field coach, was notorious for grading on extracurricular activity participation rather than test performance.

Since my brutal experiences with running the mile in elementary school, I'd hated running, but it seemed worth it to get an A in French. Because I didn't like running, I really wanted to be a hurdler, but I was too chicken to jump the hurdles. Sprinting seemed easy, nice and short, but the masses were all sprinters, and since I've never been much for following the masses, I started running with the distance group. To my surprise, I was able to keep up with the other girls both on distance runs and during intervals. One day during the first week of practice, we ran 4 miles! I thought this was incredible, but within a few weeks 6-mile runs became my norm.

This first year of track, I learned how to be a runner. In the past I'd always run fast, feeling horribly out of breath and my mouth filling with copious amounts of saliva. And I had never run more than 2 miles at one time. After joining track I learned to run at a pace suitable for the planned distance—if

I was running a 200-meter I ran as fast as my legs could travel for thirty-five seconds, and if I was running a mile I tried to run consecutive ninety-second 400s. When running 6 miles I ran at a comfortable nine-minute mile pace, which didn't leave me gasping for breath or salivating excessively and allowed for conversation.

At the first meet the coach, Barney, assigned me to run the 1,600-meter—what we colloquially called the mile—and the 800-meter. My previous personal record (PR) mile time was 8:44, which I had run the fall of freshman year during volleyball practice. I wondered whether I should tell Barney, as it seemed really slow to me. Sure, it was now a year and a half later and I was in much better shape, but the mile seemed so long.

The meet was on the 200-meter indoor track at the local college, which meant a mile was eight times around the oval. I ran a new personal best by exactly two minutes, peeing my pants the entire way. I'd kind of had to pee prior to starting the race but had no idea pushing myself so hard would make me lose control of all my sphincters.

After that first meet, Barney had me try the 2-mile, or more technically, the 3,200-meter. Now I felt really crazy. The 2-mile was the real shit—a real test of endurance. The next meet was also indoors, and therefore I had to go sixteen times around the track. I ran hard, hard enough that on the third lap my surroundings darkened. The darkness quickly subsided as I opened my mouth to gasp for air. I came across the finish line feeling like I had a fever: all my internal muscles were fatigued, and my body ached. At the same time, I was satisfied to know I was done. I'd run a 14:14. A week later I ran a 14:07.

Upon finishing each of these 2-mile races I experienced my first runner's highs. Pushing myself to my physical limit was terrible. I wanted to puke; I couldn't get air in fast enough; my vision dimmed. This is oxygen debt. Yet as awful as it sounds to those who haven't experienced it, it is wonderful. It is the feeling of complete exhaustion. It is then I know I have given a race 100 percent and am not disappointed in myself. Endurance athletes strive for that feeling. We get hungry for it and excited that we might be able to do it again. And again.

On April 23 of my first year of track, a big storm dropped 16 inches of snow. School was canceled on Monday. On Tuesday we had our first outdoor 400-meter track meet at Park Rapids. Only half the team showed up, so Barney decided I should double: run both the 1-mile and the 2-mile.

My first lap time, in the mile, was eighty-five seconds. I came across the halfway mark at just under three minutes. My lungs seared, but I was on autopilot. At 600 meters to go I pushed hard to maintain my pace, and the last 100 meters I sprinted. I came across the line and wanted to collapse. My body suffered like it had been through the wringer. My time was 6:23—a PR by twenty-one seconds.

During my hour-and-a-half break I kept warm, ate an avocado sandwich, and tried to ease my nerves. I barely felt rested when I toed the line for the 2-mile. There weren't very many 2-mile runners, so the boys and girls ran together. Two of my guy teammates—Jake and Dory, the first a foot taller than the second—lapped me on my fifth lap. Still, my time was 13:56, the first time I'd broken fourteen minutes for the 2-mile. There was a price to pay for running fast: I puked up the avocado sandwich.

The next Tuesday, we returned to Park Rapids for another meet. Now I was hooked on doubling and so again ran both the mile and the 2-mile. At each meet there was a consistent schedule of track events, set up such that distance and mid-distance runners and sprinters had recovery breaks between events. As had been the case the previous week, the mile race preceded the 2-mile by about two hours; I ran 6:21 and 13:50, respectively. Even though the margin of improvement over the previous meet was small, I had new PRs in both events.

That first year of track, I loved running. I loved the way it made me feel when I got done, whether it was a distance run, some hard 400s, or a race. It was fresh and new, and I felt strong enough to be one of the best distance girls on my team.

But I hated that for two days before a race, all I could concentrate on was how much my lungs would burn as I sucked in air. While I was in class or playing the piano, my thoughts drifted to the upcoming race and my apprehension about wanting to push my body so hard. It was two days of preoccupation during which all my waking thoughts were devoted to the knowledge that I would be performing, and it would hurt. And I hated the moments right before each race when I felt like crying and wanted to run into Mom's arms and sob like I did when I was eight years old.

My next meet was at home, again at the local college but this time at the outdoor track. Just before I toed the line for the mile, my parents showed up with my brothers and informed me Leif had gotten 100 percent on the reading portion of the Minnesota Basic Standards Test. While I had always excelled academically and was in the accelerated classes, school had long been a challenge for Leif, and he had to take remedial reading classes. I was therefore incredulous he had beaten my score by 10 percentage points!

Driven by the shock of my brother outperforming me, I raced to a new PR mile of 6:16 and followed it up a couple hours later with a 2-mile PR of 13:35. Afterward, the feelings of runner's high overwhelmed me, and I lost focus on Leif's test performance. I coughed until I went to bed. This was my first, but far from my last, experience with this cough, which made my lungs hurt and told me I had pushed hard. Running to new PRs each week left me elated and wondering what the next race had to offer.

I distinctly remember the track meet we had a week later in Detroit Lakes. We were past the midseason and only had a couple of weeks left before sections. The frequency and difficulty of intervals had increased, and our distance group was starting to come together. I was continuing to double at all my meets. There were four girls running the mile from Bemidji; three of us ran in a pack, with our teammate Sarah about 50 meters ahead. We ran the first lap in eighty-five seconds.

At 500 meters in, Barney yelled at our trio, "You belong with Sarah! Get up there with her—now!" We ignored him, continuing at our pace. We were pushing, but comfortable enough to leave something for the second half.

At the 800-meter mark Sarah ran off the track. Her effort had proved too valiant—she was too exhausted to continue. Our trio continued, silently praising our pacing. We kicked at 600 meters to go, and I ran as hard as I could. When I crossed the line in 6:11, yet another new PR, I had given the race my all. A couple hours later I ran a PR of 13:34 in the 2-mile, too.

"You're all too conservative," Barney later critiqued us. He wanted us to push harder, to run faster, but as Sarah had taught us, there's a price for pushing too hard.

It was at this point in the season I reached my plateau. For two consecutive meets my times were slower than previous meets. Running became less fun. My two-day prerace preoccupation increased in intensity with the new fear I would not be faster than the previous week. I blamed the wind. I blamed my shoes coming untied. I should have blamed my lack of ability to push myself into the uncomfortable state of oxygen debt. I started to hate racing.

Then, the week of sections, we tapered. We significantly decreased both our mileage and our interval training. My mind and legs felt fresh again. Moreover, the top female runner in the state for the mile and 2-mile would be racing with me, and I felt increased pressure to avoid being lapped—or at least to run as many laps as I could without being lapped.

Sections was held at Detroit Lakes, my lucky track where I'd had my season PRs. My parents, brothers, and aunt and uncle came to watch me run. While warming up for the mile, I once again felt like crying; there's something about racing that gets the tears flowing. I wanted Mom to rescue me from the pressure, from the self-induced brutality that awaited me on the track. I knew she understood—indeed, during a cross-country race in high school before a particularly difficult hill, I witnessed one of my teammates run right into the arms of her own mom. I think we all felt this way, because we often hugged each other before races.

After a good warm-up we went to the starting line. The faster girls got placed by twos in the lanes while the slower girls stood on the waterfall line. I lined up with my fellow teammates on the waterfall line. The gun went off, and I got in a line behind Ali, our best distance runner, running behind her and a couple other girls for three laps. The pace was fast—I was breathing hard and struggling to hold on. We hit 400 meters at eighty-five seconds and 800 meters at 2:55, putting us on pace to run a 5:50. But after the third lap, as a cheer marked the future state champion crossing the finish line in under five minutes and a cool rain began falling, my quadriceps tightened. I could no longer maintain my pace, struggling to keep running hard enough to finish in a good time. But I crossed the finish line in 6:12, a single second slower than my PR on the same track.

For the 2-mile I ran 13:40, six seconds slower than my PR, and abruptly ended my season. Sure, I got my A in French, but I wondered what I would do without track practice after school for the rest of the semester. At the same time, I was relieved to not have to race for a while.

I was in love with track. I loved the way it forced me to run long distances easy and short distances fast. I loved the power

I felt when I ran strong and could keep up with or pass other runners. I loved the runner's high I got when I forced myself into oxygen debt and the pride that accompanied my PRs.

Paradoxically, these were the same aspects I grew to hate. I often lacked the motivation to go for long runs on my own, and I usually didn't have teammates encouraging me during the off-season. The hard breathing associated with intervals and races was uncomfortable. Despite how much I loved the runner's high, my conscience told me to avoid oxygen debt. Consequently, my tolerance for it diminished, and I didn't get runner's high.

Despite my mental anguish, I joined cross-country my junior year and continued track throughout high school. The apprehension I had toward races continued.

Yet I was compelled to continue running. I had learned to run easy and could cover many miles with minimal exertion, which usually left me exhilarated. I was unsure whether I would do much racing in my future. The thoughts preceding races were difficult to deal with, but I had become addicted to that euphoria of exhaustion.

Chapter 6

Movil Maze

I learned to cross-country ski at Powderhorn Park in Minneapolis. Occupying the space of several blocks, this city park is larger than most and even has a central pond surrounded by hills. In the winter we would put our ski boots on at home and carry our skis across the street to the park, then I would follow Dad's tracks to the hills. To go down the hill I put my skis in the tracks, one slightly ahead of the other, bent my knees, and let gravity work; then I climbed back up the hill and repeated the process.

As a third grader, I proudly marched into Midwest Mountaineering, where Dad bought me new skis, bindings, boots, and poles. I liked my new equipment; the skis were mostly white with hot-pink and neon-green details, as it was the early 1990s. My bindings also had hot-pink writing. Since hot pink was my favorite color, I was happy.

In this era skate skiing was all the rage. Dad didn't skate, and neither did Leif or Mom—we all did "classic skiing." However, my new skis said *skating* on them. When we went to county parks on the weekends, I observed others skating and sought to imitate them. I tried to glide, but my skis stopped and I face-planted. A couple months went by, and I attempted again without success. A year went by, another face-plant. I didn't understand how people could glide on their skate skis.

When I was in fifth grade our class took a field trip to the local downhill ski area. Even though I never progressed from the bunny hill, I fell in love with downhill skiing. For several years I begged my parents to take me, to which Dad always responded, "I can get all the downhills I want on cross-country skis."

For the next several winters I satisfied my hunger for the speed and gravity-dependent ease of downhill skiing with cross-country skiing. I herringbone walked up hills on my skis just for the thrill of whizzing down. The winter of the Nagano Olympics, Leif and I made two downhill runs—one had a wicked corner we dubbed "Dead Man's Curve," and the other was a slalom run. We set up our poles as gates, and Dad packed down a course with snowshoes. Leif and I took turns: one of us stood at the bottom of the hill, yelled go, and began counting "One one thousand, two one thousand," and so on until the other one got down the hill and passed the finish line. Leif always beat me by a second or two.

Most frequently we skied at Powderhorn Park, where we and Dad went up and down the hill at our own pace. Sometimes we went to a trail system. When I was around nine we went to Elm Creek in the suburbs, and Mom, Leif, and I started out on a trail loop. Mom and Leif were both walking on their skis, and I was doing the same; however, it still seemed to me there should be some glide component to skiing. I tried this, and within three strides I was gasping for breath and desperately wanting to collapse in the snow. While I stopped to breathe, Mom and Leif skied away from me, not gliding but walking.

Meanwhile, Dad performed a different technique. He threw his poles forward and then shuffled to catch up to them. He didn't care about technique or going fast. He just wanted to work his body hard in the outdoors.

Neither Dad's nor Mom's technique seemed correct to me. I could walk on snowshoes. I wanted to *glide* on my skis.

Once we moved to Bemidji, Dad was excited to ski new trails. Movil Maze, our first destination, was named for its numerous trail intersections. It's laid out like a hand, with a longer "thumb" trail on the north side and an extra digit known as the "pinky loop" on the south end. Connecting trails ruin the finger analogy, and the biggest, meanest hills are not on the middle finger.

My first encounter with Movil Maze, as a freshman in high school, ended as so many of my other ski outings did at the time. Frustrated with my inability to skate ski on my skis despite them being labeled as *skating*, I quickly became upset and was left behind by Dad and Leif. When I tried to glide in the classic style, I got so out of breath I had to stop. By this time Dad and Leif had disappeared at an intersection with two possible routes to take, and I was left to head back for the car.

Leif was on the middle school ski team, which, near the end of the season, had a 3-kilometer kids' race. Leif brought home this colored piece of wax, which was slippery, not sticky like all Dad's other wax. Leif convinced him to use a scraper and remove the sticky wax from my skis, and once most of the wax had been removed, Leif crayoned on the slippery wax without an iron. Leif told me I could now "skate," and my parents convinced me to do the race. This time when I started skating, I could glide and didn't face-plant. Not only was this the first aha moment in my ski career, it was the most pivotal.

When I returned to Movil Maze I could now do a 5-kilometer loop skate skiing. My abilities had been redeemed.

My sophomore year, while still too hesitant to join the ski team, I skied almost every day at the middle school with Dad. While he was off doing his classic shuffle technique, I calculated that I could ski 6 kilometers in an hour using the V1 technique on the flats, essentially a "first gear" for slow conditions like going up hills. I knew no other technique. That February, I entered the 10-kilometer tour that was part of the legendary Minnesota Finlandia race with Leif. It was a cold day, with temperatures below 0 degrees. I wore a baggy sweatshirt and wind pants. The whole tour I raced Leif, and in the end he only beat me by a couple of ski lengths. Previous to this race he had always been way faster than me. While this was just a tour, I was sixteen years old and didn't want to be beaten by my younger brother. This was my first ski race, and though it was a rather unofficial one, it was enough to convince Mom I should get some new ski boots—some real skate boots. The women's pilot version was on sale, but since they wouldn't work with my current bindings I had to get new skis. At the local ski shop in Bemidji, the behemoth sales guy, Devin, pulled some skis off the shelf and put them down on the testing platform to fit them to me; a pair of Zeniths and a pair of Quasars both fit, with the Zeniths being $100 more. That difference was a big sum of money for our family.

"Elspeth, you'll have to pay the extra hundred-dollar difference if you want the Zeniths," Mom said. I thought about it for a couple minutes.

Then Devin cocked his head to the side and asked softly, "Do you want to be at the Quasar of your performance or the Zenith of your performance?"

I chose the Zeniths, and Mom never made me pay the $100 difference.

With my new ski equipment, I finally had the guts to join the ski team my junior year. It wasn't so much a decision to be made anymore but a natural transition following the running season. Leif was on the team, and so were two of my new friends from cross-country, Anna and Kathryn. We practiced often at Movil Maze that year, leaving school in the late afternoon and skiing until it got too dark to see.

Bruceski, as we called him, was the coach, and he taught me how to V2, a skate technique used for going fast on the flats. When I first learned to skate ski, I did so by imitation and, naturally, only used the V1 technique. I could tell other skiers did something different, but it took Bruceski to explain the difference. This was my second big aha moment in skiing. I skied around Movil Maze saying "Glide, pole, glide" as I worked on the timing of the pole plant. I rejoiced whenever I came to a hill and could V1 again.

It was at Movil Maze I put in my distance training on weekends and after school. I skied 17 or 18 kilometers a day, either skiing the outer loop twice or weaving on the inside trails, creating a real maze. Nevertheless, I got bored with the 15 kilometers of total trail.

As I got better, meaning more efficient, on the flats and uphills, I began to enjoy those parts as much as the downhills. Skiing, especially climbing uphill, uses all the muscles in the body: the force begins in the arms, is driven through the core, and results in the legs making the skis glide. There is something about pounding an uphill—being completely out of breath and really tired—that is so masochistic and so addicting. The feeling of moving myself up the hill became as addicting as the feeling of free-falling down a big hill.

One afternoon Bruceski decided we were going to do intervals on a loop that included taking the far-north "thumb" trail and returning on the next-farthest-north "index finger" trail. We divided into three groups: the boys, who had a smaller team than the girls, and two girls' groups, alternating fast and slow skiers so there was a mix in each of the girls' groups. Along the loop were cones. We started with an interval. At the first cone we skied slow and regrouped. Then, at the next cone, we started our next interval. On the 3.6-kilometer loop there were a total of three intervals.

My group went last, about three minutes behind the other girls' group. Andrea, the fastest skier on our team and a natural athlete who made state her first year skiing, and Kathryn, who could have kicked my ass had she not had pneumonia, were both in my group, along with some of our slower skiers. Erin, Kati, and Katie, all skiers who made it to state, were in the first group together with some of the other slower skiers. When it was time for our group to go, Andrea took off, making use of her talents on the flats that made up the first interval. At the end of the first interval we regrouped. The next two intervals were hillier, and by working hard Kathryn and I were able to stick with Andrea. We did the loop a total of three times. By the second loop I could tell Andrea was trying to catch the group that had started three minutes ahead of us, and she increased the pace of both our intervals and our rest. Again she took off on the first mostly flat interval, but Kathryn and I kept pace. By our third loop we were gaining on the other girls' group. We were spread out, as we had not collected the slower skiers during our rest. After the second interval on our third and final loop, Andrea kept hammering. Only Kathryn and I were left. By the start of our last interval of the day, we had made up three minutes on the other girls' group. Andrea and I passed up Katie and Kati, and then I followed behind in pursuit of Andrea and Erin. I tried hard, I skied fast, but I could not catch those two. Yet to have hammered so hard for so long was a breakthrough to the next level of my skiing—a glimpse of what might be possible.

∿∿∿

Movil Maze wasn't always awesome. Like all the other venues near Bemidji, it was on state land that was groomed, at best, weekly by volunteers. During the snowless winters of my high school and college years, Movil Maze held snow surprisingly well, but the temps would occasionally climb above freezing and then drop, leaving the trails covered in a dangerous sheet of ice. It was still better than nothing, but hardly.

December 28, 2004
On Christmas Day I skate skied. We went to Movil—not
really enough snow, so the trail was rutty. I kept stopping.
I stopped at the bottom, middle, and top of every hill! Leif
and I even skipped out on the pinky loop! We only did 13
kilometers total. I decided that severe boredom is part of
my problem at Movil.

On Sunday David drove Leif, Kathryn, and me up to
Movil. Kathryn and I did 13 kilometers again.

Year after year on Christmas break during college I went
home and returned to Movil Maze. It was either 10 degrees
below or 40 above and slushy. My mood was somber, as I
couldn't get in a good workout.

December 24, 2005
I go skating with Jill and Katie at Movil. Conditions are
slush and I seem to be struggling to keep up. We do the
north loop, the west loop, and then come back on middle
finger and call it quits: about 5 kilometers. Those girls are
so bad. "Do you want to ski farther?" I ask and they both
say "I don't care." So I'm thinking that I want to try some
hardcore workout, but they really aren't, so we just stop at
every intersection trying to make a decision and that is so,
so bad. So I come home just pissed from my lack of workout.
And the crummy snow conditions that weren't really favor-
able for much more.

In the PM I did four sets of push-ups to get to 200.
Then I did a version of my abs, which was hopefully longer
than 8 minutes. I also did leg lifts and deltoid raises, both
front and side, with the 10-pound weights.

December 25, 2005
In the afternoon Dad, Leif, and I head out to Movil. The temp is right below freezing. The tracks are solid ice and the skating lane is solid snow ice as well with its usual ruts, the hard-pack center that falls off, and crusted-over skating marks from the past few days of slush. I determined that I am a loop skier. So I skate and I go out the north loop and come back on the first finger. I decide that since the conditions are so wickedly bad I will do four of these loops. Well at least they were fast, with the biggest challenge trying to stay upright and keep a good majority of the weight on one ski only. Well, I did resort to double poling in the super-fast hard tracks part of the time. The caution downhill was wicked fast [and only during these conditions actually worthy of a caution sign], *but I still got in some V2 and V1 although the ruts in the snow made it seem impossible.*

December 26, 2005
Left with no other option, Kathryn, Leif, and I headed to Movil for a double pole workout on the snow ice. We did three loops of 7.5 kilometers each, making use of the flatter north trails to avoid the biggest, iciest downhills. I started feeling fatigue on caution hill at almost 15 kilometers. It was tough. Still, for 22 kilometers of double poling (on ice, so very easy), I should be in much more pain.
    200 push-ups: 60-50-50-40.

I constantly struggled with route choice at Movil, where every kilometer or two an intersection necessitated a decision about which way to go. I could be lazy and avoid all the big hills, but to get better I had to do hills. It was always tempting to stop at intersections and catch my breath before deciding which trail to ski next. Finally, I learned to plan a route before I started skiing.

Mostly, though, I was frustrated that I could never maximize Movil Maze's true potential without abundant snowfall and frequent grooming.

~~~

In college, I took some of my friends to Movil Maze the day after the Finlandia. The snow conditions were perfect, and we skied all the trails at least once. We were in the woods the entire time. My friends, who had spent most of their past skiing time on golf courses, were in awe of the deep forest, hills, and curves. To them it was like an enchanted wonderland. Yet to me Movil Maze had become repetitive, a place to log the kilometers with too many trail intersections. Bringing my friends here, however, made me realize that Movil was a skiing paradise. It also helped that at this point in my life I had other venues to ski throughout the winter. It wasn't until I had skied on my fair share of golf courses in Minneapolis and the exposed manufactured snow loop at Elm Creek that I recognized the true wonder of skiing *in the woods*.

Chapter 7

EDNOS

Growing up I was a skinny girl. Most of the other kids were skinny. My brothers were both skinny, too. I did my fair share of playing at the park and dabbled in sports, but I never worried about my weight or what I ate until puberty.

Suddenly, at eleven, my breasts started bouncing uncomfortably up and down without support when I ran downstairs. It was soon obvious my bust was following the maternal pattern of my family, and Mom took me to Sears to buy a bra.

My first bras were sports bras. They were constricting, requiring contortionist maneuvers to put on, and made me self-conscious. The first few times I went to the store with Mom to buy them I was mortified. When she told the sales-clerks her daughter needed a bra, I had a strong desire to hide myself in the middle of the round clothes racks.

In middle school, as I gradually accepted my B-cup breasts but not my abdominal fat, I began paying attention to what and how much I ate. At breakfast I decreased the amount of cereal in my bowl; however, I didn't understand the idea of cutting overall calories yet, so I made up for it by increasing my milk-to-cereal ratio. For lunch I had a small tray of school french fries and a carton of chocolate milk. At dinner I ate whatever Mom made—usually a healthy portion since I was hungry from lunch. At bedtime I had a snack, which always consisted of a fruit (usually an apple) and a dessert; however, I restricted myself to ice cream once a week. Still, despite my diet, my breasts continued to grow, pounds were added to my body, and my lean form was disappearing.

My lack of physical activity wasn't helping. In the fall I played soccer or volleyball, but the remainder of the year I was a slug. One summer during middle school I had good intentions about starting a running program. I'd heard Oprah Winfrey could run 6 miles in one hour and figured I ought to be able to run 3 miles in thirty minutes. My plan was to run around my city block—three times around equaled 1 mile. Each week I would increase the number of times I ran around the block by one until I could do it nine times. But like all my plans to work out in those early years, the motivation to actually do it wasn't there. I ran just one night that whole summer, and I only made it 1 mile. In those pre–high school days I still hated running.

When I commenced high school volleyball it seemed obvious that I would gain muscle and that it would make my physique more attractive. In reality I noticed little muscle-mass accumulation when I dutifully checked out my shape in the mirror each night after practice.

Playing soccer the next spring helped attenuate my weight increase. Slowly my muscles increased in size, but they were still not very prominent. My sophomore year I really started restricting my eating and joined track as a distance runner.

As I started running a lot and watching what I ate it began a downward spiral. I never missed meals, but I restricted my calorie intake more and more. The exercising eventually hit a plateau, and my running and skiing performance suffered miserably.

June 6, 2001

*In soccer practice yesterday I didn't get a workout at all.
Today I am going to run some fast intervals. Then I will
probably do a sprint workout on Friday. My breasts are
shrinking. It's all this running and then I don't eat a lot either. I've lost 10 pounds in the last six months. That's crazy
considering how much I weighed when I started to lose
weight. All my pants are huge and gross on me. My hips
and legs are a size 1 and my waist is about a size 3, but all
my pants are size 7. I have a pair of shorts that are size 9.*

And just three days later:

June 9, 2001

*I am probably too skinny. I wouldn't really mind gaining
a little weight, but I'd rather stay exactly where I am. My
waist is a good size. It got smaller. My breasts are shrinking.*

*Maybe my problem is that I train excessively. I mean
here it is summer and I'm supposed to be relaxing, but what
the hell am I doing instead? I drag my brother around Lake
Irving for a run, I do sprints around the neighborhood, I've
taken to lunges, and a bike ride to and from Target doesn't
include my workout for the day. It's 'cause I'm worrying
about track next year. I'll be fine.*

When I went clothes shopping for my junior year of high
school I fit into size 12—in girls' sizing.

That was the year I joined cross-country running in the
fall. Since track had gone well the previous year, great things
were expected from me. And for the first two weeks I did great
things. Then I ran 16 miles around Lake Bemidji, and for the
remainder of the season, when running long distances, I was
exhausted. When running fast for intervals and races, my legs
turned to lead.

I lost any desire to push myself. I placed fourth for the team during my first cross-country race, but in the second, teammate after teammate kept passing me during the 4-kilometer race, and I couldn't respond. My legs wouldn't move faster. For the third race, I was on varsity as our sixth runner. Going into the race my quads kept tightening when I ran at practice, and suddenly it seemed harder to stay with the top girls. When the gun went off, all the other girls took off, and I quickly found myself almost in last place. No matter how I tried I couldn't catch any of them. My first mile was a 6:48, the same time as my stellar first meet, but now two weeks later I found myself at the back of the pack. Everyone else was getting into better shape, and I remained stagnant. After the first mile it got worse—my quads were so tight I couldn't move them. It was too much work to stay with the other girls, and on the final hill I gave in and walked. As I came down the home stretch about a half mile from the finish, I passed one of my teammates, who had collapsed on the ground. I knew even though I would be finishing dead last in the race, I would be our fifth scorer for the team and felt all the more horrible.

It got still worse from there.

September 14, 2001
Today I am both physically and mentally tired. Yeah, I know, being worn out is a mental state, but sometimes I need to listen to my body, which is telling me I need to gain at least 10 pounds. Barney says by the end of the season we should be running 60 miles a week. The race is only 2.5 miles.

Yesterday after I raced I thought I was going to puke. For supper I had like four tater tots (Emma's leftovers with lots of grease), a tomato, and half of a peanut butter and jelly sandwich. Then I didn't feel too good. Sometimes I get real hungry, but usually when I get done with practice or running it doesn't feel right to eat. Running kinda replenishes the body of its food. I try to eat but I know I probably consume fewer calories than I burn. That is scary. Sometimes that scares me; I panic in fear my heart will stop. Then I have a snack and feel as if I have eaten too much. Then I want to exercise more. Lately it's gotten really hard to exercise, like the fuel isn't there. For me it's all mental. Mom asked me last night if I wanted to go see a psychiatrist. Can a psychiatrist change my compulsive traits? Do I want to change my compulsive nature?

September 18, 2001
Running sucks. There seems to be no point—only running all out, and I have difficulty doing so. After the last meet I didn't think it possible to get a worse time, but I did. Every race gets worse. My chin quivers and the tears start pouring. No, the tears shall not come, I am strong and already dehydrated. I don't want a headache or to feel the pressure the tears bring to my head. But the tears come anyway.

My race was so horrible, and looking back I ask why? Why did I walk? Why did I not go with those girls? Why do I not want to push myself anymore? The answer is evident and makes sense: my legs get tired. Rarely anything else—only my legs. And then I give in and walk. It is so lowly. The girls pass me and cheer me on. I know I can run faster. I have run faster before. Girls pass me and I start running ever so slowly but exerting so much effort. It used to be easier, or so it seemed. Those girls think "At least I'm not walking." At the halfway point I was about 45th. Had I not stopped to walk I could have maintained that spot. And so I reflect on my race and consider what I should have done, forgetting how tired I was at the time. I capitulated. My new motto: I will not capitulate. Next race I'm gonna get a time in the 18-minute range. Maybe I won't start as

fast. But no matter what I will not capitulate. I will not
surrender the race before the gun goes off. Nor will I walk
even one step. I will not capitulate.

The last cross-country meet of my junior year was a home
invite. Afterwards, I was too disgusted with myself to write
a journal entry. My plan was to run hard and fast, but once I
got into the race my quads wouldn't move, as if I were running
in a dream. On the backside of the course, where my parents
were cheering, there was a long, gradual uphill we had to go
up twice. I made it up OK the first time, but the second time I
started walking. Dad started jogging alongside me. It was the
only thing that kept me going. It was so embarrassing. I finished last and had added three minutes to my time from less
than two months earlier at the first meet. I was experiencing
burnout.

At practice even our easy distance days often turned into
long intervals. The goal would be to go for a 6-mile run, but
inevitably someone started pushing the pace, and then it became a race of sorts until we were almost sprinting near the
end. We were young. We lacked enough experienced seniors
to keep us going slow and keep our heart rates low on the
distance runs. We had new freshman gazelles. The fear of not
being able to run fast enough for each and every workout accumulated, contributing to my mental burnout.

For example, at cross-country camp we did a 15-mile
workout day. The idea was not actually to run 15 miles but
rather a total of two hours—to first run for forty minutes,
then thirty-two, then twenty-four, then sixteen, then finally
eight, with a half-hour break between each session. But while
the runs were meant to be easy, the fast girls would run at an
eight-minute mile pace and outdistance at least half of the
boys' team, and I felt obligated to keep up with them. Barney allowed us to bike or rollerblade one or two of the runs

instead of running, but the fastest never resorted to wheeled transportation; they were too competitive. An eight-minute mile pace added up to 15 miles in two hours—about twice as far as usual for me. Pushing all those miles was a clear recipe for burnout. Not eating enough obviously didn't help.

> *September 29, 2001*
> *Sometimes when I'm out running I get scared and doubt my ability, being as I am so skinny. I tire easily, and then I wonder if I'm killing myself because I'm too thin. Weight keeps coming off my body. I would be OK if I didn't run 30 miles every week. Last week Mom bought a scale, and after practice I weighed 96 pounds with socks, jeans, a shirt, and underwear on. On Wednesday at practice, Sherri [our other coach] asked me if I ate enough and if I had lost any weight since cross-country started. I don't know if I've lost any weight, but it seems like I eat a lot. What I eat, though, is not high in calories. Today I feel hungry all the time.*

I began wishing for time-outs during my 2.5-mile cross-country races. It seemed unfair—a stop-and-start sport such as football has time-outs. Yet the sport that really seemed to need time-outs, the sport that pits the need to go into oxygen debt against the mind telling the body to stop, has none.

∿∿∿

In February of my junior year I reached my lowest weight: 87 pounds on my 5-foot, 1-inch body. I had lost 20 pounds over a year and a half. I no longer got my period. My eating habits consumed my daily life. I was exercising a lot and not increasing my food intake to compensate. Restricting left me constantly hungry. I loved food; between meals I became fixated on what I would eat for my next meal, little as it would be.

<u>*February 10, 2002*</u>
All I can think about, all I can focus on, is food. I'm eating raisins now. I feel like I've eaten a lot today. For breakfast I had a bowl of Raisin Bran, a bowl of Cheerios, with milk and a banana. It was Jess's [a neighbor friend my same age] *birthday today, and our family was invited over there. I consumed a very small pickle, two deviled eggs, five crackers, two pieces of herring, and a few sweet pickles. Then I went home and had a piece of bread with peanut butter on it and a few apple slices. At ski school I had two mini sub sandwiches and some baby carrots. Then I came home and couldn't resist this strawberries-and-cream-cheese breakfast bar. I had a bowl of the noodle casserole leftover from yesterday's dinner, and now I am eating a small box of raisins which remains in my Halloween candy bag. I am really anal, able to recall everything I ate since I got out of bed this morning. That can't be good. Plus half of what I ate is processed, sugar, artificial, or just plain junk. Some days I consume lots of crap, which I vow to exercise off after I beat myself up over it. Then I won't eat any junk food for the next two or three days.*

Today I only skied 5 kilometers. Yesterday I skied 20 kilometers in crap snow conditions. The conditions today were perfect.

<u>*March 20, 2002*</u>
Tonight Mom made me go to the doctor about my weight issue. I do have some issues, I'm not sure how much—psychological disorders are hard to measure. On any given day I am unsure of how many calories I consume, but I have not been consuming enough lately, which is evident when I experience ravenous hunger and then try to ski 7 or 8 miles. I am an overachiever, and the "over" can be emphasized. Extreme—I go to the extreme to pursue perfection. I'm

all about practice, which should ideally lead to improved performance.

Right now I weigh about 90 pounds. Until a few days ago my daily diet consisted of two cartons of skim milk, orange juice, an orange, 1.5 cups of Cheerios, a huge leafy green salad with fresh veggies for lunch, a bread roll, some other food (cottage cheese, soup, dessert), and whatever I had for dinner. But now I have to gain 10 pounds, and I don't want to stop working out. I am a distance runner in track. I'm signed up to run the 2-mile on Saturday. I hate the feeling I get when I "overeat." Eating healthy makes me feel cleansed. I feel good. When I eat junk I imagine my arteries becoming clogged. Moreover, after I exercise I feel whole and pure and then I fill myself with food, which makes me feel impure again.

What is wrong with me? How sick am I? How sick do I sound? Am I denying to myself I have a problem? I don't want to have a problem. I don't think I am anorexic. I do not refuse to maintain a healthy body weight. Yet I burn more calories than I consume, and my breasts are getting smaller. Everybody has a weight problem. Food tempts me, and I try to control this temptation. I know I have to eat in order to exercise. I know when I do not consume enough food I am hungry and I am doing myself no good to work out. I don't want to stop exercising, which means I need to eat more—of what is my problem. I can start by eating a bigger breakfast and some more before bed. This is ridiculous, though, unless I want to be branded with anorexia. It is imperative I begin eating more.

March 26, 2002
Yesterday I had an appointment with the nutritionist. She said she would help me make healthy choices but that ultimately it is up to me to implement the healthy choices.

I was basically diagnosed with exercise bulimia. I have an obsessive-compulsive problem with exercise. It doesn't help that track coach Phelps says, "There is no secret to track and field—when you're not working out, someone else is." That may be true, but according to this statement one must work out 24 hours a day. Yesterday I went on a speed work-out—who said we have to out-train our competition? Is there no end?

Until Mom intervened I was consuming very few calories and skiing a lot, which supposedly burns 900 calories per hour. For a couple days I boosted my calorie intake, but now I'm going down again. I go back to my game again. For lunch, besides veggies and an apple, I had skim milk, a bread roll, and a half cup or less of cottage cheese. For supper I had mashed potatoes, fish, corn, and a salad and denied myself a dessert. Is this too little food consumption?

Deep down, although I wouldn't admit it to Mom, I was worried about being too thin. Yet I also liked being thin. It showed my control at the same time many of my peers were gaining weight.

∿∿∿

My first year of track, my sophomore year, I had come out strong, determined to keep up with the very best on every workout. By junior year I was deep in burnout and way too skinny. My best mile of the season was a 6:47. I couldn't push myself and thought that was the root cause. Before each race I said, "This is going to be the race. I'm going to break through this feeling of not being able to push myself, and I'm going to run fast and get a good time." But the race came, I couldn't push myself, and I was disappointed. I wondered whether it was because I was too thin or because I was burned out from training too much. I learned that in the world of individual sports, there are no easy answers. There are simply too many variables.

I wasn't the only one who burned out. It happened to Jimbob, too. And in him I saw a mirror of myself. Jimbob, a quiet, smart kid two years my junior who had his mind set on going to MIT, was having a stellar year in athletics. He quit playing soccer and ran some of the top times on the varsity cross-country team. But then he ran a superdistance week at Barney's recommendation, some 60 or 70 miles compared to the usual 30 that we normally logged, and he was never the same after. From that time on, watching Jimbob race was like watching a tortoise. It was painful. He couldn't push himself anymore.

A reflection about pushing myself surfaces in a journal entry from before my own first cross-country meet.

August 26, 2001
Tuesday is approaching, and I'm not looking forward to it. The first meet. Barney said not to worry about it, but I do. Running 2.5 miles doesn't scare me, I know I can go the distance, it's the speed. It's pushing myself for that length of time. It is essential to run the race smartly. This is my first meet ever, and I should just go out there and relax and not care about anything, but I do. I know I want to run 7-minute miles consistently. I want to finish within the top seven girls from Bemidji to secure a spot on varsity. It's pressure I enforce on myself, but if I don't, if I don't care about the race, then I won't push myself at all, and after I will be mad about my performance.

It's this last sentence—the fear about not going hard enough and regretting it later—that nags all endurance athletes.

After my burnout junior year, I vowed to have a better senior cross-country season. I had one simple goal: to be as fast at the end of the season as I was at the beginning. I believe it also helped that I began eating more and by the start of the season had gained 10 pounds from my lowest point six months previous.

The second day of practice we ran three timed miles. My times were 7:05, 7:21, and 7:21. The first one was fastest because it was both downhill and with the wind.

At the first meet of the year, I was scared shitless about racing. I planned to start in the back of the girls on our team, settle in for an easy first mile, and then begin the passing game.

Barney glared at me when he saw where I'd lined up. "I want you up there in that top five," he chided.

August 27, 2002

Yup, I thought, but in my own time. The gun went off and I was in the third line of Bemidji girls. Everybody sprinted, but I hung back and relaxed. Only Kathryn of the Bemidji girls was behind me. Before the first turn, however, I had passed Anna, Amber, and Tanya. By the next turn, a half mile into the race, I had passed lots of girls. A mile into the race I was still feeling good and gaining on that Bemidji top five, having passed Kristin, Rachael, Shauna, and Dana and many other girls with ease. Another quarter mile and I passed Sarah, then I passed Abby. At the 1.5-mile mark I was working on Becca and about to catch her. I caught her, but instead of passing her I ran with her, my mouth now open, my breathing making a rasping noise. Then I got stupid. I cut in behind Becca, shortening my stride. Barney was at the 2-mile mark telling us we had to pass girls. I don't remember how many we passed—maybe only two, but again I cut in behind her. With a quarter mile left, at the last flag, I began my kick. I knew it was an early kick, but I was determined to beat Becca. I desperately wanted the finish line. I became vaguely aware of my quads giving up the last 100 meters. But finally I crossed the white line, unable to catch the green girl in front of me. I remember wobbling from side to side, unable to walk straight, turning around to see Becca two places behind me, peeling off my label to give to the lady, hugging Becca and drooling on her shoulder. Then I walked to team camp and got my water bottle.

I was 5th for Bemidji with 40th place overall, same place as last year. My time was 18:20, a personal record and six seconds faster than last year's PR on the same course. I never got passed by anyone the entire race—I probably passed 40 girls. My first mile was 7:13, my second 7:24, and my last half 3:44, which is fairly consistent. I have found my racing style, and if I remain steady all season I will be happy, although I hope to improve. Unfortunately I do best at big meets.

A few days later I ran around Lake Bemidji—the only girl on the team to do so, *and* I beat all the guys. This 16-mile run was sandwiched between some hard interval sessions. Our next meet didn't go as smoothly as the first of the season:

September 6, 2002
Today was the Crazy Shorts race. My first mile was good, but by that second mile that back hill really got to me. My quads got really, really tired, and I was barely running down the downhills. Abby caught back up with me and I should have gone with her (OK—for next race), but I let her go and then I was so tired I walked a little and then I kept going but I was so tired . . . oh my god . . . my quads were so tired and it was hot and I couldn't kick it in. I got 10th or 11th for the team. My time was 19:39—1:19 slower than at the first meet. I am so ready for two slacker days. I didn't even make use of the downhill and kick it in at the finish. It sucked, but now at least I'll be racing JV, which I

prefer to varsity—more people to beat. I wonder how much that stupid hill, my training, and my attitude influence my performance? I wish there was a way to measure it all. So many should-haves . . . I need to get focused and get into my race better. Next race. Just relax.

The remainder of the season played out similarly. I walked some part of every race except for the first and last of the season. I distinctly remember the Thief River Falls meet—I was running well, I was racing Becca, but with 800 meters to go my will to keep forcing myself into oxygen debt gave out, and I stopped and walked.

Near the end of the season I was able to test my goal twice. First, we repeated the three individual timed miles for practice. My times were again in the low sevens, and I was satisfied I was still able to run that fast.

The last meet of the season, I was determined to be in the top nine so that I could at least be an alternate for the section team. I had little desire to finish in the top seven, however, as that would merely mean another race and another eighteen minutes of making my body suffer. During the race I was keeping up with Becca for the first mile, which we ran in 6:50. Then I let her go, but I could sense she didn't want to run one more race any more than I did. Cross-country is a tough sport. When I crossed the finish line the clock read 18:20—the same time I had gotten two months earlier in the first meet of the season. I had achieved my simple goal: to be as fast at the end of the season as I'd been at the beginning.

It seemed at this point in my life I was over my burnout. I was once again able to push myself, and just in time for my senior ski and track seasons.

There are both physical contributors to burnout, like overtraining and anorexia, and mental ones, like the inability to push far into oxygen debt, pressure from oneself and others, and the perceived pressure from others augmenting the self-pressure. This makes me think of my friend Wally, four years my junior, also from Bemidji. Throughout his middle and high school years he was the poster child of cross-country skiing. He was an exceptional skier at a young age, no doubt as a result of a father who was a ski fanatic himself, and among Wally's friends there was always a sense that it was OK if they didn't perform—Wally would pull them along. He was a talented runner as well: at age fourteen, after winning a junior high cross-country meet, he said to me, "Elspeth, running is so mental." I knew for him, skiing was mental, too, but not as much. There are even more variables in skiing than there are in running, like snow conditions and wax and hills. And the downhills can provide a sort of time-out when not too technical.

In my case, my running burnout was no doubt attributable to numerous factors. I don't know whether the eating disorder was completely to blame, but it certainly contributed. And perhaps the burnout propelled my eating disorder. Eating was something I could control, unlike my mental preoccupation with racing.

~~~

I thought I was getting better about eating enough, but the summer after I graduated high school I was running a lot and not always getting enough food.

August 6, 2003
I am too skinny again. Mom made me get on the scale this morning. I only weigh 90 pounds. I was devastated when I found this out. I haven't been trying to lose weight. It really sucks 'cause now Mom's threatening to take things away, like rowing. [I had intentions of being a walk-on for the University of Minnesota rowing team.] *I just*

hate eating past the full point and thinking about food con-
stantly. I don't think I work out that much, but apparently
I do. So now I have to gain weight again, and that means
no more flat stomach. I hate being hungry all the time, but
half the time there is no good food to eat in the house. Then
what am I supposed to do?

In college I took a class on abnormal psychology, in which I learned about *eating disorder not otherwise specified*, or ED-NOS. This disorder falls somewhere between anorexia and bulimia. I never stopped eating, but when I ate more, I exercised more. As the months of restriction wore on and I became more and more hungry, I began to binge eat. After these episodes I berated myself and convinced myself the next day I would restrict more and exercise even more. These intermittent episodes of binge eating fit neither the criteria for anorexia, as that disease is merely restricting, nor those for bulimia, as that involves a compensatory purging.

My freshman year at the University of Minnesota I continued to exercise. I became a member of the cross-country ski club and began training for ski marathons. I continued to obsess over food. That is, until the day of my first ski marathon.

In one day, during just one ski race, I became cured of ED-NOS forever. I was eighteen and doing the 58-kilometer skate race during the Mora Vasaloppet. Before dawn I woke, walked across campus, and got in a passenger van with eight other students in the ski club. I was the only girl. On the van ride my organic chemistry book lay across my lap as I took meticulous reading notes. In the town of Mora, in east-central Minnesota, we piled out of the van and got on school buses with our skis. The buses took us north, to the start of the point-to-point race. We kept driving, farther and farther away from the town, until the bus dropped us off in a field lined with flags from many nations throughout the world. Over the next several hours we would ski from this field back south to Mora. I couldn't believe how far it was.

In the starting corral I lined up even with the sign reading "Expected finish 4 hours 30 minutes." Above me flags flapped in the breeze. As I waited for the start, I wondered how I could ski 35 miles back to the town. I had never even skied half the distance before in one day. What the hell was I doing?

Before the race, for breakfast I had eaten only some PowerBar samples and a Clif Bar from the stockpile in my dorm room. We had left for the race long before the dining hall opened, and I was too cheap to purchase food. I thought what I'd eaten would be sufficient but had neglected that in addition to my usual calorie restriction, the previous day I had gone skiing in the park for a couple of hours. I was calorie deficient before the race even began.

I bypassed the first feed station. At the second I took water instead of energy drink even though I had already bonked. I kept skiing. I was hungry, but stopping to eat would waste precious time in the race, and I wanted to save my calories for more enjoyable food rather than energy drink and bananas. So although the hunger grew and grew, I never stopped to eat.

With about 10 kilometers to go we approached the outskirts of Mora and began passing houses. The empty feeling in my stomach was making me crazy. Little glucose was supplying my brain; my body had long been using my meager fat stores. I began fantasizing about skiing up to one of the houses and going inside and raiding the occupants' refrigerator in the hopes of finding food, any food, lots of food. These thoughts of pillaging were ludicrous, and yet I was so consumed with the idea of filling my stomach to satisfaction.

When I crossed the finish line after four hours and six minutes, disbelief overwhelmed me: I had just skied 35 miles! I had just finished my first marathon! Then the hunger came back. I ate the best banana of my life and then walked to the high school, where I ate a cheese sandwich and chili. It was heavenly.

The experience of racing a marathon without proper nutrition made me realize my disease had progressed too far. I could be skinny or I could be an athlete, but I couldn't be both.

Never again could I tolerate being that hungry, and so I began eating to satisfaction—and sometimes beyond—to fuel my body appropriately for my training volume. I finally built muscle mass and got strong. Since I stopped restricting food, I've never had that same desire to pillage, and I've never been quite that hungry. But every year in the Vasaloppet, when I ski by those houses, I think of my first marathon, when my desire for food became all-consuming.

Chapter 8

Making It Happen

When I was a child, Dad often took our family to the high school girls' state basketball tournament on the University of Minnesota campus. He'd park on the West Bank of the campus, where parking was free, and we'd walk across the double-decker Washington Avenue Bridge. Dad was completely enamored by this bridge spanning the tall banks of the Mississippi River; he talked incessantly about the uniqueness of motorized transport traveling across the bottom deck while bikers and pedestrians went across the top deck.

From the East Bank side of the bridge we trudged to Williams Arena. Since the tournament happened in early March, the weather was usually nippy, and there were some snow piles to dodge. I always hoped we'd arrive in time for the pregame pump-up so I could watch as the starting lineup got to run under an arch created by their teammates while "Charge" played over the speakers. I always picked a blonde with a ponytail whom I wanted to be like someday, even though I was a brunette and short and couldn't even dribble, let alone shoot a basketball. Watching those games ignited a flame in me, a desire to make it to state myself in one sport or another when I got to high school. But though I attempted to call myself an athlete by defining myself as a cross-country runner and skier, I wasn't varsity caliber.

"We're gonna make it to state in skiing," Leif kept saying the summer before my senior year of high school.

"We gotta make varsity first," I kept repeating back.

This seemed impossible. There were so many girls on the team better than me. Some of them even had roller skis and were going to training camps during the summer while all I did was run. That was before I owned my own roller skis or thought to have Mom make me some bungees or knew about hill bounding.

But somewhere deep inside me, the desire to make it to state persisted. It appeared the cards had already been dealt, and the reality was tough to bear, but I had a lot of determination.

On a cold November morning, while on a run training for the upcoming ski season, I committed myself to trying as hard as I could and pouring my heart into making it to state. As I played the oboe in band, my plan solidified. Last year I had been the twelfth skater and the thirteenth classical skier on the team. We had graduated just two seniors. We had amazing depth. We could all push each other, so our top seven were good enough to edge out Grand Rapids to make it to state. And so the plan was born: I would be good enough to be one of the seven, and as a team we would beat Grand Rapids at sections. That was how I would earn my state berth.

This plan was based on the premise that I could never qualify individually for state and the belief that making varsity would be an incredibly difficult endeavor.

The first meet of the season, on a Friday night, involved relays on the lighted trail at Bemidji Middle School. Each team member skied two loops for a total of 4 kilometers. Bruceski, the head coach, decided we could pick our own teams of three skiers. To no one's surprise, the Big Three—a trio of girls who had all made it to state individually the previous year—joined forces in an attempt to take down Grand Rapids' own trio of dominant skiers. We had two other girls' varsity teams, and I was chosen for the first JV team.

Before the race, however, Bruceski took me aside. "I have no intentions of you being a JV skier this year," he declared. "You are racing the same course as the varsity girls. If you ski faster than some of the varsity girls, you will be on varsity next race."

His belief in me built incredible confidence. It was the exact opposite of my soccer coach yelling at me to "Get in the game!" when I had that terrible headache from too many headers. As the fastest skate skier of my JV trio, I skied the anchor relay leg. While my teammate Anna was on her final lap, I took my warm-ups off and stood at the start in my spandex. I thought about the corners in the race. I thought about how I should ski in the moment and ski each part of the course as fast as possible. I pretended to be fast. I was just going to pretend I was good. These thoughts kept me warm despite the freezing December weather.

Then Anna tagged me, and I was off skiing as hard and fast as I could. I put all my weight and energy into every pole and kept my legs moving. On the second lap my skis came out from under me on a slight corner, but I got up quickly and gave some extra-hard V1s to get my momentum back. I was skiing like I was on varsity.

The results came in. They didn't seem possible—I had taken the JV field to school. My first-ever blue ribbon, and two at that: one for individual and one for the team! But moreover, my time placed me fifth among the Bemidji girls. I would be on varsity for the next skate race. My plan was working.

The next race was classic technique in Ely. Despite it being December in northern Minnesota, temperatures rose to 45 degrees for the race. The sticky yellow goop we put on our kick zones wasn't kicking for any of us. It was a terrible two-lap race. There were several striding hills, so I pretended to have working kick wax, but it was pointless. I started double poling up the hills, but the wet snow clumped in the big baskets of my touring poles, weighing them down and preventing the tips from getting the grip to propel me forward. I was coming off a cold and badly needed to hock up a loogie; with each big breath the phlegm rattled in my throat. At the end of the race I finally coughed it up. I finished ninth for the team but passed it off—it was a classic-technique race, which was not my strong suit.

Our next race was a team skate relay at Mount Itasca. Due to my superb results from the first skate race, I got placed on a team with the Big Three. We would be trying to beat such powerhouses as Ely, Duluth East, and our primary rival, Grand Rapids. I knew that to be competitive I needed some real racing poles. I junked my touring poles, with their simple loop straps and big-ass baskets, and for $100 bought new poles made from 100 percent carbon. They were incredibly light and had Velcro straps. They were so awesome I used them for both skate and classic.

The night before the big relay my stomach was queasy, and I found myself hugging the toilet. I was so nervous. But there was no way I was giving up this opportunity to race with the Big Three. My stomach settled some overnight, and I was able to choke down a little food before the race.

Each relay leg consisted of three 1.5-kilometer loops on the manufactured snow at Mount Itasca. This was my first time cross-country skiing on manufactured snow; Mount Itasca was one of the first venues in Minnesota to specifically make snow for cross-country skiing, likely because of the exceptional biathlete training program at nearby Grand Rapids. Most of the skiers on the Grand Rapids team were biathletes and trained extensively, including in the off-season.

During warm-up loops with Leif, I discovered there was a big hill with a sharp right turn coming down to where the trail runs parallel to the parking lot. Each time I went down the hill I stopped at the top and then stood up while skiing down to increase my wind resistance and curtail my speed even more. It wasn't that big of a hill, but it was the biggest I had skied on yet that year.

I skied the second relay leg for my team. I tagged off in fourth or fifth place and tried desperately to hold that position. Upon coming to the big hill for the first lap I slowed my pace slightly. I went into a tuck and surprised myself at how well I was doing when suddenly my skis slid out from under me and my body kept going.

I got up quickly and saw my hat lying 10 feet up the hill—meaning I had slid at least that far on my head down that hill. I thought about going back to get the hat, but my competitive nature kicked in.

"Shit, Elspeth, go, go, go—you're racing with the Big Three!" I shouted at myself.

It was pure hell having to do that hill two more times. I lost a few places for my team, and we were out of league with Grand Rapids and the other powerhouses. The third- and fourth-leg relay skiers were unable to make up much ground. Our team came in fourth, behind Grand Rapids, Duluth East, and Ely.

Our next race was over Christmas break at Blueberry Hills, where the outhouses have heart-shaped holes. It was a skate race with a very small field. There wasn't much snow, so part of the course had to be eliminated, which meant doing two loops. We couldn't warm up on the course, so instead we did a 1-kilometer loop five times. I kept lapping girls on this warm-up loop.

There were only a handful of other schools racing, and none of the powerhouses were present. Bruceski wanted to make sure we swept both the varsity and JV races, so he stacked the JV race pretty heavily with some of our varsity skiers. What ensued was rather embarrassing: the race turned into pure intersquad competition.

Bruceski put me on varsity. The race had interval starts, and I was one of the last skiers to start. Right from the beginning, I wasn't having a good race; I felt off-balance and almost fell backward several times. I just could not break into a good V2. Moreover, there were two gravity box hills on the course, which scared the dickens out of me. I started twenty-third in the varsity lineup, which meant I had to pass a lot of slow girls, but the trails were too narrow for two skiers, so passing was difficult. I was going up a steep V1 hill when I came up fast on another girl.

"Track, track!" I yelled, but she didn't get out of my way. I moved over as far to the left as I could, but as I was passing her my ski tip got caught in her skis, and I fell.

"Fucking shit! Get the fuck out of the way!" came from my uncensored mouth.

Next there was a big downhill with a sharp right turn at the bottom. I should've been able to step turn but ended up snowplowing around the corner completely out of control. Then I was on to my second and less eventful lap, talking to myself the whole way down the gravity box: "Elspeth, you got this, you got this." Since I had started so late in the lineup, most of the girls had already finished, and there was less congestion the second lap.

Our varsity swept the race. Our five skiers took all five top spots. I got second place behind Andrea. JV fared similarly. I beat Erin, who had gone to state the year before. I felt like a star walking to the podium to claim my red second-place ribbon. My whole life I'd been looking at the good kids on the podium at the other meets. And now here I was, one of the good kids.

Two days later we skied at the Mesabi East Invitational, the largest high school cross-country ski meet in the country.

Our team was divided between classical and skate skiers, so there were only five of us skating. I warmed up with Andrea, who encouraged me, telling me I would beat her. I think she said that to take some pressure off herself, as it's not easy to always be expected to be the top girl.

My teammate Kati, who had been vacationing with her family in Mexico and arrived at the venue only ten minutes before her start time, started two minutes in front of me. I went out hard with a skier named Danielle from Grand Rapids. I tried hard to keep her in sight, especially since she was "my girl"—the one I would have to beat at sections. I was trying so hard to keep up that as I neared the top of the uphill known as the "Triple Up" my vision started going black. I refused to back off, though, and as I caught my breath the blackness disappeared.

With 1.5 kilometers to go on the 5-kilometer course, Bruceski was standing at the bottom of a big uphill.

"Kati just went over the top! Go get Kati!" he yelled. Before the race Bruceski had told me it was my job to beat Kati. Since she started two minutes in front of me, I didn't need to even catch or pass her; I just had to make up time on her.

I dug in with a hard V1 up that hill, hoping to see Kati when I crested the top. To my dismay, she was nowhere in sight. Still I pushed hard, my lungs burning. I kept pushing and did the best V2 sprint across the finish line I had ever done, but I never caught Kati. I never even saw her.

When the results came in, however, I had beaten her by two seconds. Danielle had beaten me by about thirty seconds. Kati had gone to state the year before; Danielle and I were the sixth girls on our respective teams, and Kati was the third. She would have to bump it up for sections if we were going to beat Grand Rapids as a team.

Later in the season we returned to Mount Itasca for a pursuit race in which we did a 5-kilometer classic race in the morning followed by a 5-kilometer skate in the afternoon, starting based on the morning's results, with a combined time and placement.

January 17, 2003
Today I skied at Mount Itasca at our first and only pursuit this season. It was also our last regular season meet. The classic tracks were so beautiful. I'm convinced I'm going to dream about them. Oh, they were so deep and firm on the manufactured snow compared to the shallow washed-out tracks on the natural snow we've been skiing on. My skis stayed in them perfectly. Grandpa and Grandma L even came. That was surprising, as this was the first school event my grandparents ever attended and seeing as they didn't even go to my Mom's high school graduation. They did leave before I started racing. I ended up sixth on the team for classic, which made me very happy. Maybe it wasn't exactly my dream position, but it was pretty damn good. I had this big fall and tore up my stomach. It hurt real bad so Kathryn rubbed it with this alcohol pad that made it sting a lot, then she wrapped it up in this big bandage. It didn't hurt again, but I did realize it looked like I got my appendix taken out. The skate race sucked because the snow was so much like frozen mush. Manufactured snow acts weird. Well, it was a truly awesome course. All the hills I thought were huge at the last race had shrunk in size. The uphills were awesome, although choppy with snow. Then this girl really pissed me off. I was #138 and she was #129 [meaning she had started a few minutes before me, as it was an interval start]. *I kept yelling "On your left!" and she wouldn't move, so finally I screamed "Fucking move!" She fell on the next downhill and I thought "Serves you right." Of course, I almost fell too, and the crowd went wild. Yeah, Kathryn beat me in the skate race by a tenth of a second.*

In skiing we like to think that every second counts. So does every a tenth of a second. I ended up sixth in the skate and sixth in the pursuit among the Bemidji girls. I beat Kari, Heather, and Mandy in every race. That pretty much puts me on varsity. Of course, I still have lots of work to do because I'm not too satisfied with these results. I want to beat Kati again and be third for the team. More important, with Bryndon, Grand Rapids' top skier, in Poland [at Biathlon Junior Worlds], *I need to beat Sara and Anna of Grand Rapids so we can secure the Section 8 Girls 2003 Cross-Country Ski title. Yup, Grand Rapids is going down. I'm going to state, baby.*

Yup, the mental game, the psychology of ski racing. For me, skiing has become all-consuming in a much happier, exciting way than running. I can push myself in skiing without feeling that push. And I'm going somewhere. Schoolwork has been put on hold as I focus and dwell on skiing. Poor Mandy, she had a mega mental letdown leading into the season, and it persisted through this race. She watched all her goals dissipate this one race where she so desperately needed to kick butt. After today I understand the importance of the physical work involved to be a top-performing ski racer, but for the first time in my life, I truly believe the mental attitude is most emphasized and exists as the final determining factor. Yes, to not think about those that start behind, to forget about them and instead focus on those individuals one can catch and pass determines greatness, separates winners from losers. To always see that finish line and see no one in front. The mind is capable of exceeding the physical forces of the body.

Leading up to sections, I tried to assume the same attitude that had brought me my first blue ribbon back in December.

January 26, 2003
There are only one and a half weeks until sections. That's
when I release my ultimate can of whoop-ass and have the
race of my life. It's scary. Sections used to be eons away;
now it's practically here. I have two races this week: one is
skating at Mount Itasca and the second is classical at Lake
Bemidji State Park. This is it. Mostly, though, I need to
learn to relax 'cause I know all I gotta do is ski, and skiing
hard will come in the race. I gotta walk up there like I own
the place and pretend I am the best. I want to beat a lot
of people, and now is my chance. I have names I need to
catch that I can catch. This is it, this is the time of my life.
No regrets, no capitulating, only a go-get-'em attitude! It's
time to open that can of whoop-ass that's been building for
18 years.

In the next Mount Itasca race, we raced our section rivals,
Grand Rapids, and it didn't go well. I finished in fine position to be on varsity, but now I was thinking heavily about
state. The format of the race involved some of the team skiing
classic technique in the morning and the rest of the team skiing skate technique in the afternoon, with a combined team
score. We had stacked the classic race, and when it finished
we were ahead of Grand Rapids. Then our weaker skiers all
skated, and we weren't able to hold our lead. It seemed a bad
omen that we might not actually go to state as a team. It was
something I didn't want to think about. However, the fact
that Grand Rapids' best skier, Bryndon, would miss sections
to race in Europe provided a glimmer of hope.

A few days later we hosted a classic race at Lake Bemidji
State Park, with the team from Buffalo on the start list. They
were ranked eighth in the state.

"After tomorrow they won't be," I flippantly asserted to
my team the night before the race.

There really wasn't enough snow for a classic race, and the groomed tracks were soft and shallow. The course was 4 kilometers, and I had no expectation of doing well. I was about to line up at the back of the Bemidji row when Katie told me to get in front of her. That put me fourth in our lineup. As I took my first double pole at the start of the race, the skier figurine on my necklace, my good luck charm, bumped my teeth. Then I was off, poling hard and trying not to slow Katie up.

She passed me early, but I was hot on her tail, trying to stay with her. I felt great, really able to push my body. It was above freezing, necessitating sticky kick wax, and my kick was pretty good thanks to some orange goop I had found in our teammate David Grundy's wax box. My glide was also good. I ran up the hills, my skis sliding out to pavement at times. I kept working hard, double poling strong and running fast up the hills. My heart was pounding, but I was fifth for my team and staying in front of Buffalo's fifth girl. As I double poled down the final stretch, Bruceski was cheering, calling me the Classic Guru. It was my breakthrough classic race and defined me as a competent classic skier. Bemidji beat Buffalo that day.

And now I was on varsity—on the brink of making it to state.

With the refrain from Green Day's "Good Riddance" echoing in my head, I toed the line at sections for the pursuit race. We were at Maplelag Resort, where owner Jay Richards's meticulous grooming allowed for an exceptional course despite the scarcity of snow.

After the classic race I was exhausted. Trying to live up to my new "Classic Guru" title, I had pushed very hard. I was the fifth classic skier on our team and finished sixteenth overall. Finishing just ahead of me, Danielle from Grand Rapids had collapsed in the snow. Despite temps in the teens, I wanted to curl up in the soft white snow and take a nap under the February sun.

The results after the classic race placed Bemidji ahead of Grand Rapids. We were excited to be knocking on our rival's door, and the possibility of making it to state as a team was imminent. For most of the season we were divided: the Big Three did their own thing at practices and had their own pump-up speeches. They were elite. They had all made it to state before. They had announced before the first race they would be making it to state again, and we were welcome to join them. Now, at sections, their classic performances in the morning had already guaranteed each of them a spot at state.

This was only our second pursuit race of the year, as poor snow conditions had forced many races to either cancel or switch to skating, which requires less snow. Andrea rallied us together on the bus in between races and gave us a pep talk about how we could all work hard and qualify as a team for state.

It was a good rally. We were all enthused. We were also all very tired from the morning race.

I remember little of the skate race. I started sixteenth, a few minutes off the leaders. I held on to my place throughout the race but didn't feel strong. My body was too tired from my classic efforts. The whole race was bittersweet; I had worked hard all season and done the best I could, but my body lacked the endurance to push hard through two races in one day.

In the end, Grand Rapids was just too strong at skating, even with Bryndon absent. I finished sixteenth in the classic, sixteenth in the pursuit, and twentieth in the skate. It was odd for me to have a better result in the classic. We lost our lead to Grand Rapids during the skate and finished 8 points behind them—8 points away from qualifying as a team for state. Perhaps I should not have done the classic race, as my fifth-place finish for the team didn't count in the score; only the top four counted for the scoring. Meanwhile, I was our fourth skier in the skate, so my twentieth place counted.

Had I saved my body for the skate, maybe I could have placed higher—possibly eight places higher, as everyone else seemed really tired, too.

I was disappointed to not make it to state, something I had wanted ever since Dad had taken me to those basketball games as a little girl. But I consoled myself with the knowledge I had come closer than I'd ever imagined possible a few months earlier. I had some "would haves" and "should haves." Had I not set my expectations high, there would have been no disappointment, but perhaps no progress either. In my attempt to make it to state, I had gone from the thirteenth classic skier on the team to the fifth, and from the twelfth skater to the fourth. It was a big improvement in one year and gave me the confidence to continue skiing competitively. Our second-place sections team plaque with our team picture went on display in the Bemidji High School trophy case. At the end of the season, we ranked tenth in the state. It was a helluva good run.

Chapter 9

The Chippewa Triathlon

"The Grundy brothers were our inspiration," we told the *Cass Lake Times* the night before our first Chippewa Triathlon.

Consisting of a 16-mile canoe leg, a 27-mile mountain bike ride, and a 7-mile run, the triathlon covers a total distance of 50 miles in the Chippewa National Forest in north-central Minnesota. The fastest competitors finish in five to six grueling hours.

The summer after my sophomore year of high school, Dad volunteered for the race. He came home with the wildest of stories, for the Chippewa Triathlon is not for the faint of heart. He told Leif and me that Jim and David Grundy, brothers ages fourteen and fifteen, were so tired after canoeing and biking that they walked the run, dragging themselves along a sandy lakeshore to the finish. The Grundy brothers were our teammates in skiing, and the year after they did their first Chippewa Triathlon, we decided to take on the challenge.

Leif, Kathryn, and I formed a team for the next summer, with Kathryn and me canoeing, Leif biking, and me running. I was seventeen. Kathryn and Leif were a mere fourteen. It was at the prerace event, while picking up our bibs and reading signs that warned about "deep loon shit" at some of the portages, that we talked to the reporter. Why the three of us had come together to do this race was beyond us. It was probably a combination of our adventure-seeking natures and our inability to pass up a challenge in which the Grundy brothers partook.

I had been with Kathryn on both the cross-country running and skiing teams. She was wise and had a knack for more adventurous sports, and we became good friends.

Prior to the triathlon, my canoeing experience consisted of short family jaunts with lazy paddle strokes. I had never paddled even half the distance of the Chippewa canoe leg in one day. A couple times I tried backing out of the canoe portion, which is the real challenge of the event—not only are strength, endurance, and canoe technique mandatory, but navigational skills are as well. My parents were discouraging: "How are you going to portage the 65-pound aluminum canoe?" I had no answer. I told Kathryn, "My arms are going to fall off, seriously." But Kathryn's mom found us a lighter, faster Kevlar canoe.

We called our team Moo Juice. Together, we carbo-loaded on pasta the night before the race. By race day we thought we were ready.

Although it was before 7:00 a.m., the June sun was already high in the sky, drying the dew from the grass. I distractedly watched two of our competitors, Devon and Brett Arenz, fill empty 2-liter pop bottles with flat Coke; a series of tubing stretched from the bottles behind their canoe seats to tubing around their necks so they could drink while racing without using their hands. Their canoe was black, made of carbon, skinny in the front and back and bowed out funny in the middle to meet the minimum width for racing standards. This was a real racing canoe—the first one I ever saw. These brothers were real canoe racers, the type that engage in twenty-four-hour races and triumph, the favorites in the Chippewa Triathlon. And we were racing against them.

This was my first introduction to the highly exclusive

canoe-racing scene. Unlike 5-kilometer running races, in which the results resemble a nice bell-shaped curve, canoe race results are skewed left—only the fastest canoers race.

After a last trip to the bathroom, Kathryn and I put our canoe in the water and maneuvered to the invisible start line between two motorboats on Cass Lake. The morning was cool, and I shivered in my sweatshirt. Around us mass chaos ensued as other canoes bumped into ours and each other. Our high school principal cruised by in a low racing canoe, no life jacket covering his naked, tattooed torso. The senior class president was in another, wearing a wide-brimmed hat and a life jacket the same color blue as mine. The field was male dominated. Kathryn and I maneuvered next to the Grundys and prepared to start the race.

The gun went off. Kathryn in the stern and me in the bow, we began the 16-mile canoe adventure. Adrenaline flowed to my muscles as Kathryn and I dodged some fifty other canoes, trying to cut off time by hugging the buoys in the loop we made in Cass Lake before heading south to Pike Bay. The buoys bounced up and down in the wake of the elite canoes. As we completed the short loop in the main part of the lake and headed under the Highway 2 bridge into the bay, ours was one of the last canoes. The Grundy brothers were a mere speck on the horizon. I was already exhausted, and we had only canoed a quarter mile. My arms screamed in agony each time I lifted my heavy wooden paddle for another stroke. The real racers used carbon fiber bent-shaft paddles less than half the weight of ours. My back muscles cramped. A cheering section greeted us under the bridge; I thought about quitting.

We kept going with forced smiles on our faces as we dug our paddles into the deep water, harder and faster, but to no avail. No matter how hard we paddled we couldn't catch any other canoes. One passed us in Pike Bay as the sun beat down. Luckily, there was no wind to contend with, so the water was placid. I took a break from paddling to peel off my sweatshirt, now drenched in sweat, and feebly knotted it to a bar in the canoe, anxious to get back to paddling.

With the sweatshirt off I felt much lighter and cooler, but now I worried about my bare arms chafing against my life jacket. It was far from a paddling vest, having been purchased from Sears when I was in fourth grade. We turned east, and I got into a good rhythm, preferring the comfort of paddling on my left side over my right. A dam necessitated our first portage.

"Let's beach early and run with the canoe along the shore to save time. It should be faster than paddling," I yelled back to my teammate.

"Good idea. I'm ramming in here," Kathryn called as we crashed onto the sandy shore.

We quickly picked up the canoe and started running along the beach with it at our sides. This was a big mistake, as with every step the canoe swung hard into our hips. As we traversed a sand dune, our feet sank in, and I fell on my knees. At the end of the short portage we threw the canoe in the water; I advanced into the water next to it.

Gulp! My heart skipped a beat as I tripped and landed on the sandy lake bottom, water up to my chest. I stood up, laughed it off, and lifted my left foot high out of the water. I took a gigantic step into the canoe, and we continued on into Ten Section Lake, now with rough sand in my underwear.

We made good time crossing the small lake and soon found ourselves in a narrow channel that required us to carry our canoe over a muddy path on the left. This time we decided to take our time and walk. A few steps into the portage, however, my left shoe got stuck in the mud and came off my foot.

"Kathryn, I lost my shoe. Can you get it?" I mumbled back to her.

"Got 'em," replied Kathryn.

The portage was short, about 50 yards, and we soon had our canoe back in the water and were crossing Moss Lake. Once we were settled, I asked Kathryn about the shoe.

"What? You lost your shoe? I thought you asked me if I was still wearing mine," she answered, to my chagrin.

"Oh well. They were probably some cheap shoes anyway," I said, trying to justify my loss. I had borrowed them from Reid. "It's too late to go back now." We were hardcore canoe racers. There was no turning back for something as inconsequential as a shoe.

We continued paddling across Moss Lake, aiming for the portage trail. Four days earlier we had canoed this part of the course, anxious to see what awaited us. It was rumored there were places here with piles of loon shit 4 feet deep. We had also been warned of mosquitoes and the burden of carrying the canoe over the portages. Thanks to our practice run, we knew exactly where the portage trail went up from the lake and headed straight for that slight clearing in the trees marked with a single ribbon.

To protect ourselves from the loon shit, I had dug into my pile of knee-high soccer socks. Given our running backgrounds, we looked forward to portaging. We thought it would be a welcome break for the tired muscles in our arms and backs. This next one would be only a half mile.

When we got to the portage we drove the canoe into the shore, jumped out, and proceeded to drag the canoe farther onto the mainland as our feet slid down the bank. We passed an out-of-shape kayaker. The clay under my feet felt like Play-Doh as my shoeless foot squashed along. Our system for portaging the canoe was ludicrous: we flipped the canoe upside down and let the gunwales rest on both of our shoulders, with our heads under the canoe. The gunwales bore down on my bones, and the canoe covered my head, blinding me to the path in front of me. Fortunately, Kathryn was able to see far

enough down the single-track trail, which had been trampled
down by all the other racers by the time we got there.

She shouted directions: "Right! Right! Left! Slight right!"
Having just completed my track season, I related all distances
to the track. Racing two times around the track, the distance
of a half mile, didn't take more than three minutes. Walking
a half mile, as we were reduced to doing instead of running as
we had planned, under the heavy weight of the canoe, took
a lot longer. It felt like the longest half mile of my life. I kept
waiting for Kathryn to report a sign of blue through the evergreen trees, trying to remember landmarks we had passed on
our trial voyage. Every pine needle pricking my shoeless foot
made me hope Twin Lake was around the next bend. Kathryn remarked we were dropping in elevation. I kept expecting
the lake, but it never seemed to come—until finally it did. We
slapped the canoe half in the water, half on the bank. I flung
myself into the front, Kathryn pushed off, and we continued
on, relieved to be back on the water. We had underestimated
the difficulty of running with a canoe, for it would have been
jostling up and down on our shoulders, causing unbearable
jolts of pain. Moreover, tripping over hazards on the trail like
tree roots or down trees while running would have sent me
sprawling with a 50-pound canoe landing on top of me.

Twin Lake was blanketed with prolific lily pads and de-
void of houses and motorboat traffic. On our maiden voyage
through this lake days earlier, Kathryn and I had seen white
birds I thought were trumpeter swans. Today the birds were
nowhere in sight as we headed south to the passageway that
linked Twin Lake with its smaller sister, Little Twin Lake.
This narrow passageway was laden with tree branches, the
work of ambitious beavers. We had rehearsed this part too; I
hopped out first onto the beaver dam and pulled Kathryn and
the canoe as far as I could onto it. She then jumped out, and

together we pulled the canoe over the remaining logs. Then we scrambled back into the boat and paddled on.

Back on the open water of Little Twin Lake, Kathryn steered us toward a portage we were both reluctant to undertake following the misery of the previous one. Luckily, this portage was much shorter. I finally took the stern as we set the canoe into Lake Thirteen. I maneuvered us south and then west around a bend in the lake toward the boat ramp, careful not to hug the reedy shore too closely.

The next portage began at the boat ramp. We ignored the food station and comments about my missing shoe as we strained to get the canoe onto our shoulders. There was no time for stopping; we were hardcore, out to win, even if we were in last place. We proceeded down a gravel road, the stones biting through my sock into my foot. After a few hundred yards we cut left on a trail into the woods that brought us to Little Moss Lake. Deep mud encumbered our approach. Our feet sank into the still-freezing muck. With every step I sank deeper and deeper until the dense substance stole my other shoe. There was no stopping to retrieve it; its partner was already forsaken.

Kathryn and I flipped the canoe into the water once again, elated the portage had been brief but knowing on the other side of Little Moss Lake waited a 3/4-mile portage that would be the death of us. Little Moss Lake was small, and we quickly traversed it, scouting the portage site, as we had neglected to canoe this part of the course a few days earlier. At the start of the portage the grass we were standing on gave way to the lake. Before we lifted the canoe, our feet sank into hot puddles of water warmed by the sun. With sheer willpower we hoisted the canoe onto our shoulders, the muscles in our arms spent. We trudged down the path, my feet feeling every stick, every sharp rock cutting through my sopping-wet soccer socks. We passed a feed station, knowing if we put the canoe down, we wouldn't get it back onto our shoulders. This portage overlapped part of the bike route, and bikers yelled encouraging remarks at us. We were obviously out of any medal contention. We were just trying to finish the canoe leg. There were already people biking, and we still had a long portage and a river section ahead of us. There were maybe two or three boats behind us, one being the kayak we had passed at our first long portage.

Taking a right at a fork that left the bike trail, we entered deep woods. Mosquitoes attacked us. Their humming wings annoyed my ears, and I could feel one bite my forehead. I took a hand off the canoe to swat at it and the canoe rocked violently on my shoulders, pain shooting through my body. My back literally felt ready to break. The weight of the canoe bore into my shoulders. Mosquitoes depleting me of blood, the canoe eating my shoulder flesh, thoughts of wandering off the trail, succumbing to this endless torture, never reaching the lake . . .

"The ants go marching one by one, hurrah! Hurrah! The ants go marching one by one, hurrah! Hurrah! Come on Kathryn, sing with me. I'm gonna die if I don't sing," I called. "The ants go marching one by one, the little one stops to suck his thumb, and they all go marching down, to the ground, to get out of the rain, boom, boom, boom!"

The pain was so excruciating—the tingling and pinpricks in my scapula at the acromion process, the buzzing mosquitoes—I had to sing. Something had to keep me going.

Then, hurrah! Through the trees I saw water. The sweet, sweet water of Portage Lake. And no, it was not an illusion. Kathryn and I threw the canoe into the water. We hugged each other, cried, and screamed, "We did it! We did it!"

Getting into the canoe proved difficult. I tried stepping into the water, but it turned out to be not water at all but some quicksand-like substance. This had to be the infamous "loon shit." Kathryn and I dragged the canoe to where there was a log. I stepped on the log and got in. Kathryn rolled into the canoe as the log sank under her.

We paddled as hard as we could across Portage Lake. With our minimal practice we hadn't yet achieved synchronized paddling. In the stern Kathryn J-stroked and C-stroked as needed. Our strokes were choppy, with me digging into the water first, then Kathryn. First the canoe lurched forward from my weak paddling stroke. It stopped and then lurched forward as a result of Kathryn's efforts. On either side of us houses dotted the shoreline, and I envisioned paddling over to one of them and falling asleep on the beach. Instead, I kept paddling west, following a distant canoe.

The river flowing out of Portage Lake, which we were to canoe down to reach Steamboat Bay Lake, proved to be a pathetic stream, only a few feet wide, meandering southwest. Branches of other streams made the course difficult to follow. There were several 90-degree turns, which put us facing west. I could see the river would turn north soon, and I realized something was wrong—the map showed the river wandering south and west, but never north. Uh-oh. Now with every forward stroke we wondered whether we should really be taking two backwards. Was it possible we were heading up the wrong river? There had been no course markings since the last portage.

"If the river doesn't turn west and widen around this curve, let's turn around," I declared to my partner.

To our tentative relief the river turned west and widened, so we continued until we came to a floating bog that required us to get out and slide the canoe across tall weeds. Around us, weeds above our heads swayed in the breeze. The water on my feet felt cold, but sinking on a floating bog as I hopped between clumps of weeds was playful. After the bog the river continued north.

"Kathryn, we're still going north. Let's turn around," I

concluded. Kathryn got out her compass and verified we indeed were heading north. We were in the process of turning around when up the river came the kayaker we had passed hours ago.

"Is this the right river?" we asked the kayaker.

"Yes," he responded. We then asked him if he had done this race before; he had.

We turned our canoe back north and continued up the river. The kayaker tried to paddle alongside us, though the river was not wide enough. Kathryn and I were clearly going faster and eventually won the battle until we ran into a beaver dam. We got out on the dam to plan the portage. Up the river came an aluminum canoe with two men. There were no footprints on the beaver dam, no sign of any human passing this way. We acknowledged we were up the wrong river. I wanted to quit, just sit down and wait for some rescue mission to come save me. Instead we all turned around and started heading back the way we came, this time heading south.

I recalled the exact location at which we had made the wrong turn. There had been a fork in the river, a good half mile downstream. A wide channel led west, while a much smaller channel, barely wide enough to squeeze a canoe through, led south. Kathryn and I had made what we presumed to be the correct decision, turning west, following the larger body of water.

We took up the back of the procession as we weaved our way back to the pivotal fork, known thereafter as Sucker Turn. At the floating bog we once again dragged our canoe over the rushes, this time more in a fit of anger, frustrated we hadn't followed our intuition and turned around sooner.

As we came upon the fork I noticed that from this angle the river to the south was much wider. The kayaker and the other canoers were unsure of which way to go, so Kathryn and I led the way down the channel until we got sidetracked by some other passageway through the rushes. Ahead of us we saw bikers on a road, but it took us a long time to find the culvert under the road.

We smoothly floated through the culvert, while the kayaker fell out of his kayak and swam it through the leech-infested water. On the other side Kathryn and I had expected a lake, but we got more bulrushes. The sun was high in the sky as we spotted the last bridge connecting Steamboat Bay Lake and Steamboat Lake, the latter of which was the end of the canoe leg. I recalled from the detailed map the river we were on emptied into Steamboat Bay Lake. The bridge was directly to the west of us, yet the river branched in so many different ways through the reeds we once again had no idea which way to go. I could taste the sweetness of getting out of this blasted canoe. We were so close, but try as we might, we couldn't find our way out of this maze. I started using every expletive in the book. Seeing the bridge we were to pass under yet being unable to get there from the swamp we were in was totally frustrating. There were three main paths to take, and of the three parties, the aluminum canoe went west, the kayak south, and Kathryn and I east, navigating toward Steamboat Bay Lake and not the bridge.

Finally, our route proved correct. Before our eyes as we rounded a bend was the happiest lake I have ever laid eyes on. We then turned west to go under the bridge into Steamboat Lake. We called to the others as we raced them to the transition zone. Kathryn and I paddled with all our might so as not to be last. But as we went under the bridge, the other two boats cut us off; Kathryn and I lost a good angle as we turned north for the last straightaway on Steamboat Lake. The aluminum canoe blazed ahead of us, and the kayak hugged the shoreline. We finished last in the canoe portion.

Onshore there was much cheering, as our parents and race personnel had been preparing to send out a search party.

Apparently the sweep canoe had been through, and yet we remained missing. Kathryn and I rammed the canoe onshore. The look on my face must have been one of utter rage. I thought we had to carry the canoe onshore and run to tag off to my brother, but Leif had already been sent on ahead.

Once onshore, Kathryn burst into tears in her dad's arms. I was too irate to let anyone come near me. We had suffered terribly on the portages, taken Sucker Turn, been deceived by that stupid kayaker, and finished dead last. I wanted to scream, to curse the world, especially the idiot who hadn't marked Sucker Turn. My body was caked in dry mud and sweat, my underwear still full of sand, my socks saturated with loon shit.

Some months later, on our way to a ski race, Kathryn and I passed the wayside rest at Cass Lake, the starting point of the Chippewa Triathlon.

"Remember that place?" I asked, gesturing out onto the frozen bay.

Kathryn took a good, long look, wrinkled up her nose, and said flatly, "Hell starts there."

∿∿∿

Yet despite our frustration with our first Chippewa Triathlon, we decided to do it the next year as female doubles—meaning Kathryn and I would canoe together and from there both do the bike and run individually. We were stronger than we'd been the previous year and had practiced more together in the canoe. This time we used a canoe with a yoke, which enabled one of us to carry the canoe on our shoulders with comfortable pads. I did this for the first three portages; Kathryn helped me get the canoe up onto my shoulders by grabbing the bow, flipping the canoe over, then holding it there while I got under it. The canoe weighed half as much as me, and running with it was nearly impossible, so I was limited to the fastest walk I could muster while navigating single-track trails and big logs—one so big I had to sit on it to get over it! We were very careful to not take Sucker Turn near the end of the canoe course.

I used the hot-pink bike with 24-inch wheels I'd had since age ten for the mountain bike course. While there were some sections of single track, the majority of the course followed gravel and dirt logging roads and the paved bike trail around Pike Bay. Around six hours into the race I mentally lost it. I was near the end of the bike leg, where the course heads west into Cass Lake, while on the other side of the highway runners were heading east toward the finish at Norway Beach. There were a few scattered athletes on the course, and as I saw one of my teachers running in the opposite direction, tears poured from my eyes as I thought how beautiful it all was.

I learned that running after biking 27 miles feels awful. My quads were rubber, and it was arduous to push anything more than a trot. It was several miles before my legs felt normal and I was able to give the run any effort. The theme from *Chariots of Fire* played through the trees as I finished the 50-mile triathlon at age eighteen in seven hours and seven minutes. The canoe took three hours and thirty-seven minutes, the bike two hours and thirty minutes, and the run fifty-nine minutes.

By the third year Kathryn and I embarked on the Chippewa Triathlon, we felt cocky. We juxtaposed the ruggedness of the event by wearing hot pink. I dug out some hot-pink bandanas from high school, and at Target we bought hot-pink tank tops, hot-pink shorty shorts, and the mega find: hot-pink fishnet stockings. Being beaten by girls hurts, but being beaten by girls wearing hot pink hurts more.

Each year we did the triathlon we got smarter. I made a list of dos and don'ts: Do wear sandals for the canoe leg. Do have your dry shoes ready to go in your transition bag. Don't put on any hand lotion before the race or your hands will slip on the paddles.

I also learned not to get my feet wet before the start of the race. The water in Cass Lake is very cold in early June, hovering around 60 degrees. If I got my feet wet before the start, they would be cold and numb when I got out to run the first portage.

Kathryn and I frequently trained for canoeing on Sunday mornings. During these sessions we remarked how the rest of the world was at church while we were in the great outdoor cathedral having our own spiritual reckoning.

Three years in a row I did the entire Chippewa Triathlon course. The strategy got easier; Kathryn and I focused on the canoe. The canoe seemed to be the ultimate test, but as the hours of physically exerting myself increased, the true mental test came in the bike and the run. I did the triathlon with Kathryn for the last time in 2005, our fourth year canoeing together. By that time we were veterans wearing our "pink is power" uniforms and using a significantly lighter and faster canoe we borrowed from our friend's parents. Even though we felt experienced and hardcore, at ages seventeen and twenty, we were really just rookies.

June 12, 2005
Yesterday was the Chippewa Triathlon. Kathryn and I met our goal of canoeing faster. When we turned around partway through Pike Bay, we saw the greatest number of canoes that had ever been behind us!

I got really tired on the canoe, partly because the course was longer than last year. Our canoe time was 3 hours, 29 minutes, which is only a minute faster than last year, but then again everyone's times were really slow compared to last year.

At the portage between Moss and Twin Lakes, Jan Guenther and Kate Ellis [elite canoers, cross-country ski marathoners, and exceptional athletes who were still kicking butt well into their fifties] *came out of the woods off a trail just in front of us, as they had made a wrong turn and were getting back on course. We were awestruck following our idols and learned how they portage! They run at a steady trot holding the canoe under their arms at their sides. Kathryn and I kept up fairly well. Then those two women just took off in the lake. Another women's canoe passed us at the end of the first Twin Lake as well. We just really need a faster canoe.*

The bike went pretty well. In the first single track, trees were lying across the trail in a zigzag pattern, so I had to weave in and out, and I'm not so good at maneuvering, so that accounted for my first fall. The single track on the east side of Moss Lake was much blander than I remember. I still managed to fall. I had just bumped over a 3-inch-diameter log and then couldn't turn fast enough to avoid hitting the side of a cut log AGAIN! Next was that dreaded single track along Lake Thirteen. At the first sharp hill it said "dismount," and I debated and then finally dismounted. Good thing I did 'cause at the bottom of the hill was a deep puddle with logs floating, and the upside was mud! I was a little cautious through the trees, and one time I just stopped and my bike fell over on me. I hit the second hill just great—much easier and "weaker" than I remember.

Then I hit the MUD! It was mud like I had never encountered! The people in front of me were running with their bikes, but I found the stuff surprisingly easy to ride through. As we headed east and then back north, the trail got less muddy and I was really cruising. The mud was everywhere—caked all up my legs, spattered on my arms, and flying from my fenderless front wheel into my mouth. We had to go over this down tree with a mess of branches, and I got the bike caught on my crotch and I couldn't move my feet, so I fell again, injuring my arm. I started to cry and said "Fucking shit"; this woman in orange, who I've seen out there before, told me that swearing wouldn't help (I already know that), and then she told me how far it was to the transition zone. I told her I already knew and took off, determined not to fall biking ever again!

At the transition I took off my hot-pink fishnet socks and put on my running shoes. Then I saw Kelly Rogers and Abbi May [some more really strong women who are also really good skiers and usually beat me], *who I knew I had to beat! I took off on the run realizing I had the wrong orthotics in my shoes, so my outside toes were hitting the end and it was bad. I started running and wondered, "What's the point?" and conceded to everyone behind me. I kept up my walking/running/crying, but then when I hit the first single track I just started running and decided to not stop running until I got out of the single track. Then I caught up with these two guys and talked to them for quite a while. When I stopped to grab some water, they stopped with me. It was nice just talking on that long bout of single track. Eventually they stopped to walk and I kept going, enjoying the pine scent in the warm forest. About a half mile from the finish I started walking, then heard women's voices behind me, so, fearing it to be Abbi and Kelly, I started running again all the way to the finish line, where I sat down and took off those horrible shoes!*

I beat Kelly Rogers and Abbi May. So my time was 7 hours, 6 minutes, my PR by about one minute although the canoe route was longer. I had my PR bike time despite the mud—which I loved. And while I was out there biking through the mud and others were running with their bikes, I debated biking or running but said to myself, "This is the BIKE part! I might as well bike, and hell, when do I ever do this much riding in the mud like this?"

If it wasn't for the Chippewa Triathlon there's no way I'd ever trudge through bog mat, put my feet in dirty, slimy leech-infested water, or run with a canoe. I wouldn't ride single track, wouldn't ride over logs, wouldn't ride through sand and, yes, MUD! And after 43 miles still have the guts to run another 7. Hardcore is doing the whole Chippewa Triathlon!

Chapter 10

Mourning My Gastrocnemius

"If I couldn't run anymore, I'd be so happy I'd hop on one foot!" Dave quipped in his quintessential sarcastic tone as we bouldered in the gloomy basement of Midwest Mountaineering.

The audacity! raged the voice inside my head.

"Dave, if you couldn't run anymore, you wouldn't be able to hop on one foot!" I retorted.

Didn't Dave know I couldn't run? At least, not without limping. I couldn't even walk without limping.

I was now a junior at the University of Minnesota. My posse consisted mostly of people I had met in the cross-country ski club, and Dave was one of those people. This particular autumn we had taken up bouldering, a form of rock climbing that doesn't involve ropes, and we climbed in an 8-foot-high "cave" with cushy mats on the floor.

Dave was a year older than me and an electrical engineering major. My early impression of him was that he was a chauvinistic asshole; my later impression was that he was just a sarcastic, friendless guy. After the American Birkebeiner ski race my freshman year, I found myself in a hunting cabin in northern Wisconsin with eight guys and only one other girl.

We were sitting around the cabin—which had as many porn magazines on the coffee table as stuffed wildlife heads on the wall—all exhausted after racing a ski marathon, and Dave had the guts to say, "Girls aren't very good at ski racing."

"Oh yeah, Dave? How many girls beat you today?" Meleah, the other freshman girl, responded without skipping a beat.

My sophomore year I had been the lone girl traveling to the Noquemanon ski marathon in Michigan's Upper Peninsula. Dave was along on this trip as well. When I finished the race, he said, "Wow, I didn't expect you to finish so soon." This was before I knew Dave well enough to know he had just paid me a Dave compliment.

Now we were in the basement of Midwest Mountaineering, and he just had to remind me of the status of my gastrocnemius.

∿∿∿

At age twenty, during the summer between my sophomore and junior years of college, I decided to have a bunionectomy on my left foot. I had developed a bunion on that foot in high school and dealt with the pain for years, mostly while running. Now the pain was becoming unbearable. It kept me from running more than 7 miles. I wanted to run a marathon, but not with this bunion pain. I was too young to be in such pain and thought about surgery. Yet the decision wasn't easy.

June 28, 2005

Man, my mind is in such turmoil: to have or not to have my bunion surgery this summer. I already have my whole fall training plan done and I'd hate to have to scrap it. Four months of no running, no biking outside, no hill bounding, no roller skiing, and worst of all—no ultimate Frisbee on Fridays! What would I do? I have all these workouts planned, I am so strong now, I have worked so hard for four years to develop my muscles, my endurance, my speed, and then it

*would all go. Three hours of lat pulls—that's all I really have
to look forward to. Fridays will be so hard without Frisbee.*

*I have no obligations now, this summer, save for the
training plan, which I feel slave to. Honestly, what is wrong
with me? But really no obligations right now: no job, not
looking for a job, not in grad school, no children, just my
training plan! Furthermore—I'm young now, which means
I'll heal all the better. So yes, this should be good timing.
Just no Frisbee this fall. Murrr . . . but maybe I'll be able
to run sooner.*

My doctor in Bemidji had told me the reason I had such
a bad bunion was because my gastrocnemius muscle was too
big. He therefore wanted to partially cut my gastrocnemius
tendon so the tendon would increase in length and the muscle
would weaken and exert less force on my big toe joint.

I had the surgery in early July, which left me over six
weeks until my junior year of college started in the fall. My
left foot was swollen for months. I was in a hot-pink cast
and then a walking boot for a total of six weeks. My left calf
shrank and weakened; I couldn't flex my gastrocnemius, and
the incision looked awful. I was horribly restless and had to
start working out.

August 15, 2005
*I "swim" at 6:30 a.m. with Kathryn—mostly we kick with
a kickboard (my left ankle hurts), and we tread water
some. The weight room is closed, so I do 4 × 40 push-ups
and right leg hops. We do 8-minute abs and triceps dips. At
home I bench, lat pull, and do bicep curls with free weights.*

August 22, 2005
*Swimming at 6:00 a.m.! Felt strong but still skittish to put
my head underwater. I tried, but the water kept coming in
my nose and ears. Some treading, kicking. 8-minute abs.*

*I went to the grocery store this afternoon. I had to re-
sist the urge to go roller skiing—such a beautiful day, and
it's been six weeks. Instead I did 4 × 50 push-ups. I felt über
strong, but maybe 'cause I did them on the ground outside.
I did bungees—meant to do way more, but instead I did 50
moderate and 20 speed. Rest. 60 moderate and 30 hard—
rest—50 moderate and 30 hard; then 2 × 50 single pole
with more resistance. Then I crutched down to Pamida* [an
even cheaper version of Kmart] *with this big cast on. Not
fun. I did 2 ½-minute abs with Reid and leg lifts. Tomorrow is supposed to be beautiful again, and I might not be
able to resist roller skiing.*

Then I did something really dumb. Twice. Because I was desperate to breathe hard, to make my lungs really work, to cover
some actual distance, fast, using my own strength. I couldn't
let myself waste any more time. Because others were training,
and I wasn't. Mostly because I love making my muscles flex
repeatedly and the accompanying increase in breathing.

August 23, 2005
*I tried roller skiing. The ski boot hurt my swollen foot. My
calf pulled a lot if I skated or stepped on my left ski. I had
to double pole, but I was scared of hurting something, so I
turned around 200 meters in. I didn't do abs or bungees.*

I roller skied one more time after that. My swollen big
toe joint hurt as I crammed it into my ski boot, and there
was some pulling in my weak left calf. Then Mom called the
physical therapist and busted me. No endurance exercise for

me—no roller skiing, no biking, no running. I couldn't even walk. All I could do were more push-ups and abs and bungees.

After six weeks, I got to take the black walking cast off and fully bear my weight on my leg, but I wasn't allowed to do any activities other than walking until I could do a calf raise on my left leg. An ugly scar extended over half of my atrophied calf. When I walked, I limped, as my gastrocnemius muscle was too weak to give me a lift-off. I started physical therapy. The therapist had me try single-leg calf raises on my left leg; I couldn't do it. He had me use both legs; I felt a pop in my left calf, followed by immediate, intense burning pain. The therapist said this was scar tissue settling.

I did my exercises at home, trying to strengthen my left calf so I could support all my weight while up on my toes. I was doing calf raises when again I felt another pop followed by the same intense burning pain. I kept doing the physical therapy exercises, but my left calf didn't get stronger. I still limped when I walked.

After weeks of effort, I finally started getting some strength back in my lower leg muscles, except my gastrocnemius, but was still limping. College resumed, and by walking stairs in the parking garage I could get in some cardio. While climbing the stairs I didn't feel the weakness in my left calf. Those brief periods when I could forget about my weak calf, especially when I was working out, were precious. My mood immediately improved—I was euphoric. And then I came to a landing and had to take a few limping walking steps and was immediately exasperated that I couldn't go back and revoke my decision to have surgery.

For the next six months my life revolved around the following three sentences.

August 24, 2005
I walk with a limp—my leg and my foot are very weak. I
do not have the strength to go up on my toes . . . I can't do
calf raises.

A similar entry reveals the thoughts and frustration that plagued me. I felt helpless at not being able to change the past.

August 26, 2005
Why are good muscles so important to me? My left soleus is
going to take over for my gastrocnemius. I worked so hard
for this definition and now it has disappeared! Where is the
justice? Oh yes, I remember, justice doesn't exist. I am so
weak. I still can't walk right because I can't go up on the
ball of my foot. So sad. I am sad.

Eventually I gave up waiting for the calf strength to come back. Maybe I realized it wasn't going to—that I was never going to do another calf raise again.

September 14, 2005
I couldn't take it anymore—I went biking. I felt free . . . the
most free I've ever felt in my life!

September 16, 2005
I went to ultimate Frisbee! I limp-ran around. It sucked . . .
I got really sore hip flexors. I wish I could run like normal!

Aside from my limping, my life was really starting to work out. I had the cross-country ski marathon thing down and loved the training. I lived off the high I got from doing roller ski intervals on Franklin Hill in Minneapolis. School was starting to work out, too: I was done with physics and now taking my core biochemistry classes and enjoying them.

At work I used a fluorescent microscope and watched blood proteins circulate through zebrafish. And then there was Erik.

Erik was on the ski club. He was a couple years older than me, and, like most of the boys in the club, he was majoring in mechanical engineering. I remember he was real fast to introduce himself to me. He had unruly brown hair that was almost black, cut into a mature version of the bowl cut, and piercing blue eyes.

My freshman year, my birthday was the day before the Birkebeiner ski marathon. I hadn't done anything to celebrate, but after the race we went to the grocery store and Erik and Per, another guy on the ski club, bought cupcakes.

Erik dropped hints he was interested in me for two years. There were the aforementioned birthday cupcakes, his eagerness to engage me in conversation, his willingness to be subjected to my three-hour roller skis on Sunday afternoons in the autumn, and his quickness to follow me all over the Midwest on my quest to do back-to-back-to-back ski marathons all winter.

Those first two years I wasn't so interested in him. He was awkward in conversation and not popular among the guys. He had funny ski form, he was purposely unfashionable, and there were plenty of other guys who could ski much faster.

My junior year of college we started going to free movies together on the weekends at the student center, and afterward we talked for hours. We went roller skiing together and sometimes biking, too. This kept on for a couple of months. I had never had a boyfriend before and didn't know how to make the first move. I could only assume Erik liked me, I but wasn't sure.

October 23, 2005
Biking with Erik. We decided to go check out Hidden Falls
and find the so-called Hidden Falls. He was on his road

*bike . . . and I on my mountain bike. Needless to say I
learned how to use my left gears! We found some single
track and then the Hidden Falls . . . kinda romantic, but
nothing happened. I can't tell if he likes me like that or
not—I should probably just get up the guts and ask him
and find out!*

October 25, 2005
*Forgot to mention that at Hidden Falls, Erik challenged
me to a pull-up contest. He went first and did four, and
of course, being very competitive, I had to beat him, but
I'd never done more than three before! Well, hanging from
this rock overhang I did five! Yes, five pull-ups! So now I'm
hooked on doing real pull ups at the rec . . . no more assisted!*

I guess he thought the same about me, and in November
he was ready to see whether the feelings were mutual. One
night after the movie, we were talking, and he put his arm
around me. It made me feel all warm and fuzzy inside, and
from then we were together.

Everything in my life—school, skiing, Erik—was going
well except my gastrocnemius muscle, which wasn't getting
stronger. I kept going to physical therapy and walking and doing my strengthening exercises. When I walked, I still limped.
It was much worse when I ran. When I went downstairs and
landed on my left toes my gastrocnemius didn't catch, so
my heel just slapped the stair. My left calf was 3 centimeters
smaller in diameter than my right calf. At the end of October, after two and a half months of working my left gastrocnemius, the physical therapist had sent me back to see an
orthopedist. I was worried going into the appointment, as I
realized something was wrong, and my workouts reflected this
apprehension.

October 29, 2005
Roller ski Franklin Hill with Erik. I did more V1 than V2.
Erik remarked that it's hard to have good V2 form when go-
ing so fast. I think if I had a little better balance and practice
I could get better V2 form. Anyway, intervals seemed harder
than before, probably 'cause I was trying to keep up to Erik.

Felt slow and out of shape and horrible technique and
like I was kissing away all my dreams. Giving up . . . deter-
mination gone . . . and I didn't care. Anyway, I was trying
to study later, but my apathy was coming back to haunt
me. I think it's a good Freud defense mechanism creeping
in. Like if I don't care about skiing anymore, then I won't
care if I get bad news about my tendon. Where did my de-
termination go? I'm doing the 100-kilometer Finlandia and
I'm going to win.

Two MRIs and two orthopedists later, I was indeed dealt
some bad news.

"The MRI shows your left gastrocnemius tendon is not
connected to the soleus tendon," the second orthopedist told
me. "There is nothing we can do."

I burst into inconsolable tears. "What do you mean? I can't
have more surgery? I'm going to have to limp forever?" I asked.

"I'll talk to one of my colleagues and see if there is any
possibility," he said.

I went back to class with tear streaks on my face and big
puffy eyes. I had just broken up with my gastrocnemius.

November 3, 2005
The bottom falls out of my world. I go to another specialist
and learn my gastrocnemius tendon is permanently torn
beyond surgical repair. The doctor said I will never gain 100
percent strength in the gastrocnemius. I am crying, but I
feel it is a loss. Tears won't help. I have plans that do not

include a ruptured gastrocnemius tendon. I have no inten-
tion of quitting marathon ski racing. I'm gonna run again.
I haven't done my marathon yet.

I feel wronged, led astray . . . fucked (as I told Reid).
Mostly I'm just incredulous that this is actually happening,
that this is real. It seems impossible. I am devastated. Dev-
astated. In denial.

Two days later there was a message on my phone from the orthopedist.

"Elspeth, I talked to the other doctor. We have a plan."

While those were not exactly words I wanted used to describe surgery on my leg, it was a glimmer of hope at least.

With the doctors, I decided my best option was to have a salvage surgery. There were two plans associated with this surgery. Plan A involved suturing my torn gastrocnemius tendon into the soleus tendon, where the two come together to form the Achilles tendon. If the surgeon couldn't do that, plan B would involve cutting the soleus tendon and suturing it together tighter than originally in the hope I might be able to walk without limping.

Skiing marathons was my life, and since the orthopedist told me I could keep skiing without incurring further damage as my tendon was already ruptured, I scheduled surgery for late February after most of the ski season would be over. The orthopedist told me that if I was lucky, I would be able to walk again without limping. He said this was a humble request for a twenty-year-old. And if I was really lucky, I would be able to run again. This was the goal, the hope, the motive.

I told Erik about my predicament. He seemed optimistic, while I remained devastated. Perhaps it was my resilience and determination mirrored on his face, only this time I didn't feel resilient or determined. I felt cheated out of a life with two functioning gastrocnemius muscles.

Up until this point I had always demonstrated marked perseverance, whether it was reading my way toward 700 Accelerated Reader points in sixth grade, my drive to make it to state in cross-country skiing my senior year of high school, racing to the finish line in seven hours during the Chippewa Triathlon, starving myself through my first ski marathon, or striving to get an A in every class throughout college as a biochemistry major. But for once the hurdle was too high. No amount of willpower could compel my tendon to reconnect. I am a do-it-yourself kind of person, but this time I had to put my faith in someone else—the surgeon. I hoped Erik's optimism was a good sign, but for the next three months while waiting for surgery, I dealt with a grim reality.

My mood was extremely volatile. Tears poured out of my eyes every other day. I was inconsolable. I sat on my bed, rocking back and forth. I thought about how if I got married, I would limp down the aisle. I thought about all the marathons I could never run. I would wake up in a panic, perturbed after dreaming I could do a single-leg left calf raise. My left gastrocnemius tendon had ruptured as a complication of an elective surgery. It was like my gastrocnemius muscle had been stolen.

It was during this time I was bouldering with Dave at Midwest Mountaineering and he made his comment about not being able to run.

I thought about what I would be willing to give up to have my gastrocnemius back. I thought about Maslow's hierarchy of needs: a basic necessity, walking, had been taken away from me. I couldn't feel the love from my family and friends. I couldn't reason. Any aspirations I ever had of making it to the Olympics vanished with my self-actualization. It was a Winter Olympics year, but unlike in the past, I watched without wanting to be there; I just wanted a gastrocnemius.

Mom came to pick me up from college at Christmas break.

We had a four-hour car ride to do lots of talking, and halfway into the ride Mom brought up my gastrocnemius.

"Elspeth, I feel guilty about your leg. I shouldn't have let you have that surgery. I mean, I know you signed the papers because you're over eighteen now, but I should have discouraged you. I feel so bad, and I want to talk about it. I don't want it to be like my burns, Elspeth. I know my dad felt really bad about my burns, but we never discussed it. I don't want your leg to be like that."

I was in tears, admitting I was pissed and in denial at the same time. Worse, over Christmas break, I fought with Dad because he didn't understand that the connection in my gastrocnemius tendon was severed and I was, as far as I was concerned, a gimp.

Despite this, I became obsessed with running a marathon. While I had considered running one a couple years earlier, at the time I had decided I wasn't yet ready. Running a marathon was a future plan of mine. Now that I couldn't run, my desire to do a marathon was growing, and I was angry it might not ever be possible.

Meanwhile my leg kept getting uglier. The calf comprises two muscles: the gastrocnemius, which gets all the glory sitting up high on the calf, and the soleus, which is lower and underneath the gastrocnemius. The gastrocnemius and soleus tendons come together to form the Achilles tendon, which attaches on the heel bone in the ankle. Since my gastrocnemius muscle was so atrophied, my soleus muscle was trying to make up for it, and it just kept getting bigger and bigger. The top of my calf was shrinking while the bottom of my calf was getting larger.

I skied six marathons on back-to-back weekends leading up to my surgery. When I awoke from the anesthesia, two days after the Birkebeiner, there was pain coming from my upper calf, and I was thrilled—plan A had been effective. I made a pact with myself that so long as I was in a cast, I would do no exercise. Not even a single push-up or sit-up.

For six weeks I went around the campus in a tricked-out wheelchair with my backpack and crutches attached to the back. Mom rigged up some foam on the footrest so I could keep my leg elevated when I was sitting in class. I quickly learned which buildings had automatic door openers and how to get in and out of elevators in a wheelchair and to avoid downhill ramps, which made my hands sear with pain as I braked.

I kept my no-exercise pact with myself. Mostly. In my six weeks of no exercise, I made only two exceptions: first, I would occasionally traverse the length of my dorm hall on crutches, and second, I learned to use my wheelchair for exercise. My wheelchair was entirely hand powered, so one night I got the crazy idea to wheel up the six floors of the parking garage ramp. Erik and I rode the elevator to the bottom floor, and from there I started up. It was slow and tedious and made my arms burn. It felt wonderful.

I was in a hot-pink hard cast for six weeks, during which I mostly used my wheelchair; the crutches were for smaller spaces. I then spent six more weeks in a walking cast.

During the time I was in a hard cast I still sometimes doubted I'd ever be able to walk again without limping, let alone run. Some of my friends did running races, and I looked at the results, but as soon as I started looking at race pictures, tears filled my eyes and I got angry and had to stop.

April 2, 2006
I am laughing in a joking manner, realizing I'm spending 4 of 11 months in a cast. That's crazy, especially with all the kilometers I skied and ski races I did in between. But then the devastation of the situation strikes me and I begin to cry. I realize I don't know what the outcome of my current

surgery will be. I am trying to be optimistic—I see myself running—I so desperately want to run—but the reality is I may be spending four months in a cast only to become disabled, crippled. Last week the word of some college kid in the freshman dorm echoed in my head: "handicap." It didn't bother me because I am not handicapped . . . or am I? And then I begin crying and rocking back and forth and touching my face in a consoling attempt.

I soon discovered if I took the parking garage elevator down to level D, I could wheel from there out onto East River Road at approximately the level of the Mississippi River. Then I had my choice of either wheeling up the big hill to the east or wheeling up the big hill to the north to reach the bluff overlooking the river. The grade on both these hills was so steep the wheelchair stopped with each push forward and I had to hold on to the wheels tightly to keep from rolling backwards.

In the last week before my hot-pink cast came off I became more daring. I needed the freedom to get up and work out. The confinement of the wheelchair finally became too much, and I broke my own promise.

April 5, 2006
Abs. 40-40-40-40 (one-legged) push-ups and I feel redeemed. Then I go crutch across the bridge and back.

April 7, 2006
I go down to the River Flats to play Frisbee on crutches. I have no intent of actually playing, but I crutch back and forth like an idiot anyway for like five minutes. I don't know what people think of me. Then I wheeled up the hill. Definitely one of my top 25 athletic achievements. I hung out with Erik and we planned a canoe trip down the Mississippi. A teammate says I'm taking strength training to the extreme.

Fortunately, about the time I started doing wheelies, my six weeks were up. At this point my leg was put into a walking cast and I was told to start walking. Even though it had been a mere six weeks since I'd skied my last marathon, my left leg was completely atrophied. I hadn't straightened my left knee in over six weeks to minimize the pulling I felt on my calf. I couldn't flex my quadriceps. I had to use my crutches to get around.

Gradually I started walking. For the first couple weeks I walked a little ways and then used my crutches for a while. After three weeks I could walk as far as I wanted and not have to worry about bringing crutches with me. I eventually was able to walk to the rec center and lift. I felt so tall now that I was out of the wheelchair. It was freedom to be able to walk around. I walked for a mile with Erik, then two, then three. The bottom of the walking cast was wearing down fast.

April 30, 2006

I went to the rec—did 50 triceps dips total in five sets. I did 2 × 15 bench press and 2 × 15 upwards row. I can't believe less than six weeks until Chippewa Triathlon . . . and what have I done to train? The marathon ski season so many weeks ago, some push-ups, abs, upper-body lifting. I guess it's all canoe dependent, so if I canoe three weeks straight, the biking and running won't even matter? Ugh . . . I feel so far removed from the endurance crowd, from cardio, running, intervals, the hard shit.

I was still going to physical therapy and hoped that just two weeks after being out of the walking cast I would do the Chippewa Triathlon. I mentioned this to my physical therapist.

<u>*May 11, 2006*</u>

I walk 4 miles total because I have to go to physical therapy across the river. At physical therapy I get told not to do the Chippewa Triathlon. The orthopedist says I've come too far to screw anything up. I am devastated all over again . . . I cry to Erik and figure I can do it in my walking cast.

But the next day I emailed Kathryn to tell her I was officially out.

<u>*May 12, 2006*</u>

I call home and bawl to Mom as I decide not to do the Chippewa Triathlon. It feels like my goddamn race—we have the team name, slogan "defining hardcore, 2006," and pink paraphernalia. This race is hardcore and I feel like it defines me as such. It is a crazy insanity that is fun and pain at the same time. I have a tradition going. Not doing the race makes me feel weak and incompetent. I don't know when I'll bike or roller ski again. I feel desperate. I have never wanted or needed anything so bad in my life. Mom says it's about control. I think it's about not wanting to be labeled handicap, not wanting limitations.

Mom angered me in this conversation with her analysis of control. In truth, I was afraid. I was scared shitless that even after this salvage surgery and being in a cast for twelve weeks, my calf wouldn't be strong enough to support walking and running and biking and roller skiing. The reality was for so long in my life, my days, my existence had revolved around exercise and training for this or that race. Without it, without the endorphins and the time for me to be out by myself and think about my problems and work through them physically, I was like a lost puppy. I felt purposeless. It was not about control; it was about sanity. The sanity that physical activity brings to my life by giving me a coping mechanism.

~~~

The best part about the walking cast was that when I took it off, which I was allowed to do for showering and bed, I could actually feel the medial head of my gastrocnemius muscle when I flexed. The first time that happened was the best feeling in my world.

> *May 22, 2006*
> *Tomorrow I get the walking cast off. It has been twelve weeks since surgery—almost three months. What a freaking long haul. I've gotten so used to having some piece of plastic shit on my leg—but tomorrow I will be free!*

> *May 23, 2006*
> *I awoke from a dream that I was riding my new mountain bike. I go see the orthopedist and I get rid of my walking cast for good. I am still limping, but I get the no-restrictions go-ahead. Aggressive calf raises, mountain biking and roller skiing; however, I can't run for at least eight weeks.*

Initially when the walking cast came off, I was limping just as badly as before the salvage surgery, which was incredibly frustrating. I couldn't wait to throw the plastic walking cast in the garbage, but Erik thought it would be funny to try it on his large feet first. This whole episode of him mimicking me made me irate. After that I emphatically threw it out. Later Erik confessed the cast was impossibly difficult to walk in, and he was incredulous at how far I had walked in it.

Two days after the cast came off, I canoed with Erik from

the headwaters of the Mississippi toward Bemidji. We spent the night at a campsite accessible by a gravel road, which we went walking on. I felt like maybe, just maybe, I wasn't limping. I wanted to shout, "Two days and I'm walking!" I was so excited and happy.

Four days after the cast came off, I roller skied. At first the weakness of my leg made balance difficult, but after five minutes I told myself, "Just to go for it." I got brave and felt better. The next four weeks of my training log consisted mostly of three-a-days: biking, roller skiing, and strength workouts. Yet something was missing from my training. I pinpointed running as the missing element—before the surgeries, I'd usually alternated running and roller skiing, so if I roller skied one day I ran the next. Now I couldn't run, so I roller skied every day. Even though I was exercising almost daily, there was a big void in my life that only running would fill. There is something about running that is so pure, so complete—no equipment, continuous cardio, muscles firing—and I missed it terribly.

Two weeks after the cast came off, I roller skied 27 miles from Cass Lake to Walker, ditching Mom, who was riding her bike.

A month after the cast came off, I walked down the stairs, and for the first time in almost a year my left calf held as I put my toes onto each stair. I was overjoyed. We don't remember first learning to walk down stairs, but when it happens again at age twenty-one it's a memorable experience. It's sort of like reliving life.

I'd been told not to run for eight weeks, so I continued to bide my time walking and biking and roller skiing. As the eighth week approached, I became antsy, wondering whether my leg would be able to support the pounding of running. Finally, when I couldn't tolerate not knowing one more day, I made Erik run five minutes with me. He ran in his sandals—it was weird knowing I'd been reduced to such a poor runner that someone could keep up with me wearing sandals. Previously I had been notorious for going on long runs and leaving my companions in the dust. Now my gastrocnemius was only capable of a five-minute run. It wasn't humiliation that welled up inside me but sadness at having once been a runner and no longer being one.

While that strength, that oomph, was missing, it felt much better than it had before the salvage surgery. It felt like maybe, just maybe, that oomph would come back.

I kept running at an easy pace. Five minutes, then ten minutes, then fifteen minutes, then twenty minutes. My calf wasn't sore, and sometimes it felt as though I actually had full push-off. During this time I was working at the University of Minnesota field station at Itasca State Park, and one morning I ran particularly fast there with a couple of boys. Afterward my calf hurt badly. It was stiff and ached each time I flexed it. I worried the tendon would snap. Several times that day I reached down, flexed my gastrocnemius, and felt for my medial head. During the next couple of months, I repeated this ritual numerous times per day, always feeling the medial head bulge.

After two weeks of running at Itasca, I played ultimate Frisbee—conservatively. I deliberately never marked up so I wouldn't be compelled to sprint down the field after someone. I reached down and felt for my gastrocnemius medial head several times. I was taking a risk by playing at all, but nonetheless I had to try it to get my muscle stronger.

I returned from Itasca to Bemidji for the month of August.

August 7, 2006
Roller ski with Kathryn. Man, I'm lucky to have my gastrocnemius back.

In the weeks and months following my return to endurance activities after being out of the walking cast, this sense of gratitude became a common theme, as did my continual ritual of flexing my left gastrocnemius and feeling for the medial head.

For many weeks I plateaued at twenty minutes of running, at which point my calf would start hurting and I'd get scared and stop. Then one day I got up the courage to run through twenty minutes of pain. I rested two days and ran an old favorite 6-mile loop with Kathryn, and my calf never hurt. That was the day I knew it would never give out on me. That was the day I knew if I wanted, I could run a marathon.

Shortly after this I tried skipping while on a walk with Leif and Mika. To my surprise, I could! It was so exciting I wanted to skip everywhere. I was so happy. I wanted to tell everyone in the world I could skip, as if skipping were an accomplishment as great as going to the Olympics. For me, it was better.

In September, when school started again, I went to see the orthopedist. I walked perfectly for him and told him the previous day I'd run 7 miles.

He shook my hand and said, "Congratulations. I honestly didn't expect that result."

I almost cried. I hopped on one foot. I felt so lucky.

Chapter 11

The Big Trip Out West

In second grade, I learned that out west, in states like Colorado and Utah, there were big mountains. I became obsessed with seeing the mountains and repeatedly wrote stories about a bunny who went on a trip west and saw them. My aunt Mary lived in Utah, and I wanted to go visit her and see the mountains. My other cousins moved to Colorado, and I begged my parents to go visit them.

Over the next several years I studied a United States atlas and learned all the states and capitals and plotted routes for a big trip out west. I begged and planned and waited.

∿∿

Dad was thirty-five when he married Mom. By this time in his life he had served in the army, traveling to Korea and Iran. After he got out he went to Alaska twice. He hiked in the Bitterroot Mountains in Idaho and in North Cascades, Glacier, and Yellowstone National Parks. Dad lived for two years in New York City, which he used as a base to explore the East Coast, including Montreal and Quebec City. When he moved back to Minnesota from New York City, he biked—though by the time he got to Detroit, he ran out of time and succumbed to non-human-powered transportation.

When I begged and pleaded with Dad to take a trip out west to see the mountains, he said, "Elspeth, I've already been everywhere I want to go."

Instead he suggested we go hiking in a nearby forest or visit another Minnesota state park. This was all well and good for Dad, as it fit his minimal vacation time and budget, but there are no mountains in Minnesota.

Finally, when I was twelve, my parents appeased me with a four-day trip to South Dakota's Black Hills. To make the most of our limited time, I, as executive vacation planner, devised an hourly itinerary that included stopping at every Laura Ingalls Wilder historic site on the 600-mile drive and summiting Harney Peak, South Dakota's highest point at 7,242 feet. The hike up Harney Peak was to be my highlight of the trip.

On the second of our four days, after deviating from my itinerary with a hike in the Badlands, visiting an underground tourist-trap waterfall illuminated by colored lights, and watching Dad gawk at a steam train from the 1800s, we arrived at the north Harney Peak trailhead. We had no guidebook, no map, no compass, and no first aid kit, which is what happens when a twelve-year-old with zero mountain experience plans a hike to the highest peak in the Black Hills.

Leif and I walked at an excited pace and soon found ourselves out of sight of Mom and Dad. We stopped and waited for several minutes. Mom was slow, out of shape—and, as she constantly reminded us, she had broken two bones in her leg seven months earlier. Dad was slowed by carrying Reid, age five, on his shoulders.

We continued on in this way for 5 miles, Leif and I constantly getting ahead of the other three and then either waiting or setting back down the trail to meet up with the remainder of our party, until we ascended onto a plateau, from which we could see Harney Peak towering above us with its stone castle. From this vantage point we also saw dark clouds; no doubt a thunderstorm would soon be upon us. Dad thought a summit was possible but would require running up the steep trail. Although I desperately wanted to summit, my lungs and legs weren't capable of running such a distance. Reluctantly, I began the descent with Mom and Reid while Dad and Leif pushed for the top.

We were close to the car when Dad and Leif overtook us. They had been near the summit but had turned around, as the weather was too threatening. I was relieved they had not been successful, although in part their failure was due to the knowledge that I would have been extremely angry had they been successful. It was my first failed summit attempt.

The next day we attempted the less vigorous summit of Little Devils Tower, 2,000 feet lower than Harney Peak. This time we started earlier in the day under a clear blue sky. We also left Mom halfway up; had we done this the previous day, perhaps we would have reached the summit, as we did for Little Devils Tower. From the top we had a great view of Harney Peak, and its presence reminded us of our failure the previous day.

In the next two years we took four trips from Minneapolis to Kittson County in the far northwest corner of Minnesota. Two of these were for my grandparents' funerals; the other two were what my family considered vacations. For each trip we drove 700 miles, which meant in four trips we drove a total of 2,800 miles. I was angry—we could have easily gone to Colorado and back and seen the real mountains!

My freshman year of high school, the band went to Winter Park, Colorado, for the Ski-Music Festival. This would have been my chance to not only see the mountains but go downhill skiing as well. The problem was, of course, money: the trip cost $300. On top of the cost, there was the social awkwardness of finding a seat and bed partner, as my closest friend in band wouldn't be going. My parents supported my decision to stay home despite my wanting to see the mountains.

Throughout high school we never went on another real family vacation. We only left the state a few times: a day trip to visit family in western Wisconsin and trips to North Dakota for soccer tournaments, to play in the band during the football section meet, and to go shopping at the West Acres Mall after the annual Moorhead cross-country meet. I realized if I was ever going to see the mountains it would have to be of my own accord.

I seized the opportunity at age twenty. A group of us from the University of Minnesota ski club drove to the West Yellowstone Ski Festival the week of Thanksgiving. It was the first time I didn't spend the holiday with my family. Twelve of us crammed into a fifteen-passenger van with a pile of skis, poles, boots, and winter clothes, and on the drive west we listened to a *This American Life* episode about a guy trying to run down an antelope. I saw the real mountains and skied at 6,000 feet every day, and at one point I skied up to 9,000 feet with Erik. We skied into Yellowstone National Park, and I took off my skis and boots and waded out to a rock in the river and sat there for a picture.

The next summer, Camp Cousins, the family reunion I had masterminded at the age of eleven with my cousin, was to take place at another cousin's house in Colorado. We called it Camp Cousins Colorado. I convinced Mom to go, and it was determined we would drive there—Mom, Leif, Reid, and I. Dad stayed home to take care of the dog. Mom dubbed it "the Big Trip Out West."

Naturally, I figured if we were in Colorado, we—Leif and I, at least—ought to climb some mountains. Since we were going in June, we thought there would be snow on the higher peaks and therefore chose to climb mountains of 11,000 and 12,000 feet that would be void of snow. This was four weeks after getting out of my walking cast from the gastrocnemius salvage surgery.

We arrived at the Rocky Mountain National Park visitor center after 7:00 p.m. on our first day. The park ranger told us the 14,000-foot Longs Peak nontechnical route had just opened for the season, as the last of the snow had melted. Leif and I debated; we had no plans to climb a fourteener. Neither of us had ever hiked in the mountains before. We would have to get up early and hike while it was still dark. Moreover, Mom wouldn't let us drive to the trailhead, so we'd have to hike a longer route from our private campground, which abutted the national park land.

"Well, Elspeth, this might be my only big trip out west, so we might as well try Longs Peak," Leif finally concluded.

Our alarms went off before sunrise the next morning, and we headed out in the dark.

June 28, 2006

Leif and I got up at 4:00 a.m., and shortly thereafter we started out for Longs Peak. Even on one of the longest days of the year we still hiked, mostly uphill, for an hour in the dark. Fortunately the trail was easy to follow. I walked along eating an apple and then a banana trying to keep up with Leif. The trail was littered with horseshit. Soon we were hiking the Boulder Brook Trail, on which horses are not allowed, as it climbs 2,000 vertical feet in 2 miles. Immediately the trail gained in elevation and was steep as we followed the waterfall-laden Boulder Brook up the mountain. I was breathing hard and sweating so much I had to take off my sunglasses, as we were at 8,000 feet and gaining elevation fast. After about a mile the steepness turned into a gradual slope and I stopped breathing so hard.

For the next 3.9 miles we followed a trail with numerous switchbacks that spit us out above the tree line. I could see the arduous trail ahead of us, always heading up, up, and I was breathing hard in the thin air. I felt as if I were on the moon, capable of falling off. It was super windy, and at the trail junction where the Longs Peak Trail comes in I put on my rain jacket because it was so windy. I held on to it tightly so it wouldn't blow away. Now Leif broke away from me, and I placed my foot carefully to minimize any stretching in my left calf as the steepness picked up again. After a few switchbacks we came upon a plateau covered in boulders. Here the trail abruptly ended in a giant pile of boulders that stretched up to a rocky structure called the Keyhole. I'd never before seen so many boulders and realized this was the area marked "boulder field" on our map. It had taken us five hours to go 9.5 miles, and we gained approximately 5,000 feet in elevation in only the last 6 miles. My hip hurt, and due to my tendon situation I could not jump nor limberly pick my way across the boulder field. I knew it would be stupid to keep going, so we turned around.

I was slightly disappointed, although I really couldn't be because I'd only had my cast off for a month, and yet here I was having hiked up to 13,000 feet. It was a whole different world above tree line, and I had a new understanding of a "boulder field." There was a sweet group campsite at the boulder field. Rocks had been carefully placed to form walls around dirt areas for tents. On the way up we had seen a snowshoe hare, and on the way down we saw two marmots. Coming down the Boulder Brook Trail I really began to feel pain in my left knee. The last 2.5 miles of mostly downhill was torture for my left knee. My left gastrocnemius, which I could tell had been made stronger by the whole adventure, had given out. By the time I got back to the campsite my left knee, hip, and a silver-dollar-size blister on the bottom of my right foot all hurt so bad we decided to scrap the Flattop Mountain hike for the next day. I painfully limped around for the next few hours and then crawled into bed at 9:00 p.m. The next day we drove out of the mountains and went to Camp Cousins Colorado near Denver.

It was another disappointment, similar to failing to summit Harney Peak some nine years earlier. Two days later, however, after the soreness in my calf and the fear that I had injured myself yet again with my headstrong ways dissipated, a newfound strength emerged in my gastrocnemius.

For the remainder of the summer and some years to come, Mom talked about how she couldn't believe we had made the Big Trip Out West. A couple years later I went back to the West Yellowstone Ski Festival, so I didn't feel the Big Trip Out West was as deserving of the name. Rather, the name was more indicative that it had taken fifteen years from my first asking for a trip out west for it to actually happen.

Chapter 12

The Savanna Portage

"Erik, didn't you say there was a trail to the west?" I whined as we canoed into our fifth down tree in 100 yards on Minnesota's East Savanna River.

"I'll go check it out," he said. He maneuvered the canoe to shore and lodged it in some bushes, then got out and walked off into the woods in search of the trail.

I stayed in the bow of the canoe, speculating on how many more down trees we would encounter if we continued paddling to the town of Floodwood. At the current rate, with a tree down about every 50 feet, that would be one hundred trees a mile—at 9 miles, nine hundred down trees!

Suddenly the idea of canoeing this river seemed impossible. I could spend the rest of my life portaging over down trees in a feeble attempt to get to Floodwood.

〰〰〰

It had been a year since Dad planted the idea in my head that it was possible to canoe from Bemidji to Duluth across northern Minnesota. The route involved traveling down the Mississippi River to Big Sandy Lake, then up the West Savanna River until the stream becomes too small to navigate. From there, a walking path in the state park (the Savanna Portage, for which the state park is named) crosses the watershed divide to the East Savanna River, which flows into the Floodwood River and then shortly thereafter into the Saint Louis River. The Saint Louis River empties into the Duluth harbor. The route seemed straightforward to me until I realized that before reaching Big Sandy Lake there would be three other good-sized lakes to cross, the last and biggest being Winnibigoshish, which Minnesotans have affectionately nicknamed Winnie. On a windy day, the waves on Winnie can easily fill a canoe with water, and no amount of bailing will keep it afloat. Then, assuming we made it across the lake and all the way to Big Sandy, there was the notorious Savanna Portage. Used by traders in the 1800s on their way from the Saint Louis River to the Mississippi, the portage was now a mystery, a hint of a bygone era—railroads, then roads, had obliterated the need for such a strenuous portage. Erik and I had heard no one had traversed the complete portage in the summer for about twenty years, although there were several reports of people doing it during the winter. This didn't stop us. We never could resist a challenge.

Leading up to the Savanna Portage, we had done several canoe trips together. On our first one we paddled the Mississippi River in the Twin Cities, camping on islands for two nights. I was still in a walking cast from my gastrocnemius surgery, which made it difficult to get in and out of the canoe and sometimes nearly impossible to walk over trees and navigate through brush in the woods.

It was on this trip I learned about lightweight, quality camping gear. When I was a kid my family and I did a fair amount of camping, but with the exception of one trip to the Boundary Waters, we always went car camping, which meant the weight of our materials didn't really matter. Erik's tent was light and hot pink, and he could set it up in less than five minutes by himself. We slept on inflatable air mattresses, which were both much lighter and much more comfortable than the foam my parents had used. And Erik's sleeping bags were down filled, compressible, and much warmer than my parents' cotton giants.

May 6, 2006
Camping/canoeing trip down the Mississippi River. For dinner, Erik brought pita bread pizza with artichokes. I was impressed. Mom says a camping trip is a true test of the relationship. So far so good. He told me I was passing my camping test. It was kinda weird 'cause I knew he was testing me, and I couldn't quite decide if I was trying to show off my camping prowess or if it was completely natural.

I passed the test, and so it was off to the Boundary Waters for five days and then the Savanna Portage the following May, immediately after graduating college in 2007. In fact, I skipped graduation to go canoeing.

Our journey had begun easily, with the only mishap the first day being that we forgot the fruit. Dad got on his bike and met us on the east side of Lake Bemidji with the apples and oranges.

The first day we paddled twelve hours total. I was still using a wood paddle and Erik a heavy plastic one. There were waves on Cass Lake pushing against us, and with each swell the bow of our canoe crashed down onto the water with a *whack*, making it hard to keep a fast paddling rhythm. After this my wrists started to hurt, so on the Mississippi River between Cass Lake and Lake Winnie, I paddled stern and did little more than J-stroke when needed and some half-hearted paddling in between. This section of river took three hours, and it seemed Erik was hardly applying any power up front. I guess he was tired and hurting, too.

On the west shore of Winnie the east wind had the whole lake to make big waves, and our boat began to take on water.

We ditched onto shore and scrambled up a bank, setting up our camp in the forest, as we couldn't make the campsite a bit farther up shore due to the waves. We set our alarm for 5:00 a.m. hoping there would be calm in the early morning and we could set out on a placid Lake Winnie.

But that night the wind speed increased, and we could hear the waves crashing ashore. Because we only had nine days to finish our 250-mile canoe journey, we opted to call my parents for a ride around the lake. We initially felt pathetic for not traversing the 3-foot swells but soon felt better: it was fishing opener weekend, and we watched fishing boat after fishing boat pulling off the big lake, as skittish of the swells as we were.

Once we were back on the Mississippi River it was mostly smooth canoeing. Our second day we did only 21 miles, yet my arms were incredibly fatigued. We made up for it the next two days, however, paddling about 45 miles each day and reaching Big Sandy Lake ahead of schedule. We cruised the lake with a tailwind, then decided not to canoe up the West Savanna River, as we suspected it would be too shallow. Instead we tried our new portage wheels on a road that headed north 6 miles into Savanna Portage State Park. It began to rain, and by the time we made it to the ranger station at the state park we were in rain gear.

"We're here to do the Savanna Portage," we stubbornly declared to the park ranger.

She looked at us funny, like we had just told her a great flood was coming and she should build an ark. She could tell us little about the East Savanna River, only that there was a nice trail through the state park, but past the walk-in campsite the trail was no longer maintained. So we set off in the rain onto the Savanna Portage trail without any new knowledge.

Erik was hell-bent on using the portage wheels. At 110 pounds, I didn't object to carrying a 60-pound pack, but at 180 pounds, Erik was adamant he was not going to carry the

50-pound canoe. Unfortunately for him, the state park maintained a rather narrow and meandering trail not conducive to an 18-foot canoe on portage wheels. After several wheel adjustments and some heavy lifting to get the canoe back on course, he gave up and yoked it. It took us two "pauses," as the voyageurs called their rest stops, before we got to the walk-in campsite. The site had a dilapidated three-sided lean-to covered in moose droppings juxtaposing a brand-new outhouse. We debated calling it a day and setting up camp, but it was merely 2:00 p.m., so we headed off into the unknown. At least the sun was now shining.

The trail, albeit overgrown, was easy to follow. Only once or twice did we have to scamper over down trees. Then we started going downhill and found ourselves on planks. We continued going down; the ground got wetter, and soon our feet were in water. We inched along, careful not to fall off the planks, which we could still feel under our feet. When the water was knee deep and we were still inching along, we came to our first ditch. It was perpendicular to the trail, but we thought it might be better to canoe the ditch. And it was—for 20 feet, until we came to our first beaver dam. We thought this was an isolated beaver dam, but upon going over it, we saw another coming up in 50 feet. At the junction of two ditches, there was a snowmobile bridge and a subsequent snowmobile trail on the ditched bank heading north. We turned our canoe north, and behold: another beaver dam.

Now, I appreciate the occasional beaver dam—say, up to five in a day. They're easy to traverse and constructed of mostly harmless twigs and small branches that don't damage the canoe. After ramming onto the dam, the bow paddler gets out and pulls the canoe over the dam, trying to keep from tipping the stern paddler into the water. When the canoe feels as though it's about to snap in half, the stern paddler crawls out onto the other side of the beaver dam, and the two canoers pull the canoe over it. Then the bow paddler crawls back in, the stern paddler gives a shove and gets back in, and the canoe is back on its merry way.

But three beaver dams in fifteen minutes was annoying. I suggested to Erik we scope out the snowmobile trail on the bank. It looked like a maintained trail, so we climbed out onto it and continued portaging.

The snowmobile trail gradually became more and more overgrown. Soon we were in prickly trees and underbrush. It was on this day I learned that while rain gear is good at repelling rain, it is also a great insulator, bug proof, and tear resistant. The underbrush grew progressively thicker and progressively pricklier, but under my gear my skin made it through without a scratch.

At one point, the trail had eroded away, and we used the canoe as a bridge. After that the underbrush on the ridge thinned, and up ahead was the openness of a swamp. Two ditches came together, and we lost high ground for walking. We got in our canoe and paddled down a 5-foot-wide stream, ramming over small beaver dams for 50 yards until we pushed into a much wider channel, the East Savanna River. This looked promising until we went around a bend and as far as we could see there were trees down. The first trees were easy; they were scrawny little things, and we treated them like beaver dams. The next ones were much more challenging. They were thick, and some were above the water but too low to get the canoe under. In one case I got out and straddled a tree but then found myself helpless to lift the canoe, with Erik and our gear inside, 3 feet out of the water and onto the log. Erik portaged around and came back for me, and all the time I was straddling the tree. It was there at the fifth down tree I pleaded with Erik to find the trail he had seen on the map along this section of river.

He went on a scouting mission while I waited in the canoe, pondering on the number of down trees until Floodwood.

∿∿∿

"The first time I crossed the trail I missed it 'cause I thought it was just a deer trail," Erik reported back.

"That sounds much better than portaging over a down tree every twenty feet," I stammered. I crawled out of the canoe, and Erik helped put the 60-pound pack on my back. I took off through the underbrush, occasionally tripping over twigs while swearing under my breath. He was having a difficult time keeping up with me while portaging the canoe through underbrush and in between trees in the forest.

When I came to the trail, I was relieved to find a nicely defined four-wheeler path, much wider than a deer trail. It continued along nicely for about ⅛ mile with only two down trees, one that I went around and one that I sat on to get over. After that, the trail was abruptly lost at a swamp. We spent several dismal minutes fearing that it was a dead end and that we would have to return to the felled-tree river. But at last, there amid the swamp milkweed, we spotted the continuation of our trail, covered by a down tree.

Navigating over more wet spots and ankle-twisting tree stumps, we continued on. I was in the lead and lost the trail again as it turned toward the river, but then I got back on track. The trail, now slightly wider, appeared more promising, but it was then that Erik took the canoe off his shoulders, set it down on the ground, and said, "I'm done for the day."

"You can't be done!" I shouted. "We're in the middle of a godforsaken swamp. We don't know where we are. I'm not camping here, not in this—this swamp!"

"You can go on if you want to, but I'm not moving any farther," Erik firmly replied.

I took a big breath and sighed a big sigh. "Fine. And where do you propose we set up the tent?"

Erik maintained we were not actually in a swamp but just

on some low land. The ground was spongy, had little under-growth, and was mostly a bed of dirt. He erected the tent and put my side directly on a tree stump. We spent a rather damp night under the stars. I felt we were really lost despite the "promising" ATV trail and wasn't sure we would find these "roads" marked as faint lines on our copied gazetteer map. I was restless, imagining signals being sent from Floodwood as we were considered lost. I thought about my grandma talking about smelling ozone around this area. Grandma had equated the smell of ozone to UFOs, so I spent the remainder of the night sure we would be abducted by aliens. Then the sunlight woke me with the promises of a good day.

After a hearty breakfast of oatmeal with powdered milk, sugar, butter, and raisins, we continued down the trail, which proved much easier to follow now than it had the day before. After ten minutes we came to a fork and decided to head right, staying closer to the river. Soon we came upon another swamp crossing, this one with a defined path made of wooden pal-lets. Several of the pallets were slippery with frost; others had rotted, requiring delicate balance or jumping moves. We were glad that although this crossing was no longer four-wheeler worthy, which probably contributed to the decayed state of the trail farther up the river, great effort had once been put in to make it so, which meant it was navigable for us on foot.

A felled tree on the other side of the swamp made the trail difficult to find again for a few paces, but then a nice path led out onto what I called "the goddamn highway." Although grassy, this was a straight east–west path wide enough for a car. We turned east, heading into the sun. We passed an aban-doned house and several deer stands. Then we came upon a nice mowed field, which reminded me of the garden out on my grandpa's 80 acres. It would have been a nice camp spot had Erik given thirty more minutes of effort the previous evening.

In a few more minutes we came to the start of a gravel road that headed north. Before embarking on the 9 miles of road to Floodwood, we took a detour south to where a bridge crossed the East Savanna River, just to be sure we shouldn't put the canoe back in the water. To the southwest, the direction from which we had come, there were more down trees than we could count. To the northeast we could make out only one, but due to a bend in the river, we couldn't see very far. I thought of the portion of the East Savanna River I had seen a couple months earlier while passing on Highway 2; I hadn't been able to see far, but there had been several trees down.

"Erik, it may not be the real Savanna Portage, but it's 2007, and damn it, there are roads," I said as we put the portage wheels back on the canoe and began the walk into Floodwood. Once there, we bought a quart of ice cream at a gas station before we resumed canoeing.

We only paddled 15 miles on the Saint Louis River that afternoon, but it was 15 glorious miles without a single down tree. The day was perfect, and we found a beautiful campsite that was too good to pass up, so we stopped and dried out our tent and clothes.

The next day proved to be our final day of the trip. All day we battled a headwind, making our attempts to paddle downstream futile. At times the wind howled, pushing us back upstream through the rapids. The water level was low, and as the bow paddler I had to be on constant lookout for boulders just beneath the surface. Paddling into the wind was hard work and put me in a thoroughly bad mood.

That day we also had to portage around three hydroelectric dams—all of which reportedly had no official path. Fortunately it wasn't difficult, as Erik had procured some type of guidebook, but on all three dams he had us canoe dangerously close to the spillway. Before we found a campground for the night, we came upon an overstuffed chair sitting on an island just big enough for a chair. I got out on the island and sat on it, and from the canoe Erik took a picture of me.

At the campground we learned the weather for the following day called for heavy winds from the north—the direction we would be heading after portaging through Jay Cooke State Park. We decided we had gone far enough and called it quits, although we were both sorry to stop short of our goal. Even if we had made it to Duluth, we had already conceded to a ride around Lake Winnie. We hoped to be more successful on our next canoe trip.

We told Dad about our exploration. While we had no intention of ever doing the Savanna Portage again, we were no longer confined to designated rivers, roads, and trails, which provided us confidence to partake in our future adventures.

Chapter 13

Predicaments

It seemed I was always getting myself into predicaments—specifically, human-versus-nature predicaments. Some had the potential for death or, at minimum, suffering; others involved the weather and its lack of cooperation to suit my needs.

One such predicament occurred my junior year of high school. My family went skiing at Buena Vista, home to the Finlandia cross-country ski trails and located in a fairly remote area 15 miles north of Bemidji. The trails are divided by the highway into an east and a west section, and on this day we skied the west section for the first time. Mom and Reid skied together on a very small loop that minimized hills. Leif and Dad skijored Mika and therefore were distracted as she chased every squirrel and porcupine she smelled. I skied by myself. The trails hadn't been groomed, and I was skating, which is very difficult to do on ungroomed trails. The west side is one big loop used for the Finlandia with several cutoffs for high school races, and my plan was to ski the entire loop. I was doing well following the trail until I got out on the Cans Loop, the most distant section of trail, which is not used for the school races. I could tell I had done a loop and was heading back toward the main trail when I came upon an intersection. I could either go east, which was back toward the trailhead, or south, where a big tree lay across the trail. I chose to go east.

After half a kilometer the trail ended in a large field. Although it was 4:30 in the afternoon, the sun had already gone down, as it was only a week after the winter solstice. The temperature hovered around 0 degrees, and I knew it was supposed to be 10 below that night. It would be totally dark soon.

"If you're not gonna groom the fucking trail, then at least mark the fucking trail!" I began to sob, becoming more desperate with each tear rolling down my cheek.

"Where the fuck is the fucking trail?" I screamed, although no one could hear.

I retraced my tracks to the "iffy" junction and proceeded south this time, taking my skis off to climb over the down tree. I continued on the very defined, albeit still ungroomed, trail, constantly wondering whether I was going the correct way. After half a kilometer, I felt better when the trail turned back east. It meandered through the woods, often curving south or north. I kept skiing, frantic, my apparent options of ski or die becoming more imminent with the waning daylight. After a few more curves, I could make out ski tracks, likely from Leif and Dad, which elevated my spirits. Finally, with the last of daylight, I arrived back at the car.

∿∿

Nature has some wicked plants.

The summer after my freshman year of college I had the great idea to run around Lake Bemidji. About 4 miles in, I had to poop—and by that I mean squat in the woods and go right that minute. Almost the entire run was lined with houses, so places to relieve myself were scarce. Quickly I ducked under a pine tree in someone's front yard, which provided ample privacy. I hadn't had time to look for any big tree leaves to use for wiping, and the only thing near me I could use was a nice green plant with three leaves growing on the ground. I grabbed a handful, wiped, and then pulled up my shorts.

I finished the run in just under three hours. I was tired and didn't shower when I got home. Two days later, my butt crack really started to itch. It felt all bumpy. Then my whole abdomen became raised and red in a band slightly wider than the width of my shorts waistband. It was only when a few blisters started appearing on my torso, arms, and legs I realized the nice leafy green plant I had used to wipe had been poison ivy!

I spent three weeks in a toga, moaning, popping prednisone, and rubbing pink stuff all over my body.

∿∿∿

The girls in cross-country in high school politely described me as "well endowed." I had to wear two sports bras to support my large breasts while running—even when I weighed less than 90 pounds, my breasts were still B-cup size. While this feature may be admirable to many outside the sports world, it is a hindrance to the endurance athlete. Not only are breasts extra weight in an awkward place, but they chafe badly. The sweat from my head collects on my sports bra, first saturating the bottom band, then gradually the entire bra—and the warmer and more humid the weather, the worse it is. This wetness, in combination with the up-and-down bounce of my breasts, creates the perfect storm for massive chafing, especially on longer runs.

I dealt with this chafing for years. During the summers I had scattered open sores on the undersides of my breasts, and bloodstains were omnipresent on my bras. It finally got so bad one year that Erik remarked, "It looks like a shark tried to bite off your breasts."

He then introduced me to Body Glide. Now, before running in the summer, I liberally apply this antichafing balm to the undersides of my breasts.

Driving to the Birkebeiner my freshman year of college, Matt, the fastest skier in the cross-country ski club, devised a theory. He hypothesized the reason women could ski marathons so fast was because they could tap into the energy stored as fat in their breasts. The next day I knotted my cloth race bib tightly around my bust so it wouldn't flap during the race. When I got done with the race, I had great difficulty taking the bib off—my breasts hadn't shrunk at all during the race. Unfortunately for me, Matt's theory is wrong: women cannot tap into the fat stores in our breasts during marathons. Large breasts are indeed a hindrance.

∿∿∿

For years I struggled with the striding aspect of classic skiing, which involves getting grip by compressing the snow under the center of the ski in a movement we call kicking, and then using that force to glide on the other ski. Striding allows for gliding, unlike walking or running on skis. When I tried to stride, my heart rate skyrocketed. It was another human-versus-nature predicament in that I wasn't naturally good at striding. My struggles with the technique were likely due to a combination of bad skis, poor technique, and the wrong wax.

The quality and proper fit of a classic ski significantly impact technique. The center part of the classic ski is designed to ride off the snow during the gliding phase and then compress the snow during the kicking phase. My first classic skis were bottom-of-the-line Quasars flexed for me when I weighed 87 pounds at age sixteen. These skis, which Leif affectionately dubbed the "shitars," were of such poor quality I never felt a good compression on them. Heading into my junior year of college I made a huge upgrade by purchasing a pair of Fischer RCS classic skis, which at the time were top-of-the-line.

Besides having good skis, it's also important to be able to compress the ski at the right time in the stride. I fudged striding technique for years, often running on my skis during races and double poling whenever possible. In high school we rarely practiced in tracks and spent little time working on striding technique. In college I became determined to learn how to stride properly, but years of no snow, no tracks, getting out of breath quickly, and poor kick-wax jobs left me feeling helpless every time the terrain warranted the need to stride. My lack of coaching didn't help. Then, my senior year of college, I actually spent an hour going around a flat loop striding without poles. This had been a workout goal of mine for four years, but it took that long for the combination of a flat loop, decent kick wax, and solid tracks to come together. Later in the season I thought it had paid off.

March 6, 2007
Classic ski at Theodore Wirth Park in Minneapolis. I think I can finally stride! Well, maybe it's the skis—or at least the skis help a lot, or maybe I hit the wax right—but whatever happened, I can stride! I strided up that long back hill! Granted, it made me really tired and I stopped like three times. I think I can stride!

This turned out to just be a good kick-wax day on my RCS skis; I was really just running up the hill, not gliding. I continued working on this enigma of gliding uphill for several more years.

Then there was the kick wax, the sticky substance on the center of the ski that comes in contact with the snow during the compression to provide grip and allow the skier to propel themselves forward. What kind of kick wax is needed depends on what type of snow is on the ground, and living in Minnesota, I became familiar with many different types: fresh, dry, cold snow; fresh, wet, warm snow; old, icy snow; and slush. The drier and colder the snow, the less sticky the wax should be, and the warmer, wetter, or icier the snow, the stickier the wax. When my technique was poor, I tried using a stickier wax for the condition to get better grip. Sometimes this resulted in me running uphill and downhill while a giant pile of snow accumulated under my kick wax in a phenomenon called "icing up." I learned this was much worse than having no kick because at least when I have no kick, I can glide down the hills and double pole on the flats. This icing-up problem happened one time in the Noquemanon classic ski marathon when I had some klister—the stickiest type of wax—on my skis.

January 27, 2007
44 kilometers (shortened) classic Noquemanon. I got a good start position, but my wax was icing up in the starting gate. 20°F and new snow and I had on extra blue . . . ahah . . . must've been the old residual klister I used as binder! 100 meters into the race I had to pull off to the side to deice, which involved taking off both skis and one pole to scrape. I thought about dropping out but then thought about how much food I had consumed to prepare to race and how far I'd driven and what I would do while my teammates raced and took off. I had a pleasant 2 kilometers to myself before I passed about 150 skiers! I was proud of myself for continuing and only fell twice!

Eventually I learned klister is only for icy or slushy conditions and came to dread those conditions because klister sticks to everything. But kick waxing is only part of striding; it took me many more years before I could glide uphill.

∿

Many of my human-versus-nature predicaments concerned the weather—in particular, the amount of snow.

Bjorn, one of the best guys in the ski club, really liked roller skiing, especially up and down big hills. One year we decided to go on his roller ski route the first weekend in December. It was raining at the start, with the possibility the rain would turn to a wintry mix, and I was wearing the most clothing I had ever worn roller skiing. Soon the rain turned to snow as we roller skied through downtown Minneapolis. At first it melted as it hit the warm ground, but soon it started accumulating on the trail. At that point we decided to bail on the full three-hour loop and do a much shorter loop instead. We figured as long as we kept roller skiing it would keep snowing. And it did—to both our satisfaction and our chagrin. As the snow kept piling up, it got harder and harder to roller ski. Even though we had greatly shortened our route, we were going so slow it still took us three hours. We were forced to exclusively double pole to keep from slipping out in the more precarious skating position. Our double pole turned into a strength workout, as our small rubber wheels didn't glide well in the accumulating snow. By the time there was 2 inches of slushy snow, we were walking on our roller skis.

More often, my predicaments derived from a lack of snow. The winter of my senior year of college there was little natural snow, and I did lots of training at Elm Creek, a county park with a 2.5-kilometer manufactured snow loop. As a marathon skier, this meant 50-kilometer training days for me on the 2.5-kilometer loop (or 2 kilometers during the early season). It meant classic skiing, skate skiing, and intervals all while dodging other skiers.

December 10, 2006
*44 kilometers at Elm Creek = 22 laps. Arms still felt fresh
at end, legs killing me. Hard to power uphill in the powder.
Very warm, about 40°F and sunny, so snow very wet.*

January 13, 2007
*50 kilometers skate at Elm Creek = 20 laps! Felt pretty
good except that it was cold and I went pretty hard. It took
me 3.5 hours with a 10-minute break in which I ate a Clif
bar. With about three laps to go I ran into Craig and Erik
and I skied with them, which really helped pass the time.
Coughing a lot after, so clearly I was breathing hard while
skiing.*

The next day it was back to the same hamster loop at Elm
Creek.

January 14, 2007
*25 kilometers classic at Elm Creek = 10 laps. Felt amazingly
awesome and I felt strong despite 50 kilometers yesterday.
I went pretty easy. There were tons of kids in the classic
track and slow people, too. I think I was like the third best
classic skier out there, so I'd pass like 100 people every lap,
which meant a lot of jumping in and out of the tracks. I
gained a whole lap on Erik and then had to pass him. It's
my killer double pole.*

January 17, 2007
*25 kilometers classic at Elm Creek. Feels awesome. Took
me about 2 hours. 8-minute side abs. 60-40-45 push-ups.*

During these snowless winters, we drive long distances
to find skiable snow. The scientists call this lack of snow a
result of climate change, caused by too much carbon dioxide

in the atmosphere. Everyone seems to recall winters of enormous snowfalls, snow days, building forts in the front yard. And then winters became brown, and so to find snow we had to start driving—north, or to the lake-effect regions, or to the higher altitudes—and then manufactured cross-country loops began opening, and so now we drive to these. And as we drive an hour or more one way to skiable snow, we emit more carbon dioxide, which according to the scientists further warms the air, which will further decrease snowfall. And so the next year we drive even farther and emit even more carbon dioxide, in a vicious cycle to pursue the sport we love.

Chapter 14

Repercussions of Barney's 400s

Barney was nearing the end of his tenure when he coached me in high school track and cross-country running, but he had trouble giving up the job. His coaching reign had lasted some twenty-five years by then.

Whenever I talked to Barney, he gave me this cockeyed look I could never differentiate as sarcastic or sincere. Similarly, I could never decipher whether his deep belly laughs were cynical or heartfelt.

Rumor had it Barney had produced some great runners back in the day. In my day, however, we lacked legends. There were a few natural runners, but most of us were former soccer players, volleyball players, swimmers, and others who lacked true athleticism. Most of us wanted to make a varsity team but lacked enough hand-eye coordination to do it in our other sports.

I worked hard in practice. I ran by myself on the weekends and during the summer, and rarely did I miss a practice. Yet I still struggled to run fast. Perhaps I lacked the guts and willpower necessary to push myself far into oxygen debt, the one thing required to make varsity in running.

Like most people, when I started running fast and breathing hard and things became dim, my brain told me to slow down or stop. To be a good runner, I needed the resolution to override this warning from my brain. I needed to keep pushing forward, to not be afraid of passing out. After all, the ground was a mere 5 feet away. Some of my best races were those in which I pushed myself hard, really hard, to the point things started going dark; of course, those were the same races I thought about quitting around every corner.

Spring of my sophomore year of high school I learned how to run by doing distance runs of up to 7 miles slowly and intervals at race pace or even faster. At first the intervals were fun: 4 × 800 meters in a neighborhood, 3 × 6 minutes interspersed with a long run on country roads, 4 × 400 meters around the outdoor track. I was able to keep up with the other girls; sometimes I even outkicked them. I was fresh, I enjoyed breathing hard and getting a good workout, and I always felt strong. My times in the 1-mile and 2-mile kept improving throughout the season. The interval workouts mixed with the distance days worked to my advantage.

Then junior year I got too skinny and trained too exuberantly, and running got harder. Intervals were exceptionally difficult. When my breathing became labored, my legs stopped working. I started to dread the feeling of oxygen deprivation. I struggled to make it through a race without walking.

Barney didn't notice I was adding minutes to my races throughout the season. He didn't notice I was zapped of energy. He didn't notice my endurance was failing me—a fact I blamed on too much interval training.

I slogged through the intervals: 12 × 400s, the first six on the track, the second six barefoot around the practice football field; 4 × 600s around the soccer fields; 3 × 800s in a neighborhood with a hill. With each interval I felt slower.

September 25, 2001
Today was one of those dreaded speed interval days. No
kidding, we had to run 12 × 400 meters with three minutes
between each one. My average time was 90 seconds; not
too bad, I guess. My first one was 85 seconds and my last
two were both 88 seconds. The first 6 we had to run on the
track, and those really sucked. My muscles would tighten
up. I kept up with everybody for about 150 meters, then I
slowly fell back. The second set of 6 we got to run barefoot
in the grass! Yes—that was so much better than the track.
It was more fun, and I dreaded each one less.

Some of my teammates agreed we were doing too many
intervals. It's a bad habit to get into—running 800 meters
hard but never having to go farther. We were losing our endurance. Then Barney loaded us in the back of his 1978 pickup
truck and dropped us off 9 miles from town. We had to run
back—doing interspersed intervals. We all got tired at times.

September 6, 2002
On Tuesday, the first day of school, we had a killer of a
workout; however, we slacked off some of it. We were sup-
posed to run nine minutes at race pace, but we (the top
seven girls) went at conversation pace. Next, we were to
go at race pace for seven minutes; we went slightly faster
than conversation pace. Last we were to go at race pace for
five minutes, which we almost did. Then we did 3 × 600
meters on the track while a JV football game was going on.
Last we did 8 × 100 meter all-out sprints across the soc-
cer field. That was stupid—we never sprint in races. Poor
Scott puked, and Barney yelled at him for working so hard.
Later Barney glorified puking to the rest of us—praising
Scott for working so hard.

On Wednesday my hamstrings were really tight from the dumb sprints. Nonetheless I ran around Lake Irving with Kelly and Tanya.

Running is an incredibly tough sport mentally. When we push hard during a race, it's hard to think about anything other than how tired our legs feel and how hard it is to move the oxygen into our bodies.

One time, Shawn, the fourth-ranked runner on our boys' cross-country team, missed the bus to a meet. It's difficult to know whether this was on purpose or not; someone knew Shawn participated in the school-to-work program and was roofing a house that day. We lived in a small town, and after the bus left the high school, we drove out to the house to pick him up.

Barney sternly told him to get on, followed by a big Barney barrel laugh.

Looking back, I was in perhaps the best distance running shape of my life right after I graduated high school. That summer I spent Tuesday nights doing the Birchmont Run with the boys' track team, duking it out with my brother and Dedan, the boys' distance track coach and an army veteran, for 7 to 8 miles. We ran hard and often ended up accumulating lactic acid. I was finally peaking from my track intervals. That summer I ran a respectable 10-kilometer road race.

July 4, 2003
Before the race I really wasn't looking forward to it, you know, dreading all the hard running—that racing feel. But I had a strategy to not start out too fast and then build up. I'm in really good shape 'cause although I started pretty fast, I didn't wear out. I was trying to win my age group, 16–21. There were these three Bemidji State University track girls I knew I had to beat, but I passed them all before

*the second mile. There was a strong west wind as I ran by
the high school, but I kept telling myself to push hard now
because the wind would push me on the way back. Still, I
was getting tired, but not like "slow down a lot" tired.*

*I saw all the runners ahead of me at the turn around
and saw that I wasn't doing too bad, until I started heading back and saw Lyndsey* [an incredible volleyball and
basketball player the same age as me who also sprinted
in track] *was right on my tail. I knew then I would have
to beat her, although I immediately felt slower. I once said
that since she is such a better athlete than me, she could
beat me at any race. Well, I got real determined to beat her
and kept running real hard, only stopping to walk a few
feet by the high school, fearful she would catch me. Then I
got a real good rhythm and pace going and I flew for quite
some time. With 1 mile to go my time was 39:30 or there-
abouts. This guy passed me going crazy fast. I quickly did
the math and figured if I did an 8-minute mile I would hit
my desired time of 47 some-odd minutes. Then on the last
stretch on Fifth Street I stopped and walked a couple of
steps before resuming my pace. Three guys passed me on
the uphill before Irvine. I tried sprinting in but really only
ran hard, careful to see the time on the clock approach 47
minutes. In the end it was a very easy 10 kilometers, but
I think that's because I'm in really good shape and also it
wasn't too hot. I beat Lyndsey and even got a second-place
medal for my age group. Leif did even better, beating me by
about four minutes. He even beat Bruceski.*

This 10-kilometer race may have been "very easy" in hind-
sight, but not while running. I had stopped to walk twice,
when my mental limits kept me from pushing myself physically. My lungs had burned. I was forcing my heart rate to
go higher and higher, and it was uncomfortable. I wanted to

avoid that uncomfortable feeling, and so I quit running races.

The problem with running is that while the body phys-ically adapts, and faster and faster speeds become comfort-able, we must always push ourselves to run faster. Intervals never get easier; we force our lungs to breathe in more air than is possible while trying to keep our legs from tightening up. And so we start avoiding intervals. We say we will do them the next time we go for a run. The next time comes, and we decide to just go for an easy run. So we say we will do track workouts next year. But next year comes and we cannot get in the rhythm of running to the track.

I did one interval workout the summer after my freshman year of college.

July 8, 2004
This morning Leif and I ran up to the Bemidji State Univer-sity track, where we met Mary [a friend from high school who ran hurdles in track]. *The run up there felt slow, like my slow autopilot. It wasn't really hard to keep going, but I just felt killer slow and like I couldn't snap out of it. We started with a 200 to ease myself in. That went OK. Next we did a 300. That one felt good again, and I felt like I could have kept going. We did another 200, which felt good, and then we ran a 400. Mary didn't finish, as she puked up the strawberries she had eaten for breakfast. Next we ran a 200. I had run the 400 in 95 seconds and was going for 90. That 200 felt really good—natural and fast. I just can't believe how fast that pace is, though. It's a 6-minute mile pace, and it feels just absolutely killer fast! Next we did a mini bleacher workout. It was just that—short. We finished with one last 200. It felt really good, fast but not all out. I ran about 40 seconds. I told Mary in another month we'll have to do another track workout. Maybe 2 × 200, 2 × 300,*

1 × 400, 2 × 300, and 2 × 200. I also want to do a good 400
workout before then.

My plan was to repeat track intervals in another month—a very long break that became several years.

Years passed, and I got really good at running ten-minute miles but struggled to run an eight-minute mile. I didn't want to push myself. I didn't want to get out of my comfort zone.

∿∿

I began avoiding running intervals altogether. I figured I would just do roller ski intervals and, very occasionally, ski intervals on snow. My sophomore year in college, my first season of owning roller skis, Bjorn was president of the ski club. He sent an email recommending roller ski hill repeats on the Franklin Hill for practice.

The Franklin Hill was named for the bridge we roller skied under while going up this section of West River Parkway in Minneapolis. There was a nicely paved bike path with an adjacent walking path here, and the grade was easy enough it was possible to V2 the entire three-minute hill, as Bjorn did the first time I roller skied here.

I was incredulous. How could anyone V2 the whole hill? I was lucky to get halfway up before I lost my momentum and had to V1. And so it became my goal in life to V2 the entire Franklin Hill. It took me a year to accomplish this feat.

July 12, 2006
3 × 55 push-ups. Franklin Hill roller ski workout 10 times!
I V2 all the way up the first 6 times. I am heavily out of
breath, but the technique almost seems easy. On 9 and 10 I
was trying to stay ahead of Erik and pushing myself really

hard. I was definitely in Level 4 and almost feeling like I was ready to collapse. I don't think I've pushed myself that hard on intervals since high school! It felt really good to be able to push myself that hard.

While I continued to avoid running intervals, for several years I was able to make myself do hill-bounding intervals, in which I ran up a hill using poles, mimicking skiing, instead of just running. I could make myself do these because I only ever did them on short uphills—usually around thirty seconds of bounding time—and I always walked back down the hill to fully recover. Moreover, these intervals were designed to simulate skiing and incorporate arm power, so they were different than merely running intervals. Still, hill bounding was hard, causing my lungs to burn with the effort to get oxygen in and carbon dioxide out. By the end of the thirty seconds, I was in oxygen debt and my lungs suffered with the effort. But I knew this was only temporary.

I paid the price for my lack of running intervals, however, as my running times got slower and slower. For several years during college I thought about doing intervals but couldn't fathom pushing my body hard while running.

∼∼∼

For six years I avoided the track. Somehow my ski times gradually improved, but I was running slower than ever. I had to do something to stop this downward trend. Maybe Dedan and Barney and Bruceski knew what they were talking about after all.

One Sunday morning in July, at age twenty-four, with words Dedan had spoken to me echoing in my head—"The only way to get faster is to run faster"—I ventured onto the rubber surface with all the familiar markings for hurdles and starts for various distances. By this time I had moved to Rochester, New York. My goal was to run a sub-seven-minute mile; I figured since this was almost a minute slower than my PR, I could accomplish it without difficulty. But when I crossed the quarter-mile split mark at 2:04, well over my goal pace, I immediately gave up and vowed to begin spending more time doing track workouts.

I had read an article on interval training that was based on a highly successful collegiate cross-country ski team in Colorado. The athletes achieved remarkable success doing just twelve minutes total of Level 4 intervals per week. I set this as my baseline and began rotating between running intervals one week and roller skiing intervals the next week. I gave up on running intervals after about four sets. But I tried to keep the roller ski intervals going. By the end of dryland season, I hadn't done as many interval sessions as originally planned, but I had done some, and that was a start.

During the next off-season, at age twenty-five, I started my running intervals in April. Still focused on the far-off possibility of breaking a six-minute mile, intervals were the only plausible mechanism to obtain my goal.

April 26, 2010
Today I got up the motivation to run intervals. Since it was cold and rainy I did the intervals at the indoor track at the college. I'm not sure if it's a 200-meter track or not. I decided to do 4 × 3-minute intervals with equal rest without my heart rate monitor. At the start of each interval I felt my body transition into a faster pace as my watch began to beep. This is acceleration, I realized. In high school we rarely ran into the intervals, so the difference of running comfortable speed to fast speed felt weird, and as the interval started, I got to thinking this was acceleration. Each interval felt good. I was able to push, especially near the end

*of the interval, and yet my fast breathing didn't bother me.
This may have been because I was well rested or because I
was on a flat surface, or because I wasn't pushing all out.
But the goal of the interval wasn't to push all out; the goal
was just to run at a good 5-kilometer race pace. And to not
be so painful that I would never do another set of intervals.
At the end of the workout I was amazed at how well my
body responded, and I was eager to do more.*

Not wanting to do only one or two sets of running intervals in the dryland training season, I tried to keep the idea of
doing intervals fresh. The only way to make the body stronger
is to push it to its limits, or at least near its limits. I tried to
implement intervals as an integral part of my training—for
this year and for the rest of my competitive athletic life. I was
actively trying to change the hatred I felt for intervals that
had been ingrained in me during high school. This was mostly
from doing too many intervals instead of distance training
and continuing to push through intervals despite getting
slower. As I began my new interval regimen, the goal was to
do more controlled intervals while rested to actually make me
faster while doing mostly distance rather than speed training.

<u>May 11, 2010</u>
*Today I ran 4 × 3-minute intervals in the cemetery. The city
of Rochester, New York, is blessed to have the Mount Hope
Cemetery, an old gem with plenty of hills and gravestones
dating to the early 1800s. There is even a Civil War plot!*

*I used a total of four different hills. I wasn't sure how
long each hill would take, but I tried to do the entire interval on an uphill stretch. On the first interval at the beginning I felt fresh. I went up a section of gravel, which wasn't
too steep, but that section timed out halfway through my
interval, forcing me to keep running hard up a very steep*

section. On this very steep section I kept driving my arms forward, but the gravity effect was very strong—as if I had a 40-pound weight pulling me down. I tried to maintain my pace even though my legs wouldn't turn over faster. I noticed my heart rate monitor read 179. One more and it will start beeping, I thought. I turned onto another road, then I heard my monitor start beeping and I looked at my watch and it said 182—a new high record! I was ecstatic! It feels so good to be able to push my body to its maximum potential. I kept pushing hard up the less steep section of the hill, but after a few seconds with my heart monitor still beeping I couldn't force myself any longer, and I quit the interval a few seconds short. On the next three uphill intervals my heart rate was well into the 170s. As it would get that high my breathing became more and more labored. I was trying to suck in air fast so that I could blow it out and begin the process all over again. Near the end of the intervals I started wheezing like an asthmatic, as my airway passage isn't large enough to get in enough oxygen and get rid of enough carbon dioxide as my heart begins beating faster.

Throughout the remainder of the summer I continued to run intervals. I eventually clocked a 7:30 mile, which, although slow, felt like a major accomplishment. It was my first timed mile in six years.

After two years of running intervals in high school, it took me six years of mental recovery to fathom doing them again. Once I implemented intervals back into my running, I enjoyed pushing myself hard again. As I learned to run easy on the easy days and hard on the hard days, my love-hate relationship with running ended, and it became merely a loving relationship.

Chapter 15

Masochism

The first time I cross-country skied at Itasca State Park, I was sixteen and hadn't yet joined the high school team. My equipment consisted of glide-waxed skate skis and classic touring boots, both purchased when I was exactly half the age I was on this outing. There had recently been a snowstorm, and Itasca wasn't groomed; however, there were remnants of some skied-in classic tracks. Dad, Leif, and I started out on a 10-kilometer loop.

The scenery was stunning. We climbed a hill, went down the other side, and saw a beautiful frozen lake enveloped in a pine forest. Snow clung to the evergreen branches and glistened in the sunlight. This scene repeated itself countless times as I struggled to kick up the hills on my slippery skis designed for skating.

I wasted a lot of effort on this. I ran up the hill in the skied-in trail but had no sticky wax on my skis to grip the snow. The skin on the backs of my heels began to rub. Gradually the rubbing became pain. Before we were half done with the loop I knew big blisters had formed there; with each kick a wave of intense, sharp, burning pain shot out from my heels and nearly stopped me in my tracks.

Somewhere near the halfway mark I was able to pull ahead of Dad and Leif and ski on my own. At the crest of each uphill I was relieved to see a downhill to another lake, only to be disappointed when I saw there was yet another uphill.

I kept on, frantic, crying, wanting to scream amid the picture-perfect scenery. I didn't want Dad and Leif to catch up to me. I knew if they caught me somehow the pain would get worse and I would no longer be able to persevere. I had to keep skiing. I had to finish the 10-kilometer loop. If I stopped, I would succumb to the cold and die. So I kept going, wondering whether this searing pain was as bad as childbirth.

Finally, I made it back to the car.

When I got home and took my boots off, I could see my socks were bloodstained. Not yet ready to bear the pain of removing my socks, I waited until bedtime to tell Mom.

"You stupid child for blowing out your heels," Mom scolded as she carefully removed my socks, soaked my feet in warm water, and then replaced the flap of skin gnarled at the bottom of the blister.

For the next three weeks I walked and even ran in heelless shoes to train for the upcoming track season.

∿∿∿

Since moving to Bemidji, I had heard about the cross-country team running around Lake Bemidji. This seemed impossible to me. While not a huge lake—it's easy to see the far shoreline— it's a long lake that stretches several miles north to south.

The first time I ran around the lake it was quite by accident. It was my junior year of high school and my first season on the cross-country team, and we were running some or all the way around the lake for practice. I had intended to only run as far as the state park, about 9 miles, and then have Mom pick me up and take me to soccer practice, but Kristin, a particularly outspoken ex-volleyball player, convinced me we should run the whole way around. I ended up skipping soccer practice without telling the coach. It was the only time I ever cut practice—and it was because I was running 16 miles!

Three miles into the run I found myself on the east side of the lake on the newly paved Paul Bunyan Trail, one of the many old railroad beds in the state of Minnesota turned into paved bike trails. I was near the water, heard it lapping ashore, and could look out over the whole lake without obstruction from lakeshore properties. It was in this section I remembered Dad had once run around this lake. It had been a terrible experience involving a lot of pain, but since Dad had run the whole perimeter, it strengthened my resolve to make it all the way around the lake.

Early on I dropped the girls who were running much slower than I wanted. Most of the team had paired up—each pair shared a bike and they would switch off biking and running. Some were only biking. Others were only rollerblading. Some were only running halfway. Only a few of us hardy souls were planning to run around the entire lake.

At the state park I found myself running with three varsity boys.

Shit—what the hell was I doing?

I was still feeling good. Then the older varsity boys took off except for Troy, a freshman, who stayed with me.

Troy wasn't one for words. After a while he stopped and walked; I stopped and walked with him. Then we would run. Then we would walk. We did this for 2 or 3 miles. Then Barney drove up in his truck on the opposite side of the road with 3 or 4 miles to go to see how we were doing. Without a word to me, Troy sprinted over with newfound energy to get a ride in the truck.

I slogged on. Now I was stuck in the walk-run pattern. My shin and the inside of my ankle both pained me. My left quad hurt worse. A big blister was forming on the arch of my foot—the kind that hurts bad, but not bad enough to cry. It's also the kind I like because it goes away quickly and isn't so painful. Not like those heel blisters.

For breakfast I'd had a banana, a cup of cereal, a cup of milk, and another 120 calories of graham crackers because I was going for a run. The term *bonking* was becoming very real for me. My muscles had used up all their glucose, and there was no more to be had. But even if there had been more glucose, my muscles were too tired to know what to do with it. My legs felt like lead. I had to consciously tell them to keep moving forward. It was like I was in one of those nightmares, the kind where I try to run but just stand still, only there was no murderer chasing after me. It was just my will to keep going.

I made it all 16 miles around Lake Bemidji. It proved to be quite a stupid, headstrong endurance thing to do.

Every time I tried to run for the next several months, I couldn't make my body move—as though I were continuously running uphill on sand. My legs weren't fresh. It felt like I was pulling something behind me. Being too skinny also didn't help. That was the season I kept adding to my race times.

Yet running around the lake was a pivotal moment in my distance-running life. Two years earlier, I had thought this would be an impossible feat for me. But now I had done it.

∿∿∿

I define masochism as continuing to endure unnecessary pain when most people would quit.

∿∿∿

Three years later, just before leaving for my sophomore year of college, I ran with the cross-country team on its "run around Lake Bemidji" day. Only this time Leif, Kathryn, Jill, Jimbob, and I decided to have Dad pick us up at the state park. Earlier in the week Leif, who was in his senior year of high school, had run a PR at his first cross-country meet of the season; it seemed too risky for him to do something dumb now like run 16 consecutive miles.

By this time I had run around the lake an additional four times. Once was a summer ski practice between my junior and senior years of high school. Ice cream cake was promised at the end, and I ran with Jimbob, Bruceski, and Karen, one of our other coaches—she and Bruceski were both superb marathon runners. The entire way around the lake I kept thinking, *What the hell am I doing running this distance with a couple of people trying to break a frickin' three-hour marathon?*

Then there was running it with the cross-country team before my senior year of high school. Despite my bad experience the year prior, I had already done this run once that summer and as always was determined to run the farthest distance possible, so I ran the entire circumference. I quickly found myself alone; I may have been the only one who made it all the way around the lake. People tend to disappear on these sorts of adventures. Despite a sore hip flexor, I kept up a swift pace, finishing the run in two hours and thirty minutes. This time I tried to not let it ruin my cross-country season.

The fourth time was again with the cross-country team a year later. Leif proved to be my partner on this run, and I accomplished a new PR of two hours twenty minutes and suffered from less soreness than in previous years.

The fifth time was when I wiped with poison ivy after pooping under a tree in someone's front yard.

Now, a month after that, Leif, Kathryn, Jill, Jimbob, and I were running with a kid named Jake. He was energetic and reminded me much of myself three years earlier. He was a junior, and this was his first year running cross-country. He was rather determined to run the whole way around the lake, but we spent the 9 miles to the state park trying to convince him otherwise.

When we met Dad as planned, we all jumped into the minivan except Jake. Jake kept running. He was feeling good at 9 miles. We were all feeling good at 9 miles. The rest of us knew by 12 miles we wouldn't be feeling so good. We would be out of glucose, and our muscles would start pulling, causing funny little nagging pains.

As we drove out of the state park, we encountered Ayelsworth, the assistant cross-country coach, on his bike.

"Where's Jake?" he asked. "He was running with you, right?"

"He wanted to keep going. He's going to run all the way around the lake," Leif answered cynically.

"No, he isn't," Ayelsworth commanded. "Go pick him up."

We waited for Jake where the trail intersects the road. When he emerged, the boys went out and physically pulled him into the minivan. Jake was so reluctant to quit. We could all see it in his face—he hadn't bonked yet. We tried to convince him we had done him a favor.

"Trust us—we all have run around this lake before," Kathryn told him. "It gets miserable."

∿∿∿

The pressure I felt to get an A in every single class started in middle school and continued through grad school. It was synonymous with the pressure I put on myself to do well running. When I got a 26 on the ACT, I felt so stupid because all my classmates had gotten in the 30s even though I was getting better grades. My junior year of high school I had an English teacher who gave the most erroneous reading quizzes. His questions didn't involve the important plot points of the story but rather how many pairs of socks somebody brought on a journey or which floor of a very tall apartment building the character in the story lived on or how much the building materials for Thoreau's house on Walden Pond cost. I had an A– after the first quarter in his American literature class and vowed to start taking reading notes that included only trivial facts, such as how many days a journey took and the name of a river mentioned once in the story. It worked, and I got an A.

When I got 100 percent on a test in my Advanced Placement biology class my senior year of high school, that wasn't good enough for me because I still didn't have the highest grade in the class, and the student with the highest grade in the class got the metabolic pathways poster. So I confined myself to my bedroom on Saturday nights, learning about how DNA gets transcribed into mRNA and how the mRNA then gets translated into amino acids, the building blocks of proteins. This worked too, and I earned that metabolic pathways poster.

Throughout undergrad I spent countless painstaking hours taking meticulous reading notes. I didn't party, I had few friends, and my only real breaks from studying involved exercise. I studied my class and reading notes at breakfast, lunch, and dinner. I took what one of my friends called "head-banging classes"—hard classes like Organic Chemistry and Engineering Physics and Advanced Organic Synthesis and Physical Biochemistry. I majored in biochemistry and minored in French and chemistry, yet much of my last semester was dedicated to prerequisites for nursing school, which I had decided by then to attend.

For all four years of college, the pressure to get an A in every class was persistent. This was my own pressure; no one else had this expectation for me. Sometimes, albeit rarely, I fell short of my goal. I had what I considered a horrible semester during sophomore year: one A– and two B+s while taking Physics II and Honors Organic Chemistry lab. But for the remaining five semesters of school I got all As with the exception of one A–, all despite taking incredibly difficult classes. I spent two semesters in the fetal position crying because I didn't understand physics. I gave up trying to understand Gauss's law. After my Physical Biochemistry final I felt Schrödinger had beaten me up, and the position of an electron was still elusive; still, I got an A in that class. I graduated *summa cum laude* with a cumulative GPA of 3.905. I guess it all paid off in the end, although no one except for me really cares about my GPA. I am a perfectionist through and through.

∿∿∿

My freshman year of college, I joined the University of Minnesota cross-country ski club. Despite being a club team, we raced several marathons per year. Each January we took an annual training trip to the Birkebeiner trails in northern Wisconsin, which for the best athletes included a 100-kilometer training day and another several days of 50-kilometers and culminated in the Seeley Hills Classic ski marathon.

Dues for the club also covered entry to the Vasaloppet. Wanting the biggest challenge, I signed up for the 58-kilometer skate race my freshman year despite never having even skied half that distance in one go previously. Most of the team also skied the 50-kilometer Birkebeiner, with many club members in the coveted Elite Wave. I skied the Birkebeiner along with shorter races at the City of Lakes Loppet and the Finlandia. My freshman year I did these events to finish them rather than be competitive.

After skiing the Vasaloppet and the Birkebeiner, I was ready for a new challenge. I had logged many hours on my roller skis, so my sophomore year I did the Pepsi Challenge skate marathon and the Noquemanon classic marathon in addition to the four races I had done the previous year.

After my first few marathons my tactic switched from survival to gaining places. The morning of a race, it wasn't the distance that aggravated my stomach and made my intestines move my food through at such a rapid pace that a number two was a priority before any race—rather, it was the speed I'd have to maintain throughout the race. Any athlete knows completion is sweet and victory sweeter, but victory culminating in utter exhaustion is sweetest. To do such requires guts. It's the fear of not being able to summon these guts on a given day that makes us fret, and it's our ability to summon these guts that keeps us coming back for more.

I secretly disliked racing, and yet in the winter I did it weekend after weekend. Maybe because it gave me something to do, providing structure in my life and an opportunity to be with like-minded teammates. Maybe because I liked gliding on snow and breathing the crisp air and being outdoors. Maybe it was just for the bling—another cloth bib, another finisher's medal or age-class award. But ultimately I kept racing because in the past I had produced the guts, raced hard, and performed well, and I wanted to do that again and again. It's addicting. It's skier's high.

After I haven't done a marathon race for a year, the daunting distance and speed needed to race the event become unfathomable. On a training day when it takes me five hours to ski 50 kilometers, I wonder how I could ever have done the same distance in three-fifths of the time and how I ever can again. I fear I will never again be able to push myself that hard for three hours.

Every race is masochistic. We elevate our heart rates three times higher than normal for hours at a time. We persevere and suffer by breathing hard. The lactic acid builds in our bodies, as we cannot breathe deep or fast enough, and it makes our muscles feel like Jell-O.

My ambivalence about racing began at the same time I started racing, in 2001, when I joined track my sophomore year of high school. It quickly became apparent I had similar feelings about ski racing.

November 27, 2001

I have a problem with racing. I've never liked racing, and I never dissected the concept to know why. Perhaps it's because the contests early in my life always resulted in the opposing party or parties being the victors. Maybe from that stemmed a hatred for competitiveness from an early age, which prepared me to be a loser in society and incapable of bettering my losing status. Or perhaps I hold the winners in such regard I cannot fathom myself standing on the top. Or I am afraid of those top positions. Nevertheless, I assume myself a loser before the contest begins.

Being pitted against another human being, proving something at a set time and predetermined location, has no appeal to me.

January 26, 2002

On Thursday we had a hill workout at Buena Vista. That was fun and good. I have to get going faster on the flats. I'm getting better at pushing myself up hills, but now I gotta get the rhythm going on the flats. It sucks because now I am so excited to race, but before my race I am not excited at all. Maybe I have to look at a race as an excellent opportunity to push myself to maximum capacity. I cannot tell what I fear most, or hate most about racing, but if it is the physical harshness, then I need to learn to love that aspect—like how I am beginning to love those hills.

In the ensuing years, my feelings regarding racing didn't change. Racing wasn't something I wanted to do but was compelled to do.

〜〜〜

My junior year of college, despite my continuing desire to avoid competition, I added even more to my ski marathon schedule. I skied back-to-back races of distances from 22 to 100 kilometers over seven consecutive weekends. This was the year I skied without my left gastrocnemius.

This particular season was characterized by three overarching themes. First, I felt little effect on my skiing from my missing gastrocnemius. During this time, it was only while skiing that I didn't limp around. While on skis it was possible to forget that something so vital to me had been taken away. Second, due to the extreme lack of snow in the Twin Cities that year, I was lucky to ski three days a week and sometimes had to substitute stairs or, once, even running intervals for skiing. Third, despite this lack of training, I had my best season to date. In reviewing my training, I could attribute this to only two possible causes: early-season altitude training in West Yellowstone over Thanksgiving or forced periodization due to crummy weather and surgery.

Here is a close to minute-by-minute recap of the first race of my season, which was also my first without a left gastrocnemius.

January 14, 2006:
Seeley Hills Classic, 22 kilometers classic
I found Kathryn at the start and we lined up like old times. We lined up about 15 minutes before the start time—we should have been out there much earlier, as there were only three tracks. We lined up on the side, not in the tracks, close to the front. There were about 100 rows back, and I'd say we were about 15th. Well, I went into the race confident, focused, and relaxed. There were a lot of people and a big pileup at the start. I liked the outside right lane, but it was really hard to get out of the tracks to pass people. I never fell, which I credit to my new skis. On this one hill a guy

fell in the tracks right in front of me, but fortunately I just moved over a couple lanes and went on my merry way. There were lots of people around me and then all of a sudden at about 8 kilometers everyone disappeared and I was by myself. I wanted to beat my teammate Meleah, and she was in my sight for a while. I was racing really hard—I was in the zone, but yet I was really focused. At the turnaround Kathryn was way ahead. I was really far in front of most of my teammates, but still I didn't want any of them to pass me. A girl passed me at about 8 kilometers from the finish and I hung on to her for the remainder of the race. In the end she beat me by about five seconds. Kathryn beat me by five minutes, and Meleah had me by two. I beat two boys and six girls on my team. I would have liked to place a little higher and hang with Meleah, but I was really happy I had gotten in the zone . . . confident, focused, relaxed.

One week later, we went to Biwabik for the Pepsi Challenge ski race.

January 21, 2006:
Pepsi Challenge, 48 kilometers skate
Pepsi was cold (about 5°F at the start) but wicked fast. I was in the mood to race—lined up in the first row in Wave Two. I didn't take it conservative, either—I passed people when I could. The kilometers were flying by. Halfway through the race, I glanced at the clock after the first lap as I cruised through the stadium and it said 1:20:00. Doing simple math that would put me in under three hours. I kept going, trying to cruise and fighting on every uphill, no hesitation on the downhills. I stopped at the feed at 31 kilometers to down a water and this old guy had just caught up to me. I ditched him and he caught me again, passed me, and slowed down. I passed him back up, then he passed me up

and got a ways ahead. I chased him for 4 kilometers, caught him before the last water stop at 40 kilometers. I grabbed water on the fly and that old guy took off. I kept him in sight. And then pulled up right behind him at 44 kilometers. The race was on. I was completely warmed up—ready for anything—not fazed at all. I finally passed him with about 3 kilometers to go, so I took control. At the chalet I started V2ing and he comes up right alongside me—but I knew I could beat him in a sprint. I increased my turnover and 50 meters from the end I dropped him. I beat him by two seconds. [The results list showed he was sixty-five years old . . . I had to work so hard to beat him!] *My time was 2 hours 44 minutes for 48 kilometers! I never thought I would actually break three hours. I guess in the long run all the hard work really does pay off.*

My time in this race was almost two hours faster than the same race the previous year, when the conditions had been cold and dry powder. The following week I raced the Noquemanon in the Upper Peninsula of Michigan.

January 28, 2006:
Noquemanon, 51 kilometers classic
The farthest I've classic skied at one time this season is 25 kilometers, and by the end I was tired and my shoulder muscles were starting to hurt. I know I can make the distance—I've done the Noquemanon before, and I've done enough 50-kilometer skate skis to know the distance isn't that great. So I line up in good position, but the gun goes off and I feel like I can't double pole. Then 2 kilometers into the race I'm cruising on a downhill when my skis caught, and I was down, and all my hill confidence shattered. I fell four times before the first water stop. I completely forgot how to step turn, and on some hills it was so icy that despite

my best attempts at snowplowing I just slid. Twice I was off the trail into the snowbank. I started dreading the up-hills simply because that meant I would have to go down. It was a horrible race—my kick was terrible, my trapezius started killing at 25 kilometers. I snowplowed almost all the hills—I don't think I could have raced slower and yet I placed 9th out of 35 amongst women and won my age class.

The next week was the City of Lakes Loppet. Like most endurance athletes, I developed repetitive stress injuries, and by this point in the season I had right forearm tendinitis. Each time I poled, my right forearm seared in pain.

February 5, 2006:
City of Lakes Loppet, 35 kilometers classic
I know going into the race there will be no classic tracks and snow conditions are "iffy." I put my skis in the start-ing pen and run for a little. I start thinking about taking my warm-ups off only to discover my bag is gone! I tell the announcer my bag is missing. So I'm trying not to freak out and keep my cool and somehow in this whole mess I forget the race starts at 9:20 a.m. instead of 9:30 a.m. At 9:10 a.m. I learn my bag has been found, so I run to it and switch my mittens for gloves and then jump in the porta-potty line. So at 9:19 a.m. I run for the start, but they are playing the national anthem and I know some-thing is wrong. I get to my skis, bend down to start putting then on, and the gun goes off! But the clock only says 9:20 a.m. Oh shit, that's when the race started. I put on my skis and poles faster than ever before. I took off but had some ground to make up.
The first 5 kilometers were awesome 'cause I passed about 45 people, but I was way off the leaders. I kept skiing hard, but on the bog section it was so hilly—such wicked

turns on such narrow trail. I passed this guy and I swear he was skating. [Skating is not allowed in classic races.] *Then on this flat section there were a bunch of University of Minnesota kids cheering for me. I don't know what happened, but I fell somehow on the flats in front of those kids, which was so embarrassing. Then that guy I had just passed—well he came along and smacked his ski so hard into my tailbone it brought tears to my eyes. He must've been such a bad skier he couldn't maneuver around me. Or else he was pissed I had just passed him. Now besides the killer tendinitis in my right arm I had a wailing tailbone that killed with each step. I passed that idiot back up and never saw him again. Once I got to the lakes I realized the race was over. The people in front of me were like a minute up there and conditions were so fast I'd never be able to bridge the gap. For a while I saw no one and feared I had taken a wrong turn. I finally pulled into the finish in mega pain. Mom (I love this) had seen the results before I did. I ended up 6th out of 23 women and 29th out of 80 racers. I guess I'm pretty satisfied with that considering my start.*

The following week was the Vasaloppet. I was now in considerable pain. My tailbone hurt when I walked. My right forearm tendinitis gnawed as I gripped my poles. This is when most people would have given up and skipped the next race, but I was determined to always go the farthest distance no matter the suffering. In the end it was a new phenomenon, left soleus tendinitis, that caused me the greatest pain.

February 12, 2006:
Vasaloppet, 58 kilometers skate
The start is around 15°F. Perfect temp for spandex hat and one layer of poly under spandex. I would like great things, but I am not expecting great things. I have skated very

little in the past week. I line up at the "under 3½ hours"
fully confident I will be within that time. I have three goals.
1. Beat Emily. 2. Beat Mark. [Both my teammates.] *3. Get*
time and half medal. [Given if my time is less than 150
percent of the winner's time.]

The dynamite goes off and everyone is passing me. I
feel slow and unsteady on my skis. At 3 kilometers Mark
passes me and I refuse. Then I'm in luck 'cause two women
pass me. [Skiing with women in a marathon was very
rare; in my first few years of racing I was only part of a
women's pack once or twice, and those times were always short-lived. I rarely skied in packs at all, and when
I did they were usually made up of all or mostly men.]
I jump onto their train and soon I have passed Mark and
Emily back up. We pass some others. The women jockey for
place—I try to go with whoever is faster. Around 40 kilo-
meters to go Emily passes me leading a pack of men. "Don't
worry, Elspeth, I'll die at 30 kilometers to go," Emily says
to me. I can't figure out why she is such a consistently dumb
racer, so I decide to jump onto her pack and hang on until
she dies. Sure enough, at the hill before the water stop with
34 kilometers to go Emily dies [perhaps a more appropriate term here is bonked] *and I take off.*

Soon Pepsi man (the guy I had to outsprint) comes
cruising by me. I try to hang on to him and I can see an-
other pack ahead, but between 30 and 20 kilometers to go
I fall twice trying to catch the pack. I get angry and have to
ski by myself for the remainder of the race. Worse yet, there
is a woman I can see up ahead. By 20 kilometers to go my
left soleus is killing me. My right forearm tendinitis is still
persistent and at every pole release there is major pain. I
debate dropping out but do not know how I could deal. I
stick in for the long haul all by myself. I keep pushing so
Mark and Emily won't get me, and on straight sections I

can still see the pack I'm chasing. The pain in my soleus and arm is growing, but the kilometers keep ticking away. At 7 kilometers to go I am joined by the 35- and 13-kilometer races. So now I weave in and out of people. This makes the race more interesting. I feel really strong on the uphills— yes—really strong on the uphills. At 2 kilometers to go, I catch sight of the pack I've been chasing. At 1 kilometer to go, before I descend onto the lake, I say out loud, "Fight for it, Elspeth, fight for it" and I close the gap on the pack on the lake. I pass the woman and two men. I power up the Bell Hill—there is a fall, and I go around two men. Then I'm skiing down Main Street and I know I'm either gonna pass out or make it. I can't outsprint one more guy, but that's OK—I got like five in the last half kilometer. So I got 3 hours, 19 minutes. I'm happy with my time and half medal, and I beat Emily and Mark, but my soleus and arm both kill. I'm happy I felt strong on the uphills. That night I'm too tired to study, so I hang out with Erik in my underwear.

What I fail to report in this entry is after the race, while I limped the five blocks to the postrace celebration at the high school, my soleus burned and my right forearm screamed in pain as I tried to hold on to my poles and the tears poured uncontrollably down my face. I was miserable, not so much because I was in pain but because off my skis I was harshly reminded of my ruptured gastrocnemius.

The following week was the Finlandia. Given it was the race's twenty-fifth anniversary, the organizers brought back the 100-kilometer race, which involved two 25-kilometer laps on Saturday and the same two 25-kilometer laps on Sunday. Compelled to always go the farthest distance offered—and perhaps egged on by the fact Erik liked to ski the longest distances, too—instead of skiing the 25-kilometer race as I had done the two previous years, I quadrupled the distance.

February 18, 2006:
Day one of the 100-kilometer Finlandia, 50 kilometers skate
Brrr . . . it's cold in Brrmidji! I run for warm-up, but the
air is so cold. It's only –3°F. I feel good racing except for
the cold. I started out with a pack—pushing the pace a lit-
tle but not too much. Mark was ahead of me and I wanted
to get him, so I dropped the pack. I saw Blake through the
trees by the S-curve, but I didn't catch him. Then I started
passing the classic skiers, who had a 10-minute head start
on me. I finished the first lap and started the second lap but
struggled to stay warm as I got near the ridge on the east
side of the course. That ridge was cold. Too cold for comfort.
Then I went through the tunnel and only had a quarter of
the race left. Around the S-curve I saw Blake. Now I was
gaining on him fast. I cruised by him V2ing—he was doing
his funny skate dance. I kept hitting it hard—just cruis-
ing—knowing I had another 50 kilometers to go the next
day. I thought I had it in the bag—then I cross the "finish
line" and find out that this woman Eileen had 8 minutes
on me. I hadn't skied very hard, but the –3°F had done a
number on my lungs. I was coughing and couldn't get in
enough food.

February 19, 2006:
Day two of the 100-kilometer Finlandia, 50 kilometers skate
Leif waxed my skis, and they were rocket ships. I ran for
warm-up. Leif was my "feed" guy, although I suspected I
would only take water. My plan was to stick with Eileen for
the first 25 kilometers, then waste her. I led her for the first
5 kilometers until she passed me. Then I pulled in behind
her. 5 kilometers later, she pulled over to take a gel and I got
a 1-minute lead on her. I saw her again through the trees
on the next two laps by the S-curve, so that's how I knew I
only had one minute on her. I know my plan was to hammer

*the last 25 kilometers, but I didn't really have it in me. It
was so hard skiing by myself. It felt like a fast comfortable
pace. I hammered the last steep uphill before the windy
ridge. Leif had warmed the water, and I chugged and skied
as he ran alongside me. By Cans Loop I was getting tired.
Not bonking—just that last-interval tired. I never saw
any other racers out there until Eileen passed me with 3
kilometers to go. Somewhere in the woods Ludacris's lyrics
"Move, bitch, get out the way" blared as Eileen showed her
dominance. She gained 27 seconds on me. I love that last
3 kilometers, but there was honestly no point. My V2 was
dying. I hammered the last hill before the road. It felt so
good to still be able to hammer after 100 kilometers. When
I came in, Devin was yelling "Go Ronnannnannnander."*

My times were 3:05:46 on day one and 3:00:37 on day
two. My tendinitis still hurt like hell, and my soleus hurt, too.
I was tired. My body was tired.

But the next week I raced the Birkebeiner.

February 25, 2006:
Birkebeiner, 50 kilometers skate
*Wake up at 5:15 a.m. It was colder than expected, only 2°F
with a killer headwind. Leif and I put our skis on to ski
around. I wasn't staying very warm. Then I had to go freeze
in the porta-potty line for over 10 minutes. I took off my
warm-ups and before I could get my skis on my hands were
already frozen. We got in the gate when Wave Two went
out, but there were already so many people. Leif snuck up
through the crowd like a snake to get a second-row position. I was back in about fifth. I tried taking off my skis
to head up next to Leif, but my hands were too frozen, so
I just decided to stay put. I stood there and shook of cold
for 10 minutes in the starting gate—that's why I hate the*

Birkebeiner. There's just too many people. Then the gun went off and it was a massive traffic jam for 3 kilometers until I got to the power lines. I couldn't openly ski—I was trying to be compact. On the power line hills I started my passing. At 5 kilometers my right fingers were stinging and I had one frozen right toe. At 7 kilometers my left fingers were stinging—unthawing—and one of my left toes was numb. The uphills were all traffic jams—waiting in line to go uphill. I wanted to quit but figured that was a good sign—I usually want to quit during some of my best races.

On the High Point hill I dug in deep, and by the time I got to the top I realized I was all alone, so I must've passed everyone on the hills. A woman without a hat and pigtails passed me around 18 kilometers. I didn't think it was worth the effort to go around all the people. Another woman wearing light blue passed me, too. I was trying to pick the faster-moving lane—that was usually the one with less Wave Two and more Wave Three. I pushed the 22-kilometer hill stuck behind more people. I grabbed a gel at the OO road crossing and barely had time for water. Then the congestion died and I kicked it into high gear. Suddenly I'd lost all the drag of the throngs of people and I was free to cruise. I went without hesitation—V2ing the flats and pounding the uphills. I had some vague idea that I might bonk, hit the wall . . . but I pushed on and hard anyway—I'd done the 100-kilometer Finlandia the week before. I cruised by Emily around 26 kilometers. I was passing people left and right. I caught the light blue woman—then the pigtail woman, which made me happy. I kept cruising. I kept hammering, right up Bitch Hill. It was kinda hard, but I kept passing people. A lot of people got in my way on that climb out of the last water stop. Then I got to the lake and that wind sucked. I tried sticking on a couple trains, but I kept falling off. I still passed about 20 people. Then I got off the lake into the worst unpacked snow I'd ever been in. I kept tripping. Finally Main Street had well-packed snow and I tried to V2, but I was exhausted. Eventually I crossed the finish line—done with Birkie #3.

Two days later I had surgery to repair my torn gastrocnemius tendon. I had raced six marathon distances in six weekends, enduring terrible tendinitis for half of them.

〰

Even though I didn't like competition, I came to realize I was fiercely competitive. I discovered this one morning while running a timed mile on a straight gravel road with Erik. The goal was to see how long each mile was taking us. But as soon as the clock was running, I sped up. Then, four minutes into the mile, I started pushing. I was trying to beat the clock. It felt good. I was breathing hard, but my desire to beat the clock overrode my respiratory system telling me to stop.

I needed to remember this. In the heat of the competition, I don't care that I am breathing hard; I just want to win or to beat the next person or to beat the clock, and I am willing to work hard for this. I needed to not fixate on the effort required in the days and hours preceding the race. I needed to stop worrying about all that breathing-hard stuff and how much it would hurt. I would turn it on when need be. I would kick it into gear and push and push and breathe hard and work my muscles and let the lactate build up.

〰

In 2010, at age twenty-four, I did the granddaddy of masochistic events and convinced Erik to do it with me. We would ski the longest two-day ski marathon in the world: the Canadian

Ski Marathon, 160 kilometers of classic skiing over two days in Quebec. Erik thought me crazy for wanting to attempt it, but he is crazy, too, and agreed to the challenge. We trained all winter; we no longer considered a three-hour ski "long distance." We logged days of 50 and 60 kilometers.

That year, there wasn't enough snow for the traditional point-to-point course. Instead, the course would follow a figure eight loop in a provincial park in Quebec, with participants skiing the loop in one direction on Saturday and in the opposite direction on Sunday. Both days were to begin with a 10-kilometer stem, which would bring us from the Ottawa River up to the Laurentian Mountains. Therefore, both days would have a net elevation gain.

During this time I was working the night shift as a nurse, and in the week leading up to the Canadian Ski Marathon I worked three overnights in a row. In between shifts I slept five hours. I had one good night of sleep at home, then the night before the event we slept on the gym floor of a Quebecois middle school. The lights were left on, there were many other people, and we had to get up extremely early. Even though I was already ridiculously sleep deprived when I lay down, I only slept six fitful hours.

It was before dawn when we began. With my headlight I discerned grass poking through the snow on the starting field and several dark chunks in the snow I hoped were dirt as opposed to rocks. About 3 kilometers into the course we came to a mandatory ski removal zone, the first time I had ever had to remove my skis in an organized event. In our ski boots we traversed a slope with several ruts and clumps of grass. This start didn't bode well for the upcoming course. We put our skis back on and traversed a rocky slope that resembled the surface of the moon.

On the next uphill there were several rocks, and skiers again removed their skis to walk. Next we came to a screaming downhill. I took my turn in line but started too soon behind the guy in front of me; I snowplowed like crazy to avoid running into him, but everyone in front of me had snowplowed like crazy, too, and so the hill was sheer ice. My efforts did little to stop me, and soon I was hugging the man in front of me, the two of us going down the hill together, our skis intertwined, neither of us able to snowplow. I eventually fell to stop myself—it was the only way. I got up and continued snowplowing down the hill, but there was another lineup at the last corner and I couldn't stop, so I fell over again.

We crossed a grassy swamp, then climbed another rock-filled hill that went up and up and up. We herringboned slowly. It had just gotten light out, but at this rate I would never finish before dark. We came to another snowplowed-out hill with a corner at the bottom. I snowplowed down the whole hill and still managed to fall on the corner. It was my third fall in 6 kilometers, and I felt defeated. On the next downhill I took my skis off and walked.

I pulled into the rest stop 7 kilometers into the course with serious thoughts of quitting. There was no way I could ski another 73 kilometers at this pace or under these conditions, rock dodging and killing my quads snowplowing down hills.

"You'll regret it forever if you don't keep going," Erik told me.

Reluctantly I pushed on and in the next 5 kilometers encountered a gravel road. The event organizers had moved snow onto the side of the road, but the snow, which was sand-like in consistency, was wearing thin. The exposed gravel caught our skis. A man ahead of me going down the hill hit such a gravel spot and fell over; my choice was to further stone-grind my skis by moving out onto the gravel road, hit a tree just off the road, or somersault over him. I chose the latter in the two seconds I had to make a decision. It wasn't pretty, especially not for him, but I will say rolling over another human being is much softer than hitting the pavement.

After the next water stop something miraculous happened. The trail moved onto smooth Canadian wilderness roads, and except for two short sections, there were no more wicked downhills or rocks. I suddenly became very glad to have kept at this event. I was once again reminded of why I love cross-country skiing.

At the 60-kilometer mark, however, the brutality of the distance caught up with me. I could no longer ski so fast on the uphills; I would walk on my skis for a while, catch my breath, and then continue striding up the hill. When I tucked on the downhills, my hamstrings tightened and my back went into spasms, and so I took to standing up. My body was growing stiffer and more tired as I continued skiing. Yet I willed myself on the last 20 kilometers, thinking about how friends had told me I had "mad endurance" and remembering one friend who wrote on my high school graduation card, "Elspeth, you have the most endurance of anyone I know." Finally, we finished the first day. I was exhausted. I tried not to think about the next day, when I'd have to do this all over again in the other direction.

After just seven hours of sleep—a whole hour less than I had skied the previous day—the alarm went off. Stiff, sore, and tired, we got up off the floor, shoved as much food down our throats as our stomachs would hold, got dressed, and set out to do it all again.

The first 7 kilometers were as sparse as the previous day. I walked down more hills. The section seemed to go faster, probably because I knew what to expect and so all the rocks didn't make me as angry. We were soon back on the park roads, where my breathing labored even on the slightest uphills. The kilometers slowly ticked away.

At 30 kilometers in I did the math and realized we still

had 50 kilometers to ski. I lost it. I was tired, broken down, and had no idea how I could ski that much farther. My triceps and the muscles in my back felt like they were going to rip off the tendons. My left knee had started to hurt when I tried to stride. I ate a Clif bar, I drank more honey water, but to no avail—I had bonked. I had blown up. I wanted to cry.

Usually when I race back-to-back marathons, like the Gatineau Loppet, when I have gone 30 kilometers the second day, I only have 23 kilometers left, and it's a net elevation loss of 1,000 vertical feet. That seems doable—actually easy. But 50 kilometers of net uphill was discouraging.

I slogged on, trying to tell myself that at 40 kilometers to go I would feel better. I did, but it was thanks in part to some long, restful downhills. Then we came to a sparse rocky section before a lake and some more rock dodging. I joked, "The Canadian Ski Marathon, a $180, 160-kilometer stone grind!"

Erik and I skied our first 50 kilometers that day in just under six hours. At that point there was a feed station. I blinked back the tears; endurance events always make me sentimental. I peed for the first time in six hours and pondered whether I was hydrated enough to stave off acute kidney injury. The kidney needs to excrete 30 milliliters per hour to stay healthy. I multiplied six hours by 30 milliliters in my head and wondered whether I just peed out 180 milliliters in the porta-potty. I drank more honey water and shoved down cookies and granola bars until my stomach churned. It was hard to get in enough calories when I was exerting myself so hard.

Only 30 kilometers to go. We pushed on. *OK, I can do this*, I thought. Then we came to a long, wicked, snowplowed-out downhill with a corner at the bottom. I face-planted, and immediately tears crowded my eyes again. I started bawling like a two-year-old who needs a nap. I stood up, trying to pull myself together, but my skis were on ridges of snow, and I immediately fell backwards onto my butt. My glasses fell off my head, pain shot through my already bruised butt, and I began hollering all over again.

People stopped and asked whether I was OK. I was exasperated, I was frustrated, but mostly, I was exhausted. I had skied 80 kilometers yesterday, a new one-day personal record, and had already done 50 kilometers today. I'd had only one normal night of sleep in the past six nights. I had been staving off tears for 20 kilometers. I had hit the wall 20 kilometers ago and still had 30 kilometers to go. Sometimes, my masochism was just too much.

As I collected myself at the bottom of the hill, nearly half the skiers who came by fell as I had. This hill was dumb for a course this long, with people carrying 20-pound backpacks on rubbery legs.

I skied on. Hard. I passed people. It was a nice double pole section with the occasional gradual uphill.

Erik—who had slept much more than I had in the previous week, wasn't working at the time, and arguably was skiing at an easier pace than me since we were skiing together—said, "Elspeth, the next time you fall, you have to get up fast. You're lucky nobody plowed you over."

This sent me into another bout of hysterics. Crying and skiing at the same time was hard.

"Haven't you ever heard of the giving-up response?" I barked. "I was ready to just lie there and die, Erik."

Somehow, however, either my anger or the flat double pole section or the combination of the two willed me onward. Fortunately, unlike the previous day, which had had some climbing in the last 20 kilometers, today's course was much flatter in comparison. This helped. All I had to do was collapse onto my poles and let gravity work, although my triceps screamed at me each time I did.

On what uphills there were, I kick double poled for a while, then walked, then strided. Always there was a long restful downhill. At the last water stop, 5 kilometers from the finish, I downed more water and headed out onto the gravel road, this time going uphill. My skis stuck again, but there was no falling. Erik and I reached the finish line together in less than nine hours. I was ready to be done and not eager to do it again.

Three nights later, as I worked a twelve-hour night shift, my right triceps gave out on me. I couldn't even sign my name, a frequent requirement as a nurse. There was no way I was ever skiing the Canadian Ski Marathon again.

Previous to this marathon I had accomplished many athletic feats I deemed so difficult they seemed impossible to repeat—running a PR mile, wheeling my wheelchair up an incline so steep the front wheels came off the ground—but the 2010 Canadian Ski Marathon stands atop that list for the combination of the distance with sleep deprivation. After that, almost any other endurance athletic feat seems easy in comparison.

Chapter 16

Training Hardcore

Back when I was too skinny, I didn't like calling exercise by that name. Instead, I started calling it training. Training is exercising not for exercising itself, but working toward some goal, like doing really well at a ski race. Training was what the real athletes did, and if I called what I did training, then it was like I was a real athlete.

In high school my training was simple, mostly comprising running, skiing when there was natural snow, strength, canoeing, and biking. After my freshman year of college, the year I discovered cross-country ski marathons, my training increased in volume and became more ski specific. After deciding the only way to ski a sub-three-hour marathon was to train on roller skis, I bought a pair, just one month after my first Birkebeiner. During that era only three girls in Bemidji owned roller skis: Kathryn, Jill, and me. Together we logged countless training hours. Leif got roller skis at the same time, so we trained with him as well as with some of our other Bemidji contemporaries, including Jim Grundy and the so-called Bemidgets—Waylon, Tommy, and Matt, all four years my junior.

Long before high school I realized my physiology wasn't compatible with being an athlete. Still, once I started ski racing, which coincided with the 2002 Olympics in Salt Lake City, I wanted to go to the Olympics. I had this idea that if I trained hard enough, I could be an athlete, and I, too, could make it to the Olympics.

Roller skiing became the hallmark of my ski training. I spent many hours doing it on the Paul Bunyan Trail (PBT) along the east shore of Lake Bemidji. The PBT from the parking lot on the southern end to the northern terminus on County Road 20 near Lake Bemidji State Park and back was about 12 miles.

Another favorite roller ski route was the Migizi Trail around Pike Bay, one of the many bays on Cass Lake, 15 miles east of Bemidji. Unlike the PBT, the Migizi Trail, shaded by towering pines in the national forest, had several rolling hills and gentle curves.

My journal entries from the first summer I owned roller skis indicate my desire to reach a higher level of training and competition—likely spurred on by my reading of Pete Vordenberg's book *Momentum: Chasing the Olympic Dream*. I believed if I roller skied and ran and trained enough, I would become a better and faster skier. What ensued was a summer in training.

June 21, 2004
This morning Leif, Tommy, Waylon, and I went to Cass Lake to go roller skiing. That trail is rocking 'cause it has lots of turns, good downhills (small, so easy to handle on the roller skis), and gentle uphills to practice V2—a very difficult task on roller skis. I was really hungry by the end, probably 'cause I'd done three workouts in a row.

June 22, 2004
We ran Birchmont. I felt slow the whole run. I didn't stop until the turnaround point, and then I only stopped twice for two short walking breaks on the way back. My legs felt heavy, my quads and calves felt all rubbery—like they were

cold, which was a possibility. Anyway, my friends definitely kept me going. I had one of my best runs in a really long time.

June 23, 2004

Leif and I went roller skiing. Jim was back from Germany, and he showed up, too. We skied 15 miles total. Roller skiing is just so much better than running, but I think it's 'cause the breathing seems easier.

June 24, 2004

Leif and I ran up to Kathryn's house to go run with her. It sucked. It was about 40°F, sunny, and there was a cold northwest wind. I was wearing my black poly on top and my ski-team spandex. I was running 10-minute miles, but my body felt like I was running 8-minute miles. Yup, I just felt slow and like my legs were lead. I think I had to stop and walk twice just to get to Kathryn's. We headed west to go around the middle school loop. Man, I was dead, and so we cut back early. Once we turned south I started feeling better (really long warm-up), which helped a lot 'cause then I felt like I could run free. Also, by then I had long ditched the poly and ski pants. I was thinking running sucks and I should quit, but I can't. It's kinda like being addicted, but more like I don't want to get out of running shape. Running is so pure—the way it works the cardio system.

June 25, 2004

Leif, Jim, and I went roller skiing. When we first started it was cold and rainy, then it stopped raining and the sun came out, which made the blacktop steamy. I felt tired, and Leif and Jim were a ways in front of me. Much, much more inefficient than tired. On the way back we double poled. My arms seemed to be much more tired than on Wednesday, but they probably weren't. Double poling is just hard work.

June 26, 2004
Leif and I ran to Wilton and back. My quads felt so tight,
like how they were junior year of high school. I don't know
if it was from running on the sand, but they felt tired, and
tight so it made it hard to move. Then we ran on the road
parallel to the train tracks, and that felt much better. I only
walked a few times. I don't think the mosquitoes and sand
flies ever bothered me, and we had only four dogs chase us.
It felt good, especially for 12 miles.

"We should come up with a name for our training group. The Bemidji something," Leif said one day while we were running.

"Yeah, something about Olympic development," I chimed.

"How about the Bemidji Cross-Country Ski Projekt, with a *k* in *Projekt*?" Leif concluded.

The next summer we had thirty T-shirts made and convinced our friends to buy them—even if they didn't do much training. On the back of the shirts we put a quote from Scooter: "So beautiful to see you sweat."

A grassroots training group was born. We were different from other high school and college development programs in that we charged no fee and had no coach. Our Projekt consisted largely of a calling tree, roller skiing, and biweekly runs down a street in Bemidji called Birchmont. The goal was to get as many skiers from Bemidji as possible to become "greats," as Leif would say. And we started training like we were all going to become greats, racking up the hours roller skiing and pole bounding and lifting and running. We hosted roller ski team sprints around a median in the high school parking lot. Within five years of Leif coining the group name, the news clips started rolling in: "Jill, sixth at the state meet . . ." "Three Bemidji skiers, Waylon, Jill, and Kathryn, set to compete at Soldier Hollow representing the Midwest Junior Olympic

Team . . ." "Former Bemidji High School skier Jill makes it to the NCAA championship representing Michigan Technological University."

June 27, 2004
Today we went hill bounding up Tower Hill. It was Leif, Anna, Kathryn, Jim, and me. We used four different hills and did each hill about three times. Hill bounding is awesome, in my opinion, anyway. My arms start to kill. I never feel so out of breath until I get to the top and stop, and then it feels like I want to die. Leif says he likes hill bounding, too. He thinks we should do more. I tell him I love it, too, and I don't know why. It leaves me so out of breath at the top. I feel it in my arms—they feel cool and clammy like they want to collapse. And then I recover ever so quickly and I'm bounding again—like a kid in a candy store.

June 28, 2004
Anna (on bike), Leif, Kathryn, Jim, and I went to Cass Lake to roller ski around Pike Bay on the Migizi Trail. In the Pike Bay campground there is this downhill with a right turn onto the road at the bottom. I realized too late I was going down the hill too fast. I considered my options: go off onto the grass and make an abrupt stop, fall on the pavement, or just go for it. I decided the latter was the best option. Well, that was a good idea 'cause I cornered very nicely with Jim taking the outside. Next, I led the group for a long time. About half a mile south of Highway 2 the group jumped in front of me and I lost some momentum. The next thing I had fallen off the back of the pack. I didn't really mind, as I should be in Level 2 for the heart rate anyway. Then, at my insistence, we went into Norway Beach and then double poled back for a good workout.

June 29, 2004

Today was the Birchmont run. Before running I ate a blue cheese omelet. I know . . . I know . . . I ate too late before running and then even finished dinner off with vanilla ice cream! That was a horrible choice. My quads were so tired—feeling funny after the hill going up from Diamond Point. I was running with Kathryn and Jill and I asked to stop, but Kathryn was smart and said let's slow down, so we did. Then we walked before Thorson Hill and again afterward. By the time we got to the boat landing I had to poop so bad I had to stop at the Blue Moon bar for explosive diarrhea. Then I stuck it out and ran all the way to the last hill on Birchmont (15th Street) before I walked, then pushed it in with Kathryn. Felt good to be able to push it. I worry about my quads feeling so tired/funny/tight. I wonder if it's from roller skiing? Note: my weird hip thing didn't bother me at all. Good to push it at the end. Next week I'm going to eat earlier and stuff that is easier to tolerate.

June 30, 2004

I was told by my training partners to take a couple days off . . . so hard for me. I know I need it.

I did take a few days off, save for a bit of roller skiing and broad jumping, but it wasn't enough. At this point, very early in the summer, I was already quite burned out. Nevertheless, I pushed on, doing the 10-kilometer Tutto Bene road-running race in Bemidji.

July 3, 2004

This morning was Tutto Bene. I tried to be positive going into the race and neglect the fact I'd been running 9-minute miles. I got in the front row and everyone sprinted off the line. I didn't start too fast, and soon it seemed like I had been passed by everyone. I ran my first mile at 7:45—I hadn't run that slow in three years. It was 30 seconds slower than last year! I was in trouble and already beginning to walk. Then my heel was rubbing, so I had to stop and retie my shoe. It sucked. I ran the whole way stopping and starting—so inefficient. My running was horribly slow and not even my normal pace—so no, I wasn't running too fast. I wonder if I went out too fast, but a 7:45 mile is SLOW! After the race I talked to my former coach Karen to see if I should take a break or keep plugging along. Alas, her reply was what I wanted to hear: keep plugging away. She suggested trying some new stuff. I'm going to try not being afraid. It's just running, it shouldn't scare me. That Birchmont run—yeah, I can't be afraid of it.

<u>*July 5, 2004*</u>

We went roller skiing tonight, meeting at the high school. We (Leif, Kathryn, Jim, and I) decided to do the newly paved Carr Lake Road. It seemed Kathryn just kept flying off in front of me. I thought I was going pretty fast, too, but maybe not. We were coming back, I was flying—going good and kinda fast. Then I went out on my left ski and it was unsteady. Then I was falling—on my left butt cheek mostly. Kathryn said she saw the sparks fly. I tried to stay off my boots, but they still got a little banged up. [This was my first fall on roller skis.] *What I hate the most about falling is not that I get hurt, it's that I hurt the equipment. And I damage my clothes. My ladybug shorts got all chewed up. My roller skis didn't look too bad, but still. Expensive equipment is painful to ruin. Fortunately I didn't feel too shook up, I mean only yesterday I was figuring if I fall every 500 miles or so that's not so bad. At least I did fall on a hill, so I don't feel quite as stupid. But I still feel stupid. By the time I got back I was also in some pain. My left thumb got scraped up, so did my left arm. And my left butt (where the cheek joins the leg) is really torn up.*

July 6, 2004
Today was a miserable-looking day. It was overcast and a steady drizzle the whole day. And the daytime high was only 48°F! Mom suggested we scrap the Birchmont run and go bowling. Besides Leif and me, nine other suckers showed up hoping to be the only ones, but no, we had our best turnout yet! Well, at least we tied last week. I ran with Kathryn. Jill was running in some hot-pink capri leggings! Man, I always have my best runs when it's between 40 and 50°F and it's raining! Nothing keeps me going better than those absolutely, purely miserable conditions. I didn't walk the whole way out and only my usual twice on the way back. It rocked. Of course I was soaked through by the time I got home. I had worn Leif's ski team hat, my smiley-face mittens and black poly—both of which I had sworn I wouldn't need again this summer—and my black running shorts, which I love. My butt road burn didn't bother me too bad— only when I walked. Today it feels much better.

In the next few weeks, I took Karen's advice. I didn't stop running, but I tried new workouts incorporating running but in which running wasn't the focus. I also decided I was a skier, not a runner.

July 10, 2004
Today I tried a new/old/different workout, which I really enjoyed but shouldn't do too often. I roller skied to the high school with a backpack containing a soccer ball and running shoes. At the high school I set out on the football field running back and forth on the 10-yard lines kicking the soccer ball. I did this for 45 minutes. Keeping the soccer ball close

kept my pace down, which I really needed. It was probably my best Level 1 workout ever! So that is one of my suggestions to fight boredom and/or burnout while running. After running I went no pole around the parking lot, mostly practicing turns. I think I'm going to go do that once a week. I also found that by moving my arms without poles my speed greatly increased. On the way home I double poled.

<u>July 15, 2004</u>
Today I did, or attempted to do, the ultimate Thug Workout [a workout I read about in The Source that involves using playground equipment]. *I went with Kathryn and Leif. We started at our house and ran to the new Lincoln Elementary School playground. I did six pull-ups and that was about it. Then we ran to Anna's house and then went to the old Lincoln Elementary School playground, where I did three more pull-ups and some monkey bars. Next we kept running to Central Elementary School playground, JW Smith Elementary School playground, and Gordon Falls playground and then finally home by way of the bridge. It was a good workout and I felt very strong for the entirety— especially the bridge part. Maybe it's 'cause I've taken two rest days in the past week? I had to skip Birchmont on Tuesday night 'cause I was volunteering the whole day.*

I kept running or roller skiing almost daily for the remainder of the summer.

There's a common theme of fatigue in my entries from this time. I was trying to live the life of an athlete I'd read about in Pete Vordenberg's book and paying the price for increasing my volume too quickly.

I was desperate to become a better athlete and make the Olympics. I had greatly increased my training volume and had no coach to tell me to back off. Over the years, as my race results didn't seem to correspond with my training, it became obvious my chances of making the Olympics were minute; then I lost my gastrocnemius, and my dream faded altogether. Despite this, I saw my potential to excel as a citizen athlete. My training became less desperate and more balanced, and—likely owing to my heavy volume in 2004—I had great endurance.

∼∼∼

At the end of college my training log had similar volume, but I added in more strength workouts, biking, and canoeing. By this time my body had become accustomed to the training.

June 17, 2007: run 50 minutes; canoe 1 hour

June 18, 2007: 8 min abs, 50-40-30 push-ups, 8-5-5 pull-ups, 3 × 20 triceps dips with stair steps in between; roller ski 2 hours

June 19, 2007: run 40 min; bike 1 hour

June 20, 2007: 8 min side abs, 50-30-20 push-ups, 8-5-5 pull-ups, 3 × 20 triceps dips with stair steps in between; canoe 2 hours

June 21, 2007: run 45 min; bike 2 hours

June 22, 2007: 8 min abs, 50-40-30 push-ups, 8-5-5 pull-ups, 3 × 20 triceps dips with stair steps in between; get sick at work and puke 3 times. Take nap during lunch and don't eat. Near 3:00 p.m. I start feeling better and go to Frisbee. I eat my lunch and then play Frisbee for about 20 minutes. Canoe 40 min.

June 23, 2007: City of Lakes Tri-Loppet: canoe 5 miles, run 5 kilometers, bike 10 kilometers

June 24, 2007: bike 3 hours

June 25, 2007: roller ski 2 hours

June 26, 2007: *run 45 minutes; bike 1h15*

June 27, 2007: *8 min side abs, 50-30-30 push-ups, 8-5-5 pull-ups, 3 × 20 triceps dips with stair steps in between; roller ski 2 hours*

June 28, 2007: *bike 2h10*

June 29, 2007: *8 min side abs, 50-30-30 push-ups, 8-5-5 pull-ups, 3 × 20 triceps dips with stair steps in between; bike 1h30*

June 30, 2007: *run 50 minutes; kayak 40 minutes*

July 1, 2007: *run 1h10*

July 2, 2007: *8 min side abs, 50-30-30 push-ups, 8-5-5 pull-ups, 3 × 20 triceps dips with stair steps in between; roller ski 45 min—wanted to go for 3 hours, but it was threatening rain*

July 3, 2007: *run 35 minutes*

July 4, 2007: *run 8 miles in 70 minutes*

July 5, 2007: *8 min side abs, 50-30-30 push-ups, 8-5-5 pull-ups, 3 × 20 triceps dips with stair steps in between; bike 1h15; kayak 45 min*

July 6, 2007: *run 20 min; bike 2h30*

July 7, 2007: *bike 69 miles on mountain bike!*

July 8, 2007: *run 30 min; kayak 2 hours*

July 9, 2007: *roller ski 2 hours*

July 10, 2007: *bike 2 hours; 50-50 push-ups*

July 11, 2007: *8 min abs; 1 hour run; 8-5-5 pull-ups,3 × 20 triceps dips*

July 12, 2007: *2-hour bike; 50-40 push-ups*

July 13, 2007: *2-hour roller ski; play Frisbee for ½ hour*

July 14, 2007: Orienteering triathlon: 7 hours and 41 minutes of running, kayaking, and biking

For the remainder of the summer I continued training this way, averaging about two hours a day, and almost always felt energetic. This would be my baseline for years. Despite this, my training volume never correlated with high-placing finishes. No amount of training could make up for my poor athleticism.

I learned training wasn't only about those elusive results—winning races and being in the Elite Wave at the Birkebeiner. I enjoyed working my body and thinking about what might be possible and was infinitely rewarded.

One time I was roller skiing with the Bemidgets. I had convinced them to come to Cass Lake for a longer-distance session.

"Elspeth, you're so hardcore," Waylon said to me as we roller skied. I couldn't help but grin from ear to ear.

Near the end of a century bike ride with Erik and Kathryn, we were biking through downtown Minneapolis having already logged 94 miles. As we navigated the traffic and maze of one-way streets, all of a sudden coming toward us was a young man on a bicycle with a rose between his teeth. We thought he surely must be an apparition.

"Is that for real, or is my brain so glucose deprived I'm hallucinating?" asked Kathryn.

Another time I was skiing the Noquemanon ski marathon. Near the halfway point in the race the course climbs to its highest point. As I rounded the last bend on the hill, panting, my muscles tight, I glimpsed a man standing up high on a rock. He had a trumpet and played "Charge" as I skied by—finally, after all those years of playing in pep band for other athletes, someone was playing "Charge" for *me*!

〜〜〜

Lured by news stories of upstate New York digging out from 6 feet of lake-effect snow, Erik and I moved to Rochester, New York. I furthered my education in graduate nursing school while he worked as an engineer. I found new roller ski routes, including a loop in a suburban neighborhood with smooth pavement and hills. In a five-minute interval I could roller ski three different hills, accelerate around multiple corners, and ski downhills and flats—terrain that perfectly emulated an actual ski course.

During the late summer and fall I tried to do these intervals once a week, always alone. I set my watch to beep after five minutes and allowed myself three minutes of rest between intervals. I started on an uphill to be able to do all three hills during the interval. The first hill wasn't too bad, but my heart rate jacked up. As I rounded the first corner, pushing hard on my outside roller ski and leaning into the turn, I felt like I was about to fall over. My heart rate came down some as I skied on the flats and down a gradual hill, but then it was time to crank it back up again as I cornered into a steep hill. This was the steepest of the three, and it was always a challenge to V2 the entire hill instead of V1. My new heart rate monitor provided me instant feedback and encouraged me to push harder. At the crest of the hill I again rounded a corner, kicking off of my outside roller ski, trying to be brave enough to lean into the curve. Again I had a slight recovery as I tucked the next downhill and hoped no cars were coming in from the crossroad. Then I had one more hill to go up, this one the least steep, but it went on for what seemed like forever as my chest heaved, my legs burned, and my arms turned to lead. I couldn't wait to hear those beeps, which were like my coach, signaling me it was time to stop, recover briefly, and prepare to do this twice more.

Pushing to utter exhaustion and then doing it again and again and again feels good. When I'm breathing too hard to think, that's when I really feel alive. It makes me feel like a real athlete.

Despite working full time and completing a master's program part time while in Rochester, I made time to train. It was a priority to me and what I'd been doing since high school.

In six days I trained just over twelve hours, worked thirty-six hours, and had sixteen hours of classroom time in addition to studying.

October 23, 2011: *Get up at 5:45 a.m. to run 1 hour before working a 12-hour day shift*

October 24, 2011: *Run 1.5 hours*

October 25, 2011: *Skate roller ski 2 hours, with 3 × 5-minute intervals in a hilly neighborhood*

October 26, 2011: *Lift max 1.5 hours at rec; run 0.5 hours*

October 27, 2011: *Run 1.25 hours*

October 28, 2011: *Lift 1.5 hours at rec; 3-hour roller ski*

When we got to Rochester, we discovered Lake Ontario rarely dumps lake-effect snow on the city. Fortunately, an hour's drive south, nestled in the Finger Lakes region, was Bristol Mountain, a downhill ski resort. Up a gravel road that climbed 1,000 feet in a few miles, we reached the summit, where there was a lighted manufactured 1.2-kilometer cross-country ski loop. Unfortunately, I didn't always have an hour to drive one way to snow, and even when I did there was sometimes too much snow or ice to get up the gravel road.

The good days were those when I actually made it up to Bristol and freshly PistenBully-groomed corduroy snow met my approval. Usually after about thirty laps I was ready to go home, regardless of my original intent for the day. But one day, while training for the Canadian Ski Marathon, I got it in my head to do fifty laps—a total of 60 kilometers. During this time there was a ski lesson happening on the loop. While I skied, the participants would go one lap and then stop near the chalet to talk. They watched me go around and around.

"That girl's an animal!" declared one of them.

To me, this was a compliment. It wasn't the first time I'd been called an animal; it happened in high school as I wildly careened down the local downhill slope on my cross-country skis, forcing myself to accept the speed while defying my better judgment.

When we don't think and just do, that's what animals and real athletes do. So to be called an animal, it was like I was being called an athlete!

Chapter 17

Hardy Points

<hr />

It gets brutally cold in Minnesota. Exposed flesh freezes within minutes, the air burns our lungs, and the threat of hypothermia is omnipresent. Despite all this, ski racers continue to train and compete. It can be frustrating, as my journal reflects.

Christmas 2004

It was cold the last week. Therefore, training has sucked. My training log is pathetic! Yesterday, for example, I classic skied about 9.5 kilometers. Sad. On the 23rd I classic skied about 12 kilometers and came home and shook, and then I think I got a fever again! On the 22nd I classic skied a whopping 15 kilometers! On the 21st I did 7.5 kilometers. That gives a grand total of about 44 kilometers in four days; however, the average straight air temp was –5 to –10°F these days without factoring in the wind chill. I should add that while my fingers warmed up after about 3 kilometers (and then froze again at about 10 kilometers when I got sweaty) my toes remained frozen for about two hours at a time—not good. Definitely asking for some major frostbite!

Racing in subzero temperatures is relatively common. I'm sure we did it in high school, but those races were only

5 kilometers. Once I got to college and started skiing longer races, it took me several years to learn how to deal with competing at these cold temperatures for hours. I repeatedly developed mild hypothermia after ski races and shook to get warm.

My freshman year of college I raced the City of Lakes Loppet with the cross-country ski club. This was in the early days of the Loppet, and much of the race transpired on the frozen Minneapolis lakes.

As I skied off Wirth Lake, 10 kilometers into the race, my body heat disappeared—something I had never experienced before. With all my body heat went all my energy. The air temperature was –10 degrees, and I was only wearing a single layer of long underwear under my spandex. For the next 25 kilometers I struggled to keep going, wondering whether I should drop out and get help for my hypothermia. I later learned this happened to my teammate Dave, too, and he did drop out.

The course returned to the woods, where the wind didn't bite as hard and the sun provided some warmth. I went around a bend and people cheered.

"Your spandex is making me hot!" they shouted in reaction to our gold-maroon-and-black spandex suits with stars and stripes. I briefly felt a bit warmer, then the last half of the course we skied on exposed frozen lakes again, and as before I lost all my heat. Upon finishing it took me an hour of shivering inside to get warm.

Three years later it was again quite cold for the City of Lakes Loppet. Despite warnings that bare flesh would freeze in ten minutes at that day's wind chill reading, I found myself underdressed again.

February 4, 2007
Freezing cold race. Around –9°F at race start with wind chill about –30°F! It was frickin' cold! I was trying to stay

warm the whole race—well—only thinking about it half
the time. It went pretty fast. I went with nothing on my
face and didn't get frostbite, so I feel pretty hardy about
that! I died the first 5 kilometers despite a decent warm-up!
That air just burns the lungs. I was tasting blood and didn't
give a shit about going fast. At 10 kilometers I started feel-
ing good and passing some people! Then I realized how
short the whole thing is. I fell over at the last aid station
'cause there was a paper cup in the tracks. My knees and
stomach got all bruised up. I double poled hard up the fin-
ish and beat two close competitors! Then I started shaking/
chattering 'cause all the tents were freezing cold! Finally
some guy brought me in to the heated medical tent—they
thought I was really out of it at first—but it was nice to
just shake somewhere that was above 20°F!

At the end of the race I had gone into the changing tent.
It was barely warmer than air temperature; by the time I
switched out of my boots and put on my street shoes, my
hands were too frozen to change my other clothes. The food
tent was located outside, and there was another poorly heated
expo tent, but when I was all sweaty and it was below 0 degrees it was very difficult for me not to get hypothermia. I
shook for half an hour in that medical tent before I got warm.

After this race my lungs felt raw each time I took in a
deep breath. Erik's mom thought I had gotten frostbite in
my lungs—something I didn't even know was possible. I kept
coughing, a good sign I had skied hard but also a reminder of
how harsh these temperatures can be.

∿∿∿

When Dad did the Finlandia in the early 1980s, it was a
two-day race of 50 kilometers each day. It commenced in the

town of Bemidji and followed a course north across Lake Bemidji, through Lake Bemidji State Park and other county parks,
across more frozen lakes, and eventually finished for the day
at Buena Vista. The next day the skiers made their way back to
Bemidji, repeating the same course in reverse.

In the intervening twenty-five years, the course had
moved entirely to Buena Vista and been shortened to 25- and
50-kilometer races over just one day. In 2006, there was the
special 100-kilometer anniversary race. I had to do it, even
without my gastrocnemius. Perhaps it was because I had
taken to doing the longest race possible at every event; perhaps it was because Dad had done it back in the day. I convinced Erik and a couple other University of Minnesota ski
club teammates to join me in the 100-kilometer and more to
do shorter races.

Temperatures were expected to be "below the donut," as
forecast by Too Tall Tom Szymanski, the expressive meteo-
rologist out of Fargo. The wind chill would be –25 degrees on
Saturday, with a possible reprieve on Sunday. I skipped my
biochemistry class on Friday to travel to the race, thinking,
Who skips a class to ski 62 miles in subzero temperatures? Midwest ski news site Skinnyski.com was calling all hardy skiers
to do the Finlandia. Although most cross-country skiers are
hardy, that doesn't mean all of them are; two skiers from the
University of Minnesota who had registered for the Finlandia
backed out upon hearing the forecast.

The night before the race, over a carbo-loading dinner at
my parents' house in Bemidji, my teammate Blake devised the
hardy factor scale. Blake, who was from Fargo and had served
in Iraq in the National Guard, had started cross-country skiing and the same year racing marathons. His scale wasn't well
defined; someone skiing the Finlandia that year automati-
cally had a hardy factor of about seven, but those of us doing the 100-kilometer had a hardy factor of one hundred. As

we discussed further, it became easier to quantify in terms of points. Not showing up for Frisbee due to rain was −10 Hardy Points. Swimming in a river in the middle of winter was +10 Hardy Points.

On day one of the Finlandia, I blasted a techno CD on the short drive to the start. We arrived with an hour to go before the 100-kilometer race; the thermometer read −5 degrees. The wind was howling out of the northwest. I stayed in the warm van, listening to Scooter and trying to get pumped up enough to brave the frigid air and bone-chilling winds.

The course was made up of two 25-kilometer laps each day in a figure-eight pattern, which meant I would be going by the finish line seven times before I was done. While this left plenty of opportunity to drop out, it would be all the harder to keep going, especially if I succumbed to hypothermia.

For the race I wore my spandex racing suit with two layers of long underwear on top and just one on the bottom. As expected, the wind was brutally cold, especially as I crested the ridge near the end of the loop on the east side. As I climbed up on the ridge, I talked to myself: "Think warm thoughts, Elspeth." I knew if I lost my body heat up there on that ridge—if the wind just whipped through me—I would have to admit defeat. I crested up and over the ridge twice that day, using all my brain power to feel warm. Somehow thinking warm thoughts kept the wind from taking my heat away, and I made it safely off the ridge and onto the more sheltered west side to finish my 50 kilometers on day one. Afterward, while eating my recovery meal in the famed Lumberjack Shack, I shook to get warm.

By Sunday, temperatures had barely warmed, but the wind had died down. There was nothing hardy about day two's weather conditions—the only Hardy Points to be garnered came from having raced 50 kilometers the previous day. Conditions were perfect. I was alone in the woods for most of the race, gliding peacefully on fast snow. There was no wind, and the February sun had enough power to keep me comfortably warm despite the temperature hanging around the donut.

～～～

In 2007 Erik and I returned to the West Yellowstone Ski Festival over the week of Thanksgiving. Our friends and fellow club members Emily, Craig, and Dave all wanted to go too. We decided to get one hotel room, as Emily liked to sleep on the floor; her mattress at home was an inflatable camping pad. The five of us drove the 1,000 miles west from Minneapolis to West Yellowstone.

As we pulled into the hotel parking lot, Dave had a surprise for us.

"Uh, guys, I decided to get my own room," he said.

Dave proceeded to sleep on both of the two beds in his room, use housekeeping, and take two showers each day. In our room we had a roller ski drawer, took ten showers total among the four of us over the course of a week, and had more fun. We usually walked to the ski trail together and skied together. Sometimes we saw Dave at the communal breakfast, and sometimes we skied with him, but usually he went too fast for us to keep up.

Each night we had dinner together.

"So, Dave, how was your ski today?" Craig asked at our meal on Friday, after we hadn't seen Dave all day.

"I didn't ski," he replied. "I stayed in bed all day."

The other four of us sat in stunned silence.

Maybe all the solo training and going hard all the time was burning Dave out.

～～～

In 2008 I signed up for the Pepsi Challenge 48-kilometer skate ski marathon, but because it was expected to be –20 degrees without factoring in the wind chill, the race was canceled. I was secretly thrilled. Despite calling myself a hardy skier, I had honestly never skied at temperatures colder than –10 degrees, and at that temperature only for short periods of time. I had been worried about the Pepsi course as well—it was a two-loop course, and both loops ended with 5 kilometers of downhill. I had serious doubts I would be able to stave off hypothermia with wind chills approaching –50 degrees on the exposed descent.

Being as Pepsi was canceled, the club held a classic distance practice at Elm Creek. The thermometer read –5 degrees as we put on our skis. I wore my new hot-pink balaclava, compliments of Erik's sewing talents and some leftover spandex fabric from an early-1990s sewing project.

"No hat, Elspeth, just the balaclava?" Blake asked.

"Yeah, it's not that cold out here," I replied.

Only a handful of us showed up: Erik, me, Travis, Bjorn, Blake, and Mark. Dave, we concluded, must be at home in bed watching TV. Minus 10 Hardy Points for him. I was the only girl, so I expected the boys would drop me. I'm sure they expected the same. I had perfect kick, probably because the snow was so cold it was like skiing on sandpaper. I started out in the lead, double poling until the first uphill, when the guys passed me; I felt good, and the boys didn't get too far in front of me. I worked hard on the next downhill and caught up to them. On the next hill I stayed with Travis and Bjorn, skiing immediately behind them.

As we completed the loop, I watched how Travis and Bjorn kicked—they both took enormous strides, which didn't look so much like striding but more like running. I figured if I took big strides, I could be fast like they were. And that's just what I did—I started taking enormous strides and stayed with them. When they turned around and saw I was still matching their pace, they looked surprised. Maybe the altitude training in West Yellowstone was paying off.

I matched their pace for a second 10-kilometer loop. I felt amazing. My great kick due to the cold weather and my determination to ski despite the cold had led to a breakthrough in my classic skiing. I also thought I had learned the secret to classic skiing uphills: just take big steps, like running but with really big strides.

∿∿

That winter, 2007–2008, was a cold one. A few weeks after Pepsi would have taken place, temperatures were predicted to be in the negative teens for the Vasaloppet. Again Skinnyski.com called all hardy skiers to Mora but also advised them to cover up all exposed flesh with moleskin, buffs, or Vaseline. There are traditionally three long races at Mora: the 58-kilometer skate, the 42-kilometer classic, and the 35-kilometer skate. Due to the forecast air temperatures, all races were changed to 35 kilometers and had the same starting time. After suffering soleus pain while skating the previous two years, I decided to do the classic race this year.

At dawn on the day of the Vasaloppet, Emily, Erik, and I walked over 1 mile to the fifteen-passenger vans. My glasses instantly fogged up upon leaving the house, which had never happened to me before. As we walked by the tall buildings on campus, the wind picked up, bringing water to my eyes. Vapor rose off the open waters of the Mississippi River as we crossed over it on a high bridge. The world was silent and steamy.

Once we arrived in Mora, we clamored out of the warm van into the cold air. We picked up our bibs at the local high school, and there was much discussion about how many layers of clothing to wear. Some were racing in spandex, perhaps adding a vest on top. Some were racing in their ski jackets and pants. None of us had ever raced at such cold temperatures; most of us had never even skied at these cold temperatures. After we made what we thought would be our final clothing selections, we got on school buses, which transported us north to the start of the point-to-point race. Usually when we got to the start the bus drivers opened the doors and made everybody get out. This year they let us stay on as long as we wanted. Erik and I dawdled on the bus.

I finally went outside to warm up. On bottom I wore thick socks, nylons, long underwear, spandex, and my ski pants. On top I had a bra, two layers of long underwear, spandex, a vest, and my heavy winter jacket. I wore liner gloves and lobster mittens. The night before, I had scraped every particle of sticky wax from my kick zone and had only applied a very thin layer of green kick wax made for frigid temperatures. For glide on my tips and tails I had applied two layers of Extreme White Racing Wax—a concoction made in Minnesota for cold weather.

I decided to put my skis on and do a warm-up. My skis barely moved. At temperatures in the minus teens, the snow was very rough and the coefficient of friction very high.

Then it was time to take off the warm-ups. I got my thick winter jacket off but somehow couldn't bring myself to take off my ski pants. I decided to just keep them on for the race. We all got in line, and the national anthem played. The air temperature was –15 degrees; the wind chill was –38 degrees. The wind blew at us as we shivered to "The Star-Spangled Banner."

The gun went off, and for the next 35 kilometers I sweated, and sweated, and sweated. I had overdressed, a feat I hadn't thought possible at –15 degrees. Moreover, the snow conditions were so incredibly slow we all had to work hard to keep our skis gliding. A few others said they had also overdressed.

At each of the water stops there was a fleet of buses to pick up skiers who were hypothermic. One of our skiers, John, who was wearing only his spandex suit, later said he thought about getting on the bus at every stop. Thinking back to the City of Lakes Loppet my freshman year of college, I sympathized.

"I know how you felt. You will learn," I told him.

Everywhere around me, skiers were unrecognizable under their many layers of clothing and moleskin. Many of those dressed in spandex had bulky undergarments poking through. The winner wore both ski pants and ski jacket. Most people wore masks or moleskin and resembled looters more than skiers.

When I crossed the finish line in downtown Mora, the race against hypothermia began. I was so sweaty that it would come soon, so as fast as I could, I got my skis, my poles, my race bag, and myself to the high school to change clothes and stay in the heat.

I had a phenomenal race that day. Early on, two women passed me, but I was able to stay on their train. It was one of my first times skiing in a train of only women skiers. I worked hard to ski with them and then eventually passed them, finishing in 6th place among the women and 53rd of all 233 classic skiers.

I also racked up the Hardy Points for the day, but not Dave. He didn't race due to the cold temperatures. He missed out on a lot of Hardy Points.

Chapter 18

Moose Crossing

In early 2007, a lack of snow caused most ski races to be canceled or drastically altered. The Vasaloppet was changed to laps on the lake. The Birkebeiner was shortened to half the normal distance and made into a tour. The Finlandia was the same length as usual, but we had to do four laps of the more wooded west side of Buena Vista.

Dad skied the Finlandia 25-kilometer classic race. His race started thirty minutes before mine, and I'd forgotten he was even racing when I came upon him during my first lap. I passed him rather unexpectedly after the Wall. I tried to figure out where I would see him on the next lap and whether I could see him on all four of my laps. I realized there was one lap on which I wouldn't see him, but I could make it my goal to finish before him.

Each time I shouted words of encouragement as I lapped Dad. It kept my race more interesting. In the end, I passed him three times and still beat him by twenty minutes despite the fact I'd skied twice the distance and he'd had a thirty-minute head start. I attributed this to poor technique, outdated equipment, the heavy sweatshirt he wore instead of spandex, and his use of sticky wax from tip to tail. Had I thought harder, I would have realized the real cause was something else.

For the past few years Dad had been reporting a lot of mucus when exercising. He blamed this on chronic bronchitis, although he had never been a smoker. He said he couldn't push himself hard anymore.

∿∿∿

Mom, Leif, and Reid came to Minneapolis to visit me in August. I was expecting them on a Thursday afternoon; my plan was to leave work early so I could spend the late afternoon and evening with them. I even thought Leif and I could go for a three-hour roller ski.

Not ten minutes before I was about to leave work, I got a phone call. It was unusual for me to get phone calls at work, though I had made the mistake of giving Mom the number, and she had called me in June to tell me not to exercise because the Twin Cities was under a smog advisory.

"Hello, Elspeth, this is Judy Grundy," said the voice on the other line. Yes, it sounded just like Judy Grundy, but what was Judy Grundy doing calling me at work? Judy was a family friend in Bemidji, and her son, Jim, had found my number on the internet.

"Yes, Judy?" I responded, rather confused.

"Your Mom isn't at home?" asked Judy.

"No, she and my brothers are coming down to Minneapolis to see me today."

"Oh, well, I hate to be the bearer of bad news, Elspeth, but your Dad was on a bike ride today, and he collapsed." My heart flipped inside my chest. "Elspeth? Elspeth are you still there?"

"Yes, I am." I could barely find the words to speak.

"Do you have a cell phone?"

"No, I don't, and neither does my mom. I'm going to go to my apartment now. My family should be there, and we'll try calling you as soon as I can get to a phone." As usual, we were technologically behind the times. Moreover, the landline at my apartment had just been disconnected because I was moving in two days. It had been my intention to get a cell phone that coming weekend.

My hands shook and my body was clammy as I picked up the phone to call Erik before I left work. Unlike me, he had a cell phone.

In a rush, I told him about Judy's call. He told me he hoped everything would turn out all right.

My stomach knotted. I told my boss what I had just learned and then left on my bike. I don't remember much about biking home. When I got to my apartment, I was relieved to see Mom and my brothers yet didn't really want to share the bad news.

"Why the long face?" Mom asked as I stopped my bike and got off.

"Judy Grundy just called me at work. She said Dad collapsed on a bike ride," I stammered.

After that it was confusion.

Dad had been biking around Lake Bemidji that afternoon on a ride promoting bike trails with a couple of politicians, Frank Moe and Jim Oberstar, and several other Bemidji bike enthusiasts. Included in the milieu were family friends John Tibstra and Judy's husband, Bill Grundy. The group had started at the infamous Paul Bunyan and Babe the Blue Ox statues on the south side of the lake and from there biked east, then north toward the state park. At the top of the big hill at the state park, known as Rocky Point, the group stopped for a water break. It was there that Dad, while getting off his bike, had collapsed.

We called cell phones of friends who were with Dad. CPR was initiated, a defibrillator brought, a fleeting pulse, the ambulance arrived . . . and there was nothing they could do. Mom, Leif, Reid, and I were helpless from 200 miles away hearing the story on various breaking-up cell phone lines. Bill and John were too distraught to talk. Finally, it was Frank Moe who called and said Dad had died.

It was horrible. I didn't even cry; none of us did then. We were in shock. It was so unexpected. We were in disbelief. I wondered what to say. I wondered what to think. I wondered what to feel. But mostly, I wondered how many times I had to pinch myself to make it real.

I called Erik to tell him the final news.

"When is the funeral?" he asked.

"I dunno," I said.

"Is there anything I can do for you?"

"I dunno," I said.

"Should I come up to Bemidji?"

"I dunno," I said.

It was hard to think about anything. Suddenly I realized the decisions about a funeral would be up to Mom, Leif, Reid, and me, and I felt too young at twenty-two to make these plans.

We drove to Bemidji, stopping at a restaurant on the way there. "How are you guys doing tonight?" the waitress asked.

"Good," we all mumbled. When she was out of hearing distance, we joked, "Well, about as good as we can be considering Dad just died."

As we drove north, I was reminded of a trip a decade previous. We drove all night after Dad got off second shift to visit my grandparents in Dad's treasured far northwestern corner of Minnesota. I was dozing around 5:00 a.m. We were still driving north, just north of Thief River Falls on Route 59. Suddenly Dad slammed on the brakes, abruptly waking me up.

A moose was crossing the highway.

A decade later in Bemidji, I wasn't sleeping well either. When my head hit the pillow, the tears spilled out. I got up early in the morning to be with Mom, who I knew hadn't slept well either.

~~~

That morning, Friday, we went to the hospital to be with Dad. The autopsy later confirmed what Mom already suspected: Dad had died from a massive heart attack. While waiting for the chaplain to come talk to us, we saw copies of the *Bemidji Pioneer* newspaper scattered around. "Local man collapses while on a bike ride," read the headline.

> *August 10, 2007*
>
> *There was a beautiful article sans the title written up in the Bemidji Pioneer about Dad. I know it would've done him proud because it did us proud. It had all the facts straight, it was so perfect—even mentioned Dad wanting a bike rack at the new government center.* [Coincidentally, two days later while we were walking around town, we discovered that there was a bike rack in place at the government center.] *We said goodbyes to Dad at the hospital. Only Mom saw him, but Mom covered him up and we all went in and said the Lord's Prayer. I really wanted to go hug Dad and bring him back to life and tell him he was a great dad and that I thought he was the best ever, but I couldn't bring him back to life, so I just walked out of the room hoping he knew that I thought the world of him. Then we went to the funeral home, where I insisted I be listed before the boys under the "survived by" section in the obituary (something feminist, but I am the oldest), and the guy wrote a really good obituary with our help editing. It was really hard getting the clothes Dad died in from the funeral home.*

Usually when one of us made the paper, whether for a sports write-up or the picture of Dad running Mika across a Mississippi bridge, we plastered it to the fridge. Not this time.

Judy made us her famous Grundy bars: three layers comprising a moist graham-cracker-like crust, a layer of chocolate, and a layer of caramel on top. For four days I ate Grundy bars for breakfast, lunch, and dinner. I ate the caramel off the top first, the sweetness melting in my mouth. Next I ate the crust. I left my favorite part, the chocolate, for last. The only good thing about Dad dying was eating all those Grundy bars.

I already missed Dad.

I'd been embarrassed of him at more than one point over the years. One day in high school, for track practice we ran 4 miles from the school to the local college and then got a ride back. On the way back I found myself in the car with Jessica, Ashley, and Lyndsey—all popular jocks who got voted as homecoming royalty. As we drove down Fifth Street in Bemidji, we crossed the street leading into my neighborhood. There, riding home from work on his last Ronnander Recumbent bicycle, was Dad.

"What kind of bike is that?" asked Ashley. I kept silent. Mortified. If only they knew that was Dad!

Now I would suffer through endless embarrassment to have him back.

All day the day after he died people kept coming to the house and giving their condolences and bringing us food. I didn't go running or roller skiing, and the lack of exercise contributed to my somber mood. We sat around and cried a lot and tried to decide how to have a proper funeral, which was a challenge seeing as we didn't belong to a church. My parents had both been baptized into the Lutheran Church. Dad's parents had attended church all their lives, but Dad had a falling out with organized religion and stopped going. Mom's parents never attended church regularly, so Mom's religious education had been in the public schools, which at that time had daily prayer.

My brothers and I weren't baptized, and growing up we

only attended church for weddings and funerals. I didn't believe in God or heaven. I knew of people who had died suddenly, from heart attacks, and others who died slow deaths of cancer. I concluded it would be better to die suddenly even if it left things unfinished.

I wondered what death was like. For the people who believe in heaven, it seems easy to imagine death. Then there's Pascal's wager. Pascal said it's better to believe than not to believe due to the consequences of not believing, but I can't believe in something that doesn't make sense to me. I think when we die, we go back to where we came from, which is an unknowing, unfeeling, unconscious oblivion. I think it must be so because I don't know anything from the time before I was born. And it seems if there's no beforelife, then there should be no afterlife. This concept of where we come from, of unconscious oblivion, stymies my intellect, although I think it must resemble sleep without dreams. What is it like to no longer think? To no longer be? I realize I will not always be here, but then what?

Now Dad was no longer here.

Despite his falling out with religion, he had recently been reading the Bible before bed. Mom knew a woman who was a nondenominational minister, and she agreed to officiate the funeral.

∿∿

On Saturday I decided to get happy. Something about the sad faces and constant tears just wore me down, and I couldn't be like that anymore. Given exercise almost always makes me happy, I asked Jill to come roller skiing with me on the Paul Bunyan Trail. I didn't want to talk about Dad. Instead, we talked about our summer training, our jobs, and Jill's plans to ski for Michigan Tech.

~~~

On Sunday I went to church. Under the cathedral of the great blue sky, Kathryn and I paddled in Dad's heavy aluminum canoe across Lake Irving and up the Schoolcraft River into Lake Marquette as we had done on many previous Sunday mornings. There is something about the stillness of the water, the repetitive rhythm of the paddling stroke, and the solitude of being in nature that makes the whole experience rather spiritual. It was on this canoe I expressed my gratitude surrounding Dad's death.

I felt so thankful for having twenty-two years with Dad. For his having died doing something he loved so much, among friends. For the fact he had lived fifty-nine years, full years of travel and adventure. Dad did a good job of making use of opportunities. He took several backpacking and canoeing trips in his twenties and thirties and had seen the world while in the service. He married Mom and had us three kids. And I think we mostly made him proud.

My paternal grandmother got dementia in her seventies. Dad thought he might also get dementia and often joked that when he got really bad, we should send him for his last ski. Dad died in August, so there was no snow. But for a man who spent so much time in nature, it seemed natural he should die doing something he loved outdoors. He was on a bike ride promoting bike trails and the development of more of them in the great state of Minnesota. Dad was a huge bicycle advocate, and although he loved winter and skiing more, he had to settle for a last bike ride.

~~~

We had Dad's funeral in the backyard. The flowers in Mom's garden created a beautiful backdrop. The service was at noon on a sunny Monday. Our family sat on the patio, facing the house; the backyard gradually sloped up to the alley from the sunken patio, creating a natural amphitheater. Erik sat on my left and Leif on my right. Neighbors provided chairs for some two hundred guests. Mika attended on her tie-out. She demonstrated unusually good behavior, as if she, too, were sullen for the service. I kept myself preoccupied by focusing on an ant crawling up Erik's mom's leg so as not to start crying.

The attendees slanted younger than what should be seen at a funeral, where white hair usually dominates the crowd. There were the middle-aged folks, friends of parents, and a disproportionate number of high school and college students, my brothers' friends and mine.

Afterward, with all the family present, I had the overwhelming feeling Dad would really have enjoyed this day. He loved seeing his brothers and extended family, and it felt wrong he couldn't participate.

∾∾∾

Even though I felt immense gratitude that Dad had died doing something he loved and that he'd lived a very full fifty-nine years, he still died prematurely. True, he died before he became old and frail and could no longer use his machine, his body, to its full potential. But it also meant Dad wouldn't be around to see me get married or Leif graduate from college. He wouldn't be there when Reid graduated from high school, or even on Reid's sixteenth birthday. It seemed unfair. After all, Dad died less than ten years after his own dad, nine years after his mom, and just three years after my maternal grandpa. Dad was always incredibly fit; he had an exemplary active lifestyle, and he ate things like oatmeal, wheat germ, and more than his fair share of fruits and vegetables.

In the days and months after Dad died, my thoughts about him were pervasive.

August 21, 2007
30-min run with soccer ball, so slow and Level 1. 8-5-5 pull ups; roller ski 2 hours. While at work I think a lot about Dad. It just kinda plagues me. I can't stop thinking about it, yet I don't feel like crying.

Following a string of many two-a-day workouts, with running in the morning and then biking, strength, or roller skiing in the afternoon, I wrote the following in my training log.

September 26, 2007
40-40-30 push-ups. Attempted to go for a two-hour roller ski, but it ended up being one hour because, as Leif would say, "I just wasn't feeling it." Mostly I feel like all I do is train as of late, and it feels like to no avail. I ran into Bjorn roller skiing—he was going for a half-hour double pole—it makes me think I train too much or that I'm really ineffective. I feel sad tonight about Dad . . . he will be missing out on so much, like my wedding. It still feels so unreal and not possible except I feel like crying all the time. It cuts so deep. How is it possible?

I also thought about the good times with Dad—that hardy Swede who used to have spit-rolling contests at recess when it was –40 degrees, who raised me to be hardy, too.

June 21, 2004
Yesterday, I was thinking of running in the afternoon, but it turned out to be a really hot day. Well, not hot in the general public's opinion, but I consider 70°F and sunny to be hot. Anyway, when Dad came home and it was Father's

*Day, we went "baja-ing" [off-road mountain biking].
We parked at the north Three Island County Park parking
lot and took the snowmobile trail north. The trail was in
pretty good shape except at the bottom of a few hills there
was some mud. If there wasn't too much mud and I was
going fast enough, I could get through it, but a few times
it was really muddy and I came to a dead stop. I was sinking fast, and my shoes got all muddy. Once Dad hit some
mud and went flying off the front of his bike. Sometimes I
had to get off and walk my bike up a hill, or the grass was
really tall, and since the ticks have been so voracious this
season, I kept having ticks crawl up my white socks. It was
dumb, but I'd have to stop and get them off, which only allowed the opportunistic ticks to further bombard me while
the mosquitoes bit into me hungrily and the sand flies
buzzed in circles around my head. I called the bugs a triple threat—mosquitoes, sand flies, and the ticks. Finally,
we came out on the nice dirt forest road that we run on at
cross-country camp. That's my favorite road ever that Barney took us running on. There are some really good hills on
that road. Dad and I rode west to the boat launch at Larson
Lake, then turned around and biked east all the way to the
paved road—'cause to hell if I was going to go back on that
tick-infested snowmobile trail.*

∿∿∿

In the year after Dad died, we planned to distribute his ashes
in his most beloved places.

In October we went to Itasca State Park to spread some of
the ashes by the Big Red Pine. Every time we went to Itasca
State Park, Dad wanted to stop and go look at the Big Red
Pine. He would walk up to it, put his hands in his pockets,
hike up his pants, push out his stomach, stick his tongue out

of his mouth, and just stand there and look at that tree till the cows came home.

As was typical for me, I combined this mission with an extraordinary training opportunity, so Erik and I roller skied the 35 miles to Itasca State Park from Bemidji over fairly hilly terrain. When we got to the Big Red Pine, we learned it had been decapitated in a storm the previous summer, around the same time Dad died. It was ridiculously metaphorical. Mom dispersed Dad's ashes as I choked up and tried to emotionally distance myself so as not to break down into tears. I tried not to think about never seeing Dad again and everything he'd miss and everything I'd miss sharing with him.

A few months later, in winter, we went to Three Island County Park to distribute more of Dad's ashes in the small river that runs near the ski trail. Our family always thought this was the most picturesque park to ski in the Bemidji area. The ceremony was short, owing to the cold temperature, and left little time for emotional sentiment, but I still blinked back the tears while skiing back to the car.

After Dad died, I perceived life differently. I tried to take advantage of more opportunities and to really make things happen. Cost had always been an issue. But now I forgot about cost and did what I had always wanted to do, like go to Europe and move away to New York. In the coming years I went so many places and did so many things. I wanted to call home and tell Dad I had just paddled around Manhattan or summited some mountain or seen Quebec City, but I couldn't.

It took us almost eight years to make the trip to Kittson County to deliver Dad's ashes to his parents' cherished 80 acres. It had been over a decade since we last walked the trails, now owned by my uncle; I had run many thousands of miles since then, and the trail system seemed much smaller than my eight-year-old's memory. However, the wood ticks were significantly more ubiquitous. Eventually we decided to leave some ashes in the south clearing.

By this time the years had passed. The emotions were significantly subdued. I had become accustomed to Dad not being around. But I still wanted to tell him about all my adventures. And I still felt compelled to go on these adventures—to explore new rivers and climb mountains and hike new trails. I got my adventurous nature from him. And I try to make my life as full as possible because ultimately Dad taught me life is short.

Chapter 19

The Axe

———————

Perhaps one of the most coveted prizes in citizen marathon ski racing is the axe. While many races offer giant cowbells, Swedish Dala horses, or plastic trophies, the Finlandia gives its winners double-bit throwing axes hand-painted by local artists.

Many adventures in my life have been like winning the axe.

∿∿∿

When canoeing a river, most people paddle downstream and shuttle upstream, which involves two cars and lots of driving. Dad had a better idea.

Dad's shuttles involved a bike. From our cabin on the Rum River we canoed a 3.6-mile section of the river several times. Dad would get up early, put his bike in the car, and drive to the takeout spot. Then he biked back to the cabin to join us. We then paddled downstream to where our car was waiting for us. Using a bike eliminated most of the driving and any need for a second vehicle. Besides, we were a one-car family.

Once Kathryn and I started canoeing together, we got more creative. We always dreamed of point-to-point runs but rarely had the opportunity to do them. One time, we employed a running shuttle to return a canoe we had borrowed.

We canoed from Kathryn's house on Lake Marquette down the Schoolcraft River, through Carr Lake, then down the Mississippi River, across Lake Irving, and across Lake Bemidji to the canoe owner's house. We then ran the 9 miles back to Kathryn's house clad in life jackets and carrying canoe paddles.

Then Erik and I discovered the ultimate in canoe shuttles: the roller ski shuttle. Like the running shuttle, all the equipment needed for roller skiing could fit in the canoe. But on roller skis, we could go much farther and faster than running.

We first tried this on the Cannon River in southeast Minnesota. We were searching for a place to stash our canoe on a side river near a waterfall when Erik got down on his knees. He grabbed my hands tightly and looked into my eyes.

"Elspeth Kate Ronnander, will you marry me?" he asked.

I was shocked and had had no idea the question was coming. Although Erik had been driving around with a mysteriously shaped package all weekend, it was many times larger than any normal ring box. I instantly said yes.

Then he took me back to his car, where he proceeded to pull out the contents of the mysterious package. I was dumbfounded as a carbon paddle emerged—Erik had gotten me a carbon paddle instead of an engagement ring. I had talked incessantly about how much I wanted a carbon paddle, and I guess since I talked so much about carbon paddles and not rings, he thought it made more sense. I agreed. It was kind of like winning an axe.

〰〰

Eventually I went under three hours in the canoe portion of the Chippewa Triathlon. It happened with Erik in a solo Wenonah canoe. In triathlons there are usually no strict rules about canoe length and width. Pretty much anything goes—including rigging a solo into a tandem.

We spent the day before the race putting in foam seats and foot braces and water bottle holders and paddle clips. The end result was a seat I couldn't crank on too hard, a footrest a little too far in front of me, and a sitting position much lower than ideal that quickly made my arms burn with fatigue. But the boat was fast, no doubt, and we used carbon paddles. We had the best starting position we had ever had, and on the last lake a broad smile filled my face as we drafted two teams of men's racing canoes!

∿∿∿

In high school and throughout college, I started running and walking and biking and sometimes even roller skiing or canoeing for transportation. This wasn't a novel concept; Dad championed this his whole life. I liked telling people, "I ran to the store . . . literally." Consequently, I ran home with all sorts of awkward packages like brie cheese, earrings, and shoeboxes while satisfying a primordial urge most people never enjoy. It's fulfilling—not only because I don't require a car but because using my body I can travel farther and faster than most people imagine possible. It also gives me a destination and thus a break from my usual challenge of deciding where to run. Once, in college when I was working as a teaching assistant on the University of Minnesota's Saint Paul campus and living near the Minneapolis campus, I used running as a mode of transportation.

December 14, 2006
I went roller skiing for two hours in the afternoon when it was 45°F and sunny. 60-40-45 push-ups. Felt very, very hard after the roller ski. Proctored and graded biochem tests in Saint Paul—didn't get done until 10:30 p.m. (buses only run every half hour at this time back to the Minneapolis

campus, and I had just missed a bus), so I decided to run home—only took 25 minutes (at 5-kilometer pace)—less time than the bus. I felt like the Kenyans running from point to point as transportation. Maybe it'll make me faster!

As a climactic thing to do, my friend Emily joined me for a 6-mile round-trip run from the Minneapolis campus to the Saint Paul campus to turn in my senior thesis. I thought it made more sense than taking the bus.

∿∿∿

I never considered myself a tomboy, but in retrospect I was never good at styling my hair, my stint with makeup lasted exactly one and a half years, and I could never understand the phrase "Diamonds are a girl's best friend" because I think diamonds are ugly.

The day before my sophomore year in high school started, I painted my toenails. Remnants of the polish still remained on the last day of the school year. Since I hadn't bothered to even remove the nail polish, let alone put on another coat, I decided to give up on nail polish, whether finger or toe, indefinitely.

The monkey bars and rings were always my favorite playground equipment. When I was a kid, I did both until my hands tore open and the stinging of the popped blisters made me quit. My hands were calloused all summer every summer, and I was always disappointed when a blister developed and the pain kept me from swinging like a monkey for a few days.

Somewhere in there I became obsessed with working out. First I started doing abs—just sit-ups at first. Then, in eighth grade, our volleyball coach did fifteen real push-ups. I couldn't even do one, so I got determined. I started with the "girly" push-ups—the kind where the knees rest on the floor instead of the toes. Soon I could do one real push-up. Then it was two, and then three, and then fifteen, and then four years later I did sixty-five and beat all the boys on the high school ski team!

I became obsessed with muscles, too. My senior year of high school we dissected cats in anatomy, and separating all the forearm muscles increased my obsession. I started lifting, mostly when we had a few minutes during practice. Spring of my senior year, Leif convinced me to lift three days a week, so I did this for a few years in college.

November 8, 2005
Lift arms at rec. Start with upwards row and bicep curls with bar with 10 pounds extra. This guy walked up to me while I was resting between sets and asked, "Are you using this?" When I was like, "Yeah," he gave me the most incredulous look ever! Who says girls can't lift?

While dating Erik I realized we were going to go head to head in a lifelong pull-up contest. I had done my first two pull-ups in physical fitness testing in fourth grade. At the time I recall being quite aghast at being able to do pull-ups, as most other girls couldn't. I also remember how powerful doing a pull-up made me feel. When we moved to New York, I used the clothesline poles in the backyard as my practice, and Erik rigged himself up a pull-up bar—a tree branch anchored into the Vs of two adjacent trees and secured with twine.

"Eight!" Erik said as he walked up the stairs one night.

"Shit, really? Man, now I gotta go do eight!" I exclaimed and immediately went outside to equal the effort.

A couple weeks later I was feeling particularly good during a set and did nine.

"Guess what?" I asked Erik when I came up the stairs.

"You did nine pull-ups," he said with a smile on his face. Then he was out the door to match me.

For several years my goal was to do ten pull-ups. In 2012, after graduating with my master's degree, I finally accomplished it. At this point I was able to consistently do more pull-ups than Erik and began to frequently challenge my male skier friends to pull-up competitions in which I would often tie, if not beat them, even though they could kick my ass in ski races. Doing pull-ups still made me feel very powerful.

ᜫᜫᜫ

In early high school, Leif got nicknamed Cool Runner because he never looked like he was pushing himself—he always seemed relaxed, like he was just running easy, and his times reflected this effort. He ran his 5-kilometer high school cross-country races in nineteen or twenty minutes.

Leif's senior year, after putting in a good summer of running and another good summer of roller skiing, he was ready to leave Cool Runner behind. I had the pleasure of watching him race the first cross-country meet of his senior year.

August 31, 2004
Leif did absolutely awesome! He started off in the front (probably 30th), and I was like, shit, he's not gonna be able to maintain that. Well, second lap he was trailing end of first pack and looking good. Derek was a little in front of him. Third time Leif is on Derek's heels. The winner got 16:43, then here comes Leif, just playing with kids on his kick, and he goes and pulls off 16th place and 18:17—a PR by a minute. He got a medal, and I was so proud of him!

ᜫᜫᜫ

During the 2008 Noquemanon ski marathon, I skied a large portion of the race by myself, which was common for me during marathons. I blamed this on few participants and my inability to be aggressive and take risks at the start, which resulted in me losing the pack I should have been skiing with and therefore skiing the remainder of the race playing catch-up. And so it happened that I got passed once 5 kilometers into the 50-kilometer race and only passed about ten people myself thereafter. At 20 kilometers to go, I was passed and didn't see another soul until the end of the race. At 8 kilometers to go, I took a nasty fall. It left me with a sore knee, a sorer breast, and a shoulder injury. Nevertheless, I kept going, and after a few kilometers the knee stopped bothering me and I was feeling good again.

"Go get 'em!" the road-crossing volunteer cheered enthusiastically at 1 kilometer to go.

"Get who?" I mumbled. "I haven't seen anyone in 19 kilometers."

But then I looked up, and there was a figure striding away a third of a kilometer in front of me. I did a double take. Wait, was this figure wearing a bright gold hat? Wait, was the figure wearing the same spandex as me? Was that figure my teammate Jordan?

"Fuck, Elspeth, just go, go, go!" I commanded myself. And I went. I double poled as hard as I could after 49 kilometers of skiing. The whole time I was speculating whether the figure in front of me was Jordan. It was my goal to beat him, even though I'd been told to not base my performance on others' results.

The figure turned the last corner of the race, and I temporarily lost sight. But I kept on double poling, and when I made that last corner and came into the straightaway, there he was barely 30 yards ahead. It was most definitely Jordan. Instead of double poling, which was the much faster technique on this section of flat ground, he was striding. He was barely moving.

I knew I had to make my move hard and fast with the

finish line in sight. I had to pass Jordan and get across the line before he had time to mount a sprint.

I slid my skis into the far track and accelerated. As I passed Jordan, a spectator yelled, "Twins!" and Jordan turned his head to see me burst past him in a blaze of stripes. Jordan's dad caught the moment on camera. I misjudged my need to sprint, as Jordan had nothing left in him, and he continued to slog away with his stride across the line as I broke my momentum with a hockey stop. It was a total axe moment.

∿∿∿

There are a few diehards who do the Finlandia year after year in hopes of winning an axe. Leif is one of those diehards. He got second one year and has been fifth or sixth too many times to count. Each year he skis the 25-kilometer classic thinking this will be his year to win the axe. Others hop between the different race distances and techniques, either in optimism that one of the races will prove the lucky one or else to collect an axe in each race.

In 2006, when I entered the 100-kilometer Finlandia, I figured I had the axe in the bag. I doubted any other women would be so foolhardy. But I was wrong—two others showed up, and I only beat one.

In 2008, temperatures were balmy for the race, with the start expected to be around 10 degrees. There was enough snow for a full course, and so we raced two 25-kilometer loops. I checked the starting list for the 50-kilometer. There were just five of us women: Mur Gilman, who had won the Birkebeiner back in 1981; Montana Faulke, my tireless teammate two years my junior who rarely trained and therefore slogged through many a four-hour marathon on sheer will and determination; Diana Munger, wife of the infamous John Munger (creator of the City of Lakes Loppet) and mother of two daughters, who could ski a marathon well under four hours; Lisa Boulay, the most outspoken four-and-a-half-hour ski marathon single-sticker of all time; and me.

I knew the field was all mine. Waves of anticipation mixed with pressure came over me. This was gonna be my year to get the axe. And Dad wouldn't be there to see it.

The gun went off, and I found myself near the back of the pack in the male-dominated field. We took off toward the lodge, and as we got to the top of the gradual downhill, Mur passed me. This was unacceptable. I quickened my pace to stay with her. Soon we were ascending Sunnyside, a green downhill ski run. Now I was stride for stride on the steep hill with Mur. I started feeling dizzy and light-headed but promised myself the feelings would soon pass. The hill leveled out, and I kept up a hard V1 to stay just behind Mur. As the trail left the downhill area, I moved in front of her and gradually pulled away.

Now on the east 13-kilometer loop of trail, I was ever conscious that Mur might be just behind me. I tried to resist the urge to turn around and see just how much distance I had made on her. It was in these 13 kilometers I realized my skis were painfully slow; I had missed the wax badly. After religiously checking the weather on Thursday night I had waxed expecting temps around the donut at the start. But the temperature was already 10 degrees warmer than predicted and steadily climbing, and I began to panic, as my skis were waxed too cold. I was suffering from a high coefficient of friction, and my skis weren't gliding well. I knew Mur was close behind.

The 25-kilometer race started fifteen minutes after mine. I heard the lead racers coming up behind me and moved into the classic track to double pole. Phil Rogers led a pack of five. He was a beast with the most ripped quads of any male skier in Minnesota, only rivaled in recent years by Matt Liebsch.

"Go Phil!" I yelled as I slogged on in the classic track.

The lead 25-kilometer pack turned a corner and was

quickly out of sight. My skis dragged on a slight downhill. I decided to get back in the track and double pole. On top of the ridge on the east side, John Munger was waiting to cheer for his wife. I wondered how much time I had on her. Usually I beat her by an hour, but my skis were so slow I wasn't sure I could keep my lead.

I kept going. I started on the second loop and skied up the demanding downhill run. As I felt the high coefficient of friction pushing against me, I worried again about Mur gaining on me. I also worried about Diana Munger. By now my left soleus was sending sharp pain spikes up my leg, and I was happy to double pole in the classic track—skating really stretches my soleus. When I left the track to skate again, my soleus burned and I wanted to cry, but I skated on, assuming skating would be faster than double poling.

As I started my final loop on the west side, I saw Mark Morrissey, a Finlandia board member, filming me. Usually I would feel so honored to be filmed, like a Hollywood star, but my skis were so slow I felt stupid. I kept trying hard on the final 12 kilometers of the course, motivated by the constant fear Mur would pass me and I would be powerless thanks to physics. Damn physics again. It made me want to curl up in the fetal position, but I pushed on despite the burning in my soleus and lungs.

Finally, I crested the last hill and skied through the tunnel. Mur was nowhere in sight, and I double poled the last straightaway to alleviate my pain.

It was the first time I had ever won a ski race. Mom and Erik were at the finish as well as a few scattered spectators and race officials, but there were no crowds to cheer me on. There's no pomp and circumstance at the Finlandia.

I beat Mur by twenty minutes. There was no podium finish picture, as the women's winners were too spread out. My time was a very slow three hours and twenty minutes. It felt like one of the longest races of my life—leading from almost the start with the ever-present fear of being overtaken. Having missed the wax made my victory harder and therefore slightly sweeter.

At the awards ceremony, there was a special recognition for Dad: the Finlandia presented the Bryce Ronnander Lifetime Achievement Award to our family. In a subsequent year, the award went to Bruce Adelsman, creator of Skinnyski.com, the most comprehensive and navigable cross-country skiing website on the planet. I thought a lot about what to say for the acceptance speech. In the end I said something simple: "Dad was a skier. He got my mom to ski. He got us kids to ski. I went to the University of Minnesota, and I got a lot of college kids to come ski the Finlandia. That's how one person makes a difference."

Later, wearing my black Bemidji Cross-Country Ski Projekt T-shirt, I got up to accept my axe for winning the 50-kilometer Finlandia.

It seemed paradoxical that I would win my first marathon title at the Finlandia, a race with history so dear to Dad, six months after he died. It seemed so unfair that a man who had enjoyed the successes, accomplishments, and activities of his children could no longer partake himself. I would miss Dad celebrating my wedding, Leif's state canoe victory, and Reid's many graduations, but winning the Finlandia was the first big landmark event I didn't share with Dad. He would have been so proud.

∿∿∿

Despite winning a marathon title, I was hungry for more. I wanted more success in more competitive races. After winning the Finlandia I still wasn't convinced I was an athlete. The field there had been weak and consisted of a mere five female skiers, none of whom had qualified for the Elite Wave at the Birkebeiner in recent years. I wanted more proof all the training was paying off.

Two weeks later, I went to a rather low-key race, the River View Loppet in Brule, Wisconsin, and skied the 12-kilometer classic race. While this race largely attracted a high school crowd, a few local shufflers showed up, as well as some competitive citizen racers.

Before the race I noticed one particular woman who appeared to be in her thirties or forties. She looked fast in her team spandex, supported by one of the local ski shops. She looked fit and wore a spandex hat, too. She was obviously going to lay the smackdown on me. At least I wouldn't be cherry-picking.

The race had interval starts. I quickly forgot about this fast woman in the spandex as I focused on getting a good start and passing Harriet, an older woman in a big purple jacket on touring equipment with her name displayed on her bib, by the second uphill. I was breathing hard and working hard, and as the first part of the course was mostly uphill, I was tired. Then there was a rolling section, and I struggled to get my breath back and do more double poling. I kept working hard and pushing on the uphills. Still, there seemed to be lots of room for improvement, such as getting more out of each stride.

When the results came in, I was only four seconds behind the fast chick in her ski-shop spandex. It was races like that in which I realized that I, too, could be good and that I, too, could be somebody's idol one day.

Chapter 20

Epitomizing Determination

The day of our wedding, May 3, 2008, was forecast to be 38 degrees and raining, fitting the pattern for the spring we had been experiencing. It had snowed every other week and rained in between, and we would go a week at a time without seeing the sun.

"It's gonna snow the week before our wedding," I told everyone. It did. Although Minneapolis only saw a few flurries, Bemidji got buried in 18 inches.

We had an outdoor wedding at Fort Snelling State Park, on an island near the convergence of the Minnesota and Mississippi Rivers.

The morning of the wedding, Kathryn, Erik, and I got up early to go for a 6-mile run. Two miles in, the sun streamed through the clouds. Four miles in, the clouds were breaking apart. By the end of the run, the sun was high in the sky, and there were no clouds in sight.

I feared that after getting married, I would quit all my endurance adventures. I had little time to worry about that. Following the reception, Erik and I canoed off into the sunset, 6 miles down the Mississippi River to an old tugboat that had been converted into a bed-and-breakfast. Just Married signs garnished either side of our canoe. As we paddled, we got cheers from a barge heading upstream, a train, fishermen on the shore, and several prom dinner cruises.

Our friend Craig bought me a road bike for a wedding present, and I was charged with using it to commute 15 miles each way for the next week. During our honeymoon in Europe, Erik and I hiked 100 miles around Mont Blanc in just nine days with 30,000 feet of elevation change. We moved to New York and climbed the highest mountain there and in Vermont, New Hampshire, and Maine on very steep, rocky trails.

We forgot how dumb it was to do back-to-back-to-back ski marathons. One Saturday, we did the Lake Placid Loppet, a grueling two-lap course with more elevation change than the original Olympic marathon course. The following weekend, we did both the classic ski and skate ski marathons over two days at the Gatineau Loppet. The next week, we flew to Minnesota and drove to Wisconsin to do the Birkebeiner. The tally: four ski marathons in three weeks.

With Erik I managed to summit all of the mountains we attempted to climb, and four years into our marriage, we completed a 300-mile hiking trip in the Sierra Nevada, summiting Mount Whitney, the highest peak in the continental United States, along the route.

Erik became the catalyst to achieving my dreams. He knew how to climb mountains successfully. He wanted to get better, faster, and stronger at skiing. He wanted to go on long canoe trips, too.

∿∿∿

In 2009, Erik and I skied the 53-kilometer classic on Saturday and the 53-kilometer skate on Sunday at the Gatineau Loppet in Quebec, again keeping our goal of always competing in the longest possible distance. The course was the same both days: after making a 10-kilometer loop to the south of the start, the out-and-back course climbed above the Ottawa River for 20 kilometers and then returned to the finish. It was like no course I had ever skied before. Once we were on the out-and-back section, the hills just kept coming. Unlike the Birkebeiner, which has more numerous steeper hills, the hills on the Gatineau course climbed relentlessly for 1 to 2 kilometers at a time without a break.

It was a strider's dream—but I was a terrible strider. I owed my classic prowess to double-pole courses; my classic striding technique was inefficient, leaving my lungs screaming. I knew my strides lacked glide, and this was wrong. My striding mimicked running on my skis. I needed to glide.

I thought back to my childhood and that experience skiing with Mom and Leif at Elm Creek. They were walking on their skis while I was determined to glide, but trying to glide left me panting. I stopped and caught my breath, and they passed me. I was trying to glide on my skis and was irate that Mom and Leif, who seemed to be just walking on their skis, were going faster than me. Save for now knowing how to double pole, I felt like my nine-year-old self again as I skied the Gatineau Loppet, getting all out of breath trying to glide on my skis.

Fortunately, a few days after the race, a friend who was a good skier told me that when I brought my foot forward during the recovery phase, I put it down too soon, and it made a slapping noise—accounting for my lack of glide. Over the next couple years, I worked on changing my striding technique by slowing my stride and going through the new motion. I worked on bringing my foot into contact with the snow later and farther in front. Then I practiced this at faster speeds.

I have no recollection of my pride at first learning to read or write, despite the pivotal role both reading and writing play in my everyday life. But one of the joys of adult learning is being better able to appreciate our aha moments. The coordination required to change my striding technique was frustrating at times; other times I thought I'd never grasp the technique, but I kept practicing.

At last, I mastered it. It was so exciting. I watched videos of the Norwegians stride-gliding up the hills. And now I could glide up the hills, too. Gradual hills at first, then steeper and steeper ones.

Two years after I first learned how to fix the flaw in my technique, I did the same race that had initially caused me so much trouble. The Gatineau Loppet was the biggest race in Canada, and I was the eighth-fastest female skier. That was striding success—until the next aha moment.

∿∿∿

At sixteen I wrote in my journal:

> *October 4, 2001*
> *Someday I'm gonna run a marathon. I'll train three days a*
> *week: two days running 5 miles or less, another day doing*
> *16 or 20 miles. My goal will be to get under four hours.*

In the ensuing ten years, I suffered from burnout, then a severed gastrocnemius tendon, and finally fear. Twenty-six miles is a long way to run, and I feared I couldn't cover the distance. I feared injury. I feared not making my time goal; I desperately wanted to break four hours and only had plans to run one marathon. So I delayed.

During the year my gastrocnemius tendon was torn, I fixated on not being able to run a marathon. Once my leg had healed and I could run without limping, it seemed stupid to let the fear of not getting my ideal time prevent me from actually running a marathon.

I was spurred to finally make the idea a reality in 2010

when Kathryn started talking about running the Quebec City Marathon. Since I couldn't let her run a marathon before me, I started looking into courses. While I liked the idea of running a race in a French-speaking city, the Quebec City Marathon course wasn't to my liking.

Remembering watching the televised Montreal Marathon in the past, I looked up that course. I immediately fell in love with the winding route, which traverses islands and bridges on the Saint Lawrence Seaway, eventually culminating in a finish in Olympic Stadium. The finish around a track was really the selling point for the race, although the promise of a wicking T-shirt and finisher's medal were also good incentives. The race was slated for September, which seemed like a great cool-temperature month for running a marathon.

I could no longer let the fear of not getting my desired time prevent me from running a marathon. After all, when I couldn't run without limping, I'd wanted more than anything to be able to run a marathon. I had lamented for months about how my body might never be able to run 26 miles, and now here was my chance—I couldn't let some fear like not breaking four hours prevent me from putting my reconnected gastrocnemius to the ultimate test.

Unsure of how my body would hold up for the race, I did some marathon preview training. I hadn't run more than 13 miles at a stretch since regaining my gastrocnemius and hadn't run more than 9 miles in a few years. I gradually built up my distance for a few weeks, and when I could run 16 miles, I stopped, confident that with training I could run 26.2 miles.

I signed up for the Montreal Marathon in January 2011. A few days later, I learned the finish had been changed from Olympic Stadium to a nearby park. This was upsetting, as I really wanted to finish by running around a track, Olympic style. Now I would have to content myself with the T-shirt and medal.

My training for the marathon went well, and I worked up to a three-and-a-half-hour run by myself. The week before the marathon, I did a 16-mile run, which left me feeling strong, and two 10-mile runs, which didn't leave a single part of my body sore. I had been popping iron supplements since donating blood the first week of my marathon training and felt ready.

My goal was still to break four hours, although from my training runs with my GPS watch I knew this would be a difficult goal. The day proved to be warm and very humid, with temperatures ranging from 70 to 80 degrees.

I started with a valiant attempt at breaking four hours, aided by a 100-foot downhill over the first mile. For the first 6 miles I was in sight of the 3:45 rabbit. I got to 8 miles at 1 hour, 10 minutes and was pleased with my efforts. Then, things started to fall apart. My breathing, which had seemed easy in the beginning, now felt too laborious. People were passing me. I began getting chills, and my fingers swelled. I gradually backed off the pace until I was barely moving by mile 14. Whenever I started to run faster, I started to breathe harder, and then I started to panic.

I kept up this slow jog for many miles. I was glad there were masses of other people running to keep me going. I couldn't will myself to go any faster. It was like a switch had been flipped, and I couldn't run normally. Sometimes I had to stop and walk. Erik ran with me for a while between miles 18 and 24. I'm not sure whether it helped or not. When he left me with 2 miles to go, the distance remaining seemed like an eternity. He told me to gradually pick up the pace more and more, and that had been my goal, but I just didn't have it in me. Finally, however, with half a mile to go, I broke through the wall and could run fast again. I weaved in and out of the throngs of people and was happy to be passing many half-marathon runners. Lengthening my stride felt amazing. I felt so strong. I really enjoyed that last half mile.

I finished the marathon in 4 hours, 16 minutes. I was obviously disappointed and immediately started planning to run another marathon—this one perhaps with a stadium finish—to try again to break four hours. I was proud I had made a solid attempt in the beginning but blamed my lack of speed training on my hands swelling and my pace dropping considerably. In the end it was hard to say whether I went out too fast, and that ultimately prevented me from establishing my "cruising speed" through the middle half of the marathon, or if I would have gotten progressively slower no matter my starting pace.

Six years earlier, I couldn't run without limping. I couldn't even walk without limping. I was fixated on the fear of never being able to run again, let alone run a marathon. Had I been told then that six years later I would run a 4 hour, 16 minute-marathon, I would have cried with joy. I would have been so happy. With my time I beat "Barney's Bulge" by finishing in the top half overall, for women and for age class— not bad for someone who established themselves by saying *I am not a runner*.

∿∿∿

Her senior year of high school, in English class, Jill had to write an essay about determination. She wrote about me. She said I epitomized determination.

October 21, 2005
Only girl at Frisbee on cold, rainy Friday. The guys are getting better about passing to me. Then I missed like four Frisbees in a row. Some boy threw me this really bad pass, and I heard that jerk Wittig yell, "Turnover time!" and I got really determined to catch the Frisbee . . . and I did with only one hand!

∿∿

In the summer of 2013, I planned a Harney and Longs Peak revenge trip with Erik, who hadn't climbed either mountain previously.

Our planned route to Harney Peak was significantly longer than either the north or south common routes and involved an overnight hike on a loop. We began hiking in the early afternoon. On the way to the trailhead we had driven through a thunderstorm, and we planned to camp on the way up to the peak before we gained too much elevation.

Before long, we climbed well above the water sources. The clouds dissipated, and we met some hikers coming down the trail who told us there was a cistern on the top of the mountain from which we could get water. We decided to push for the summit and have our dinner on top of the mountain. Near the top, the elevation gained quickly, but much more gently than the mountains in the East. There was a stone fire tower at the summit, and a cistern had been built just below to collect rainwater for the fire watchers. We used this water to make our dinner and enjoyed two hours of evening light, blue skies, calm winds, and a family of mountain goats on the top of South Dakota's highest point before descending a legal distance below the summit to dry camp. It ended up being an easy summit bid despite the initially threatening weather.

Two days later, we drove to Colorado and up to Rocky Mountain National Park. We began hiking from the trailhead at 4:00 p.m., heading for the Boulderfield. We first hiked on the Boulder Brook Trail, the trail I had found to be so steep seven years earlier. As we ascended it now, it surely felt steep as it climbed 2,000 feet in 2 miles, but I had forgotten how it leveled out after the first mile.

After ascending the Boulder Brook Trail, we continued hiking up a trail with multiple switchbacks that climbed a truly modest 500 feet per mile until reaching the Boulder-field. During this section of trail, we arrived above tree line and enjoyed expansive views. On the final switchbacks, we got close to a herd of grazing elk.

We camped at the Boulderfield at 12,700 feet, then, the next morning, continued upward. Having hiked boulder fields in the Alps and the northeast United States by that point, the Boulderfield was pretty easy, and before long we arrived at the Keyhole, a saddle separating Longs Peak and the adjacent peak to the north.

The view on the other side of the Keyhole was vertigo in-ducing, and I thought about turning around but knew I would regret it forever. Instead I got determined and started along the edge of the cliff called the Ledges. Along the Ledges we passed a couple college guys; one remarked on my good climb-ing skills. I told him about all my experiences hiking out East. As I said this, he was likely thinking this was a joke, but in reality climbing mountains out East—even if their summits sat below the elevation where we had parked our car in Colo-rado—had really prepared me for this section of trail.

In the Trough, a scree field, we gained serious elevation. Others used climbing helmets, but Erik and I didn't know this and weren't wearing any. We had to be ever aware of falling rocks knocked down by other climbers as we ascended. The last part of the Trough involved some bouldering moves be-fore we came to the Narrows, which was more hiking along a cliff. On the final section, the Homestretch, we again gained quite a bit of elevation as we walked up a very steep granite slab. This rock was so steep, with seemingly so many conse-quences if I slid out, that on the way down I would scoot most of this section on my butt.

The view from the top was well worth the effort, and there wasn't a cloud in the sky. It took Erik and me several hours to hike round trip just from the Boulderfield. After summiting

Longs Peak, I knew that seven years earlier, when Leif and I had decided to turn around at the Boulderfield, we had made the right decision. Despite the substantial climbing skills I had gained in the intervening years, I still found Longs Peak challenging.

∿∿∿

Four years after getting married, Erik and I moved back to Minnesota, where we bought a house 6 miles from my work. On Mondays I biked to work in the morning and ran home in the evening. On Tuesdays I ran to work, then biked back home. The other days I usually biked both ways. Using human-powered transportation to get to and from work made me feel I had achieved self-actualization. Dad was right: the body is a machine, and it likes to be worked. And I still didn't know my own strength.

In my first ski marathons back in Minnesota in 2013, I didn't place where I wanted, though I did manage to win the 50-kilometer skate Finlandia in a sprint against Eileen, who had beat me handily in the 100-kilometer in 2006. It was my second go in a row at that distance and my second axe in as many tries. That sprint finish was so exciting it kept me up all night. Still, my poor performance throughout that season motivated me for a hard year of training.

One day in October of that year, Erik and I did uphill roller ski intervals. I used roller skis with faster wheels than Erik. The 1-kilometer route snaked up a hill with four 90-degree turns and a flat section in the middle and climbed 100 feet up the Mississippi River bluff. On the first interval, I showed Erik the route and stayed in the lead. I got to the top in 4:02 with my lungs burning. It seemed impossible I could go that hard for the next two planned intervals.

On the next interval, Erik knew the way. He took off, but

I gained an advantage on the first big left turn with my mad cornering skills. He caught me on the flat section, but I was able to stay with him on the corners and steep V2 section. We finished the second interval dead even in a time of 3:49, thirteen seconds faster than the first.

Now my lungs burned even more, and I could tell the effort was making me very tired. In addition, I had gone for a 7-mile run earlier in the day. I was breathing hard, gasping for air, feeling the hunger in my lungs.

On the third interval, Erik pulled away from me, but I worked hard to get in front of him before the flat section. He again pulled away from me on the flat section, but I again made up for it with good cornering skills and my strong V2. He was able to catch me on the last V1 section near the top, and I couldn't quite stay with him to the crest of the hill. Still, my time was very fast at 3:47, moving an average of 9.5 miles per hour. My maximum heart rate peaked at 181. I was heaving, my lungs exhausted, yet it felt wonderful to still be able to push myself that hard and to keep up with Erik and really push him to the top.

I had gotten the taste for finding my limit, the so-called runner's high or skier's high, in high school, and it was still driving me to train and compete. It was addicting to push to that limit. But since I had never broken the six-minute mile or made it to state in skiing, I had some unfinished business. I was still hungry to find my limit—to learn my true potential and prove, at least to myself, what I was capable of achieving.

In 2014 I did better in my ski marathons. After skiing 43 kilometers of the Finlandia not knowing about my female competition from the year previous, I learned to pay better attention at the race starts, especially in the smaller races. I practiced this early in the season when I did a small race in Wisconsin. A few weeks later, as I prepared to start the Finlandia, this time the 25-kilometer classic, I looked for the female skiers around me. I spotted a woman from the University of Minnesota cross-country ski club, Katelyn, who I knew had made Elite Wave in the Birkebeiner the previous year. I wanted to win, to get another axe and prove I could win the Finlandia based on skiing prowess rather than attrition alone.

I began to feel more confident in my ability to win, as it looked like only Katelyn and a high school girl would be my main competition.

"Judging by my competition, I think I'm going to get fourth," remarked my old teammate Travis.

I am going to win, I thought.

The gun went off, and soon Katelyn and I were in the lead. I made a distinct pass to drop a guy with poor technique, and Katelyn stayed behind me. Then the positive self-talk began: *I want to win. I want that axe. I want it more than Katelyn.* I tried to conserve energy as I led and began planning where on the course to make my move. As the race progressed, Katelyn took the lead, and after a few more kilometers I found myself herringbone walking up a steep hill behind her. I had more positive self-talk: *She's getting tired, and I'm still fresh.* I was still debating where I could make a solid pass, as I didn't want another sprint finish.

I pulled ahead of Katelyn on the next downhill. As I began climbing in the lead, I recognized this was the last big uphill before a few kilometers of flat. Moreover, Katelyn wouldn't know this, as she hadn't skied the course before, so I put in a surge and was able to drop her. I still had a few kilometers to go in the lead and kept pushing hard. In the end I beat Katelyn by two minutes and learned about evaluating my competition, positive self-talk, and confidence.

The next week, on my eighth Birkebeiner, I felt poised to qualify for Elite Wave for the first time. For the second year in a row, I was racing the classic technique, and only the top twenty women qualified for Elite Wave in the classic race. I was in Wave Two, having qualified for that wave the previous year skiing out of Wave Four. My plan was to start in the front row of Wave Two among the men. If anyone said anything about starting at the front of the wave, I planned to tell them about my axe collection—a collection I had added to the previous week after winning the Finlandia 25-kilometer classic.

My plan was almost foiled by a big traffic jam and bus-unloading delays on the way to the start. My warm-up was running half a mile from the bus drop-off area to the start in my ski boots, carrying my skis. With less than three minutes to spare, I crawled under the starting-line flags and lined up in the front row of Wave Two.

The gun went off, and I soon realized the cold, new snow was incredibly slow. As we began climbing, however, my kick was excellent despite not having had time to test my kick wax. I tried to stay with the front of Wave Two, but some got ahead of me, and we spread out in the early hills. I tried to work on gliding with striding, but around High Point I resorted to some shorter running strides. This is also when I began passing skiers from Wave One, which had started 15 minutes ahead of me. Just before OO, a Wisconsin county road that crosses the Birkebeiner trail near the halfway mark, I passed my first Elite Wave woman.

Just past OO I passed Dave, who had skied out of Wave One. I had already beaten him twice that season; both times he had started behind me and stayed behind me. Now, for the first time, I was passing him.

"Go, Dave Dawg!" I cheered. What I really wanted to say was, "So girls are slow, huh?"

After OO I passed more Wave One skiers and Elite Wave women. Around 42 kilometers, I got tired. I yo-yoed with Wave One men on the last big uphill, lacking the energy to leave them in the dust. There was a brutal west wind, and I worked hard to catch a pack in front of me that I planned to ride across the lake to the finish. That plan was thwarted when half the pack stopped for beer at the start of the lake. I tried taking the lead with my strong double pole but moved slowly with the headwind and slow sandpaper snow. A Wave One man took the lead and quickly strided away from me as I double poled behind him. Usually double poling was faster than striding on a flat lake, but not this day with the wind so strong and the snow so slow. I resorted to striding and kick double poling, even though this made my left gastrocnemius hurt—which still scared me, since it was my "fake" calf. I hoped I had given enough of an effort to make the Elite Wave.

When the race was over and I finally checked the results, I saw I was in sixteenth place! The coveted Elite Wave had eluded me for so long, but after eight tries, I had qualified.

∿∿∿

By age twenty-four, I finally believed I was smart, but I still wasn't sure I was an athlete. To me, athletes were the kids in high school who had made varsity as underclassmen and whose photos were plastered across the sports pages in the newspaper week after week. I wasn't one of those kids.

The question was, just what did I have to do to consider myself an athlete? If I had failed at being an athlete in high school, could I make up for that later in life?

Throughout my twenties, I still hadn't answered that question, so I simply did what I'd always done: I kept training. While the "real" athletes collected fans and accolades, I amassed sore muscles and self-doubt. As the years wore on, my drive and dedication persevered, so was it fair to validate my athleticism based on that even if I wasn't on top of the podium? Sure, I could do ten pull-ups, but was that all it took to be an athlete? I felt like an imposter. Had all my training been wasted time if I could never be satisfied with my mediocre accomplishments?

In response to my doubts, I trained ever harder—skiing in subzero temperatures, doing thousands of push-ups, completing punishing runs through thunderstorms.

And why was it so important for me to be an athlete, anyway? Since elementary school, I had put athletes on a pedestal that I myself wanted to climb onto. Was it all because I wanted recognition? If so, from whom?

Despite qualifying for the Birkebeiner Elite Wave a further three times after my first success, at age thirty-one I was still struggling to define myself as an athlete.

Then, one late May afternoon, while Erik and I were canoeing down the Rum River, we encountered a mature maple tree felled across the entire river. The thick trunk lay across the right half, and the canopy, consisting of multiple foot-thick branches, sprawled across the left half. It seemed impossible to make it through, as all the branches were either too low to paddle under or too high to lift the canoe over. Most people would have paddled over to the bank and portaged around the tree. But that seemed too easy. We needed a challenge.

We paddled toward the canopy to try shoving the canoe under one of the branches close to the water while we climbed over branches higher above the water. While Erik, in the stern, balanced our canoe in the current, I clamored out and held myself in the air by bracing my arms on two branches. Then I pushed the canoe down, deeper into the water, and forward with my legs so the canoe could go under the low branch. After I got the bow under the branch, I raised my upper body into the air and then lowered it to get into position so my feet could rest on the gunwales to ram the canoe farther under the branch. This was a whole-body effort, requiring upper and lower body strength and core stabilization, and yet it was effortless for me. I suddenly realized what I was doing likely looked quite difficult, but for me, it was easy. It was natural. And I was good at it.

If only Adrienne could see me now, I thought. Would my soccer coach, who had sidelined me from the high school team, think I was an athlete? This thought from the bowels of my psyche shook me up, but I had an answer.

It didn't matter what Adrienne or anyone else thought. It only mattered what I thought.

As Erik and I paddled downstream, away from the down tree, I realized I had found the proof for which I'd been searching all these years. My self-doubt vanished. It must've gotten hung up in all those maple branches. With each paddle stroke, my confidence grew.

As I looked back upstream, I saw countless hours of training, adventures filled with mud and bugs and all the hazards Mother Nature had blasted at me, companionship, obstacles, victories, and my refusal to ever give up. It had all been worthwhile. I believed in myself now.

Finally, I had become an athlete.

Epilogue

November 2019

Dear Dad,

After living in Rochester, New York, for four years, Erik and I moved back to Minnesota. I got a job as a nurse practitioner at Hennepin County Medical Center, fulfilling my childhood notion of adulthood by working in downtown Minneapolis amid the skyscrapers. We bought a house in Saint Paul, in what Erik calls an upper-middle-class neighborhood, two blocks south of Summit Avenue. The neighborhood has beautiful old houses, and I can walk around and admire the architecture just like I used to do as a kid.

In spirit, I'm more of a Minneapolis girl, but I fell in love with this old house with its arched doorways, modern kitchen, and southern exposure. Then I discovered we can see the Minneapolis skyline from our front bedroom. That made me so happy. I fell in love with that skyline as a girl, and I've never fallen out of love with it.

Our house is exactly 3 miles due east of where we lived by Powderhorn Park. We still shop at Hi-Lake, and our old Knox off University Avenue is still there, but now it's our Menards. I remember that one time you bought a big sheet of plywood at Knox and strapped it to the van. When we were coming home over the Lake Street Bridge, it almost flew off the roof. You had to roll down the window and hold on to it with your strong arm.

You wouldn't believe the price of our house. Your eyes would get so big, and you'd admonish me for spending such an outlandish sum, but I promise you it's quite affordable given our income. We paid for the neighborhood; the house, built in 1924, only has 1,800 finished square feet. It's a modest home with only one living room, one eating room, and three bedrooms. And the basement is unfinished, with tall ceilings for ski waxing.

While you might not like the price of our house, you would like the location. It's perfect for bike commuting to downtown Minneapolis, my primary mode of transportation to work. I take bike lanes to the Marshall Avenue–Lake Street Bridge, then go north on the West River Parkway trail to downtown. All but one block of my bike commute is on trails or bike lanes!

I don't always bike commute, though. I am fortunate to live on a limited-stop bus line, which picks me up down the street on Cleveland Avenue and drops me off in front of work. Taking the bus has gotten more popular. And those "empty seat" buses have fewer empty seats these days. :) I take the bus in the winter when it's colder than 15 degrees or there is considerable snow and ice on the roads and bike trails.

I often run to and from work as well. The shortest running routes are 5.2 miles and take me forty-five minutes when I'm moving well. Of course, it takes me an hour or more when there is snow and ice. If I desire a longer run, I take West River Parkway all the way south to the Ford Parkway Bridge and then run back north along East River Parkway or run up the Mississippi River awhile before I cross the river and head toward home. I prefer running to biking, although it's slower. During the nonsnowy months of the year, once a week I bike to work, run home that same day, run back to work the following day, and then ride my bike back home. When it's snowy, I sometimes take the bus to work and run home or run both ways.

Occasionally, I run home through south Minneapolis, by

Powderhorn Park and our old house—a literal run down memory lane. Our block feels so small; I easily cover the length in a minute or so. The neighborhood is really cleaned up now. It's so safe, not at all like it was in the '90s, when you would go to SuperAmerica to get milk at night and I'd worry you'd be shot and never make it back home.

Somebody told me recently that Powderhorn Park is the most up-and-coming neighborhood in America. This ripped a hole in my heart. The summer between seventh and eighth grades, I would stay awake at my window facing the alley, waiting for you to ride up on your bike after your second shift at exactly 11:27 p.m. Once you were safely inside the house, I would go to bed. I never told you this.

You were so strong and brave and cunning, riding home in the dark on your bike without lights so as to go unnoticed by any troublemakers and frequently changing your route whenever you sensed danger. I always felt so safe when you were around. So protected.

Mom's doing OK. She still lives in Bemidji, in the Painted Lady. Buying that house with cash was probably the best financial decision you ever made—knowing you and Mom were both frictional workers.

She misses you. She'll never marry again. She'll never replace you as her best friend. She never wants us to say anything bad about you. She knows you did the best you could, even when you left your government job when we were just kids to pursue your dream of building and selling bikes.

Sometimes I think about those times in childhood you infuriated me by calling me a princess because I wanted nice things, or soft things, like to not walk to school when it was well below 0 degrees or raining, to have indoor plumbing at our cabin, a closet, a piano. I knew enough even back then to know that I wasn't really a princess, not with my postage-stamp-sized bedroom and the constant reminders from you that "money doesn't grow on trees." In many respects I've been trying to disprove this characterization ever since.

I think about this when I'm running or biking when it's 38 degrees and raining and I'm on the brink of hypothermia. There's no choice except to keep going.

I think about this when traversing boulder fields on my way up mountains, shoveling heavy snow, breathing hard in races, portaging through mucky swamps, or going a week without a shower. No, Dad, I am not a princess.

And I think about this when I run home from work when it's –17 degrees with a wind chill approaching –45 degrees. My coworkers think I'm crazy, and even more so when they see how little I'm wearing. But when I'm running with the wind, it makes all the difference. I stay warm and have an enjoyable run. You were right. The body can handle the cold much better than the car.

I told Leif the apple doesn't fall far from the tree.

Alas, Dad, I am not the hardcore bike commuter you were. I don't bike year-round, though there are many other hardy bike commuters in the Twin Cities who do. They all have studded tires or those newfangled fat bikes. I could outfit my bike with studded tires but choose not to, partly because my bike would get corroded by the salt, partly because I like running, and ultimately because winter is for skiing.

But you were truly crazy, bike commuting all winter without studded or fat tires. Somehow you never slipped out on ice, and you pedaled even through the deep snow. I don't know how you did it. You are the hardiest person I've ever known and ever expect to know.

Bike commuting has drastically changed in the Twin Cities since those days. Back then, everyone thought you were crazy for doing it. Now there are numerous bike trails beyond those along the Mississippi River. Most begin in downtown Minneapolis or Saint Paul and extend into the suburbs in nearly every direction. There's another trail in south Minneapolis called the Greenway, which follows the old train line running west to east in the trench just north of the old Sears tower. You would love it. I can imagine you biking up and down that trail, your tongue hanging out to the side and a huge grin stretching from ear to ear.

There are bike lanes on so many city streets, too. On Park and Portland Avenues, the city took out a lane of traffic to create a bike lane with a buffer zone on either side: one for traffic and one for parked cars. Oh man, Dad, I think the era of your "automobile welfare" is nearing an end. I just wish you could see it now—you'd be calling this "bicycle welfare"! Oh, you'd love it.

Not a day goes by that I don't see at least one bike commuter, even during subzero temperatures with lots of snow and ice. And when the tulips emerge, the bikers are out in full force. There are too many to count during the summer on my bike commute.

Something else amazing has happened: bikers are becoming more respected by motorists. Where the bike trail intersects streets, the bikers have a stop sign; however, daily I witness cars actually stopping for bikers to cross! I don't expect the cars to stop, but the fact they sometimes do is a miraculous change.

Recently, on a cold day in November when the wind was howling out of the north, I ran home from work along the bike trail. As I was running, numerous bikers were passing me despite the temperature hovering around 20 degrees. It was then that I realized, a smile slowly spreading across my face, how much has changed since you were an oddity and a pioneer in the Minneapolis biking scene, because now biking in the Twin Cities has become, dare I say it, mainstream. I guess you were just ahead of your time.

On my early-morning bike commutes, I often encounter

an older gentleman biking. He's around the age you would be now. He says "Good morning—God bless" to everyone he meets. He's out there no matter the weather: rain, cold, snow, ice. Indeed, it seems the worse the weather, the more likely I am to see him. Every day that I meet him, it makes my day better and puts a smile on my face, but especially on those dark, cold, wet mornings.

There's something about him that seems familiar. The early mornings, the bicycle, the way he seems to embrace the most inclement conditions.

Oh, Dad, maybe it's you.

Love always,
Your Princess

Acknowledgments

I want to thank Pete Vordenberg and John L. Parker Jr., whose respective books *Momentum: Chasing the Olympic Dream* and *Once a Runner* impeccably captured the agony of endurance training and racing and provided me models and the inspiration to do likewise.

Thank you, Mom, for *everything*. It was so special to collaborate with you on my book cover. I know all my artistic talent, cleverness, and wit is from you. Dad was wrong: only one in a million of your ideas are bad. :)

Here's a shout-out to my bro Leif, my number one fan.

A special thank-you to my youngest brother, Reid, who provided an insightful first edit on a very rough draft. He did what my writing group recommends: he critiqued the writing, not the writer, and did so with unprecedented wisdom despite being just a teenager at the time.

Thank you to my husband, Erik, for providing a second edit and expertise in vocabulary. He was never shy about telling me when I had used the wrong word. He deserves more appreciation for answering my constant questions of "Does this make sense?" and "Should I take this out or leave it in?" as well as being the sounding board for all my self-doubt.

Thank you to my family, my friends, and everyone with whom I've ever crossed paths. Many of you have roles in this book; the others are there in spirit. Because this isn't fiction, I didn't develop my characters—you developed me.

Thank you to the staff at Beaver's Pond Press, who made me feel heard.

And last but not least, I thank my fellow members of the Merriam Park Library writing group (Elizabeth, the Jims, Dorothy, Lakin, Lyn, Linda, "the Twins," Bob, Frank, and Dick) for their camaraderie and excellent editing. Along with Reid, they developed my manuscript into a much better book than I could have ever done alone—often offering the same critique he had, which was finally enough to persuade me to make changes (sorry that I couldn't listen to you alone, bro). They not only provided constructive criticism but also helped me learn more about myself in the process. In particular, I want to recognize Lakin, who aided me in crafting a most beautiful ending to my story.